Professional
Education
in the
United States

Professional
Education
in the
United States

EXPERIENTIAL LEARNING, ISSUES, AND PROSPECTS

Edited by Solomon Hoberman
and Sidney Mailick

With contributions by
Robert H. Ebert, Frederick M. Hart,
Elaine Marshack, & J. Michael Norwood

Westport, Connecticut
London

Library of Congress Cataloging-in-Publication Data

Professional education in the United States : experiential learning,
   issues, and prospects / edited by Solomon Hoberman and Sidney
   Mailick ; with contributions by Robert H. Ebert . . . [et al.].
      p. cm.
   Includes bibliographical references.
   ISBN 0–275–93386–5 (alk. paper)
    1. Professional education—United States. 2. Experiential
learning—United States. I. Hoberman, Solomon. II. Mailick,
Sidney, 1923–   . III. Ebert, Robert H.
LC1059.P75   1994
378′.013′0973—dc20   94–1148

British Library Cataloguing in Publication Data is available.

Library of Congress Catalog Card Number: 94–1148
ISBN: 0–275–93386–5

First published in 1994

Praeger Publishers, 88 Post Road West, Westport, CT 06881
An imprint of Greenwood Publishing Group, Inc.

Printed in the United States of America

∞™

The paper used in this book complies with the
Permanent Paper Standard issued by the National
Information Standards Organization (Z39.48–1984).

10 9 8 7 6 5 4 3 2 1

IN MEMORIAM

Solomon Hoberman died on April 14, 1994, when the manuscript of this book was finally reviewed and prepared for publication. I had the good luck of working with Sol on many projects for the better part of thirty-four years. Sol was a most brilliant man. He would present his arguments with clarity and grace, and once when I asked him to, he presented the opposite position with equal merit. Sol had great integrity. In all of our work together, I never saw him choose the easy road when the more difficult one was the one to take. We all mourn the loss of a good man. However, his memory will spur us on to attempt to fulfill the ideals he believed in and lived by.

—Sidney Mailick

CONTENTS

PREFACE

This volume consists of discussion, analysis, and recommendations for improving the quality of education for the service professions. Nathan Glazer, quoted in Schon (1992), has distinguished between professions that have "a fixed content of professional knowledge . . . [such as] . . . medicine, law, and business" and those, such as education and social work, without "a fixed and unambiguous end in a fixed institutional setting." We do not believe this is, for educational purposes, a useful distinction. We distinguish between research and service professions. These considerations tend to make us focus on conflict between research and teaching in allocation of priorities and on the use of natural experiential education. We hold that service and research professions require different kinds of education.

There have been a number of studies of professional education for these professions in the past fifty years. However, in no case has a study led to significant changes in educational objectives or approach. The professions themselves have come under increasing attack and scrutiny during this period. We present a new analysis of the variables that influence educational effectiveness and link professional education and services.

The discussion and analysis are directed primarily to policy makers concerned with the effectiveness and cost of professional education and professional services. Because resolution of the issues have significant consequences for the entire population, the materials presented are of value to public policy makers and beyond them to the public that pays for the education and services. The effect and importance of nature and costs of medical and social services are obvious. But legal and managerial services have no less effect on the political, social, and economic well-being of our society.

While four professions are discussed, findings and recommendations apply in large measure to every profession. To some extent they also apply to professional education and services in societies other than our own. Too often the relationship between such educational variables as content and teaching approach and such service variables as quality and cost is neglected. While our focus is on content and teaching approach, other variables affecting education and services are also considered.

Each contributor to this volume emphasizes the role and importance of natural experiential education—education in which practice is integral to the learning process. We feel that this discussion is of particular importance: for while all research points to the value of this educational approach, it is insufficiently employed for the integration and transfer of learning, and when used its potential is rarely achieved.

Other issues discussed include objectives of the different stakeholders; priority for research or teaching; faculty selection, training, and promotion; student characteristics; importance of interpersonal relations; assessment of professional education; relationships between the professional school and the university; relationships with other professionals and paraprofessionals; and research related to professional education.

The problems and issues that we deal with are not new. Thus, with respect to the teaching/research conflict, N. Annan (1992) has pointed out that J. H. Newman in his classic text "Idea of a University" (1973, p. 9) "insisted that teaching was more important than anything else, so important that perhaps research should be carried out in institutions outside the universities." While some issues and recommendations are not new, we believe that the analyses are. Each contributor has used and supervised others in using natural experiential approaches. Review of the literature indicates that it is a learning approach that many educators want to improve and to use more effectively.

The content area that we emphasize is relationships with others. The professions that we have chosen to examine in depth are medicine, law, social work, and management. These are fields in which the work of practitioners involves extensive relationships with others including clients, fellow professionals, and paraprofessionals.

The discussions, analyses, and recommendations regarding professional education are not based on new, empirical research for this book. They derive from firsthand experience in the design and conduct of programs for the education of professionals and from knowledge of the descriptive, critical, and research literature.

Part One provides a frame of reference for analysis of professional education. Chapter 1 is an introduction to the characteristics of professional education and to the discussions that follow. Chapter 2 is a brief discussion of learning theory and of natural experiential education in particular. Chapter 3 is an introduction to the nature and development of the service professions, to professional education, and to some of the criticism of professional education. Chapter 4 is a brief overview of education for the four professions that are later discussed in detail. Chapter 5 contains a presentation of other factors that affect and are affected by the educational approach.

Part Two is the heart of the book. It consists of four independent sections. Each is devoted to education for a single profession. Each contains analysis and recommendations for strengthening professional education in a specific field.

Part Three is an overview of professional education based in large part on a synthesis of the four sections in Part Two. Commonalities and differences are identified and their importance discussed. In addition, there are brief discussions of issues that were not considered in the plan for the book, but whose importance became apparent during our discussions and analyses. In the final chapter, recommendations for strengthening education in the professions are developed and defended. The need for further study and analysis is discussed and promising areas and approaches identified.

Many variables affecting professional education are discussed. Do the objectives and expectations of society and of school faculties differ and have to be reconciled? Should the roles of professional organizations and government in determining how professionals are certified be changed? Do we need to change the current educational model, which is based on providing the same undergraduate education for all students and the same professional education for a wide range of professional tasks from pure research to general practice? Our focus is on learning and transfer of learning. However, this does not indicate lack of concern with issues relating to quality and cost of professional services. Thus, Robert H. Ebert's discussion of medical education has great relevance with respect to the continuing debate on the cost and quality of health services.

We were fortunate to enlist contributors who are distinguished educators and professionals in their respective fields serving as faculty, deans and administrative officers of professional schools, practitioners and consultants. Each has had extensive experience using experiential approaches and have given great thought to the other issues that affect the cost and effectiveness of professional education. All are familiar with the literature, studies, and recommendations relating to professional education in their fields.

The contributors discuss the aspects of education that they consider important and discuss how education affects the quality and cost of professional services. Each chapter is an important analysis of historical development and the state of professional education and contains new insights, cogent criticism, and valuable recommendations for improving education in a major professional area. Each chapter contains contributions that are of importance for analysis of services as well as education.

We hope some readers will be motivated to make increased efforts to improve professional education. Some may discount our analyses, conclusions, and recommendations. Some will use them to make only minor, cosmetic changes. This would be unfortunate. In a report by the Stanford Research Institute, it has been said that significant changes in higher education are not incremental but sudden—and not normally initiated within the educational system (Hartle, 1977, p. 199). Our review of the literature leads us to a different conclusion. While we are a long way from resolving all the problems that critics have identified or from even getting most administrators and faculties to consider seriously the issues, there are educators in every profession who see the need and are willing to work for reform of education in their fields.

We thank our contributors Robert H. Ebert, Frederick M. Hart, Elaine Marshack, and J. Michael Norwood for their outstanding contributions to the improvement of professional education and for their patience and good humor in responding to our comments. We also thank William Pincus, Stephen Stumpf, and Martin Begun for reviewing and commenting on the content and form of different chapters; their views were extremely helpful. We thank Bahman Ghaffarsamar who worked most effectively on many phases of this book and the index would not have been as good or as complete without the work of Nathalie Pochat. And we thank our editors, James Dunton and Arlene Belzer, for their confidence in us, patience, and good advice.

Above all we thank Mildred Mailick and Dorothy Hoberman for reading copy, commenting on style, and providing the support needed to complete this work.

Part One

SECTION I: FRAME OF REFERENCE

Solomon Hoberman and Sidney Mailick

1

INTRODUCTION

The welfare of a society depends to a remarkable degree on the dedication and competence of its corps of "service" professionals in maintaining and improving the quality of life. Professional education determines the quality of services provided. One indication of the recognition of the importance of this education is the great number of studies and papers dealing with the subject. This book is a contribution to the continuing effort to make professional education more efficient and effective.

WHO ARE PROFESSIONALS?

Professionals are the most highly educated and trained persons in the work force. There are close to 12.5 million professionals in the United States (Carnevale, 1989). These men and women are in occupations that provide services of the greatest importance to society and for which there are few criteria and standards and little but anecdotal information to judge their effectiveness. Members of a profession form a community with similar education, training, and practices as well as commonalities in culture, tradition, language, and qualifications, which are in large part a consequence of their professional education. Virtually all have at least a baccalaureate degree. Most professions require formal graduate work either before or during employment as a professional.

Professional education is directed toward helping students acquire special competencies for diagnosing specific needs and for determining, recommending, and taking appropriate action. Professional education is also expected to socialize students in the "thought processes" of the profession and to inculcate them with its customs, ethics, working relationships, and the behaviors expected from members of the profession. Professionals expect—and are expected—to have a great deal of autonomy in their jobs, to have a minimum of supervision, and to make decisions on the basis of their own professional competence.

The recruitment, education, and indoctrination of this elite, in the long run, determine the spirit of the society. The professional schools not only recruit, educate, and qualify professionals to provide specific services, but they are also the major research centers and producers of new theories and technologies. In the course of educating students and reviewing the performance of practitioners, professional schools set and oversee the maintenance of standards for professional conduct.

Social importance and concern is shown by state supervision and the licensing of practitioners. Some state governments require continuing education for maintenance of the license. However, "professionals hold an extraordinary power of definition; the most successful (physicians are a prime example) have established the right to set the very terms of the problems and services involved in their sphere of work" (Thorne, 1973, p. 36). To a greater extent than in the past, this mandate is being challenged. We will consider the role of professional education in provoking the challenge and determining the responses.

THE SERVICE PROFESSIONS

Formal school-based professional education in the United States is less than 200 years old. Before the beginning of the nineteenth century with very few exceptions all school-trained professionals in the United States were trained in European schools. In the early period professional schools were freestanding. They were considered to be "trade schools" by university academics, one notch above schools for mechanics. Only later in the century did universities sponsor professional schools. And, only in the twentieth century have they achieved status with other studies.

In practice, service professions apply learning from one or more sciences. The sciences have been traditionally designated as natural and social. For the purpose of discussion of the professions, Simon (1957) makes a distinction between natural and man-made sciences. In a sense, he distinguishes between the type of phenomena studied. Another categorization distinguishes between the hard and soft sciences. These distinctions hard and soft, pure and applied, natural and man-made have an effect far beyond classification. They carry in their training an academic hierarchy, with the natural, hard, pure having greater prestige and the education and practices of these having greater validity than those of the soft, man-made, and applied. The invidious comparisons have strongly influenced the selection of faculties for professional schools and the nature of professional education.

Professional training in the natural, hard sciences is in great part built on natural experiential learning in either laboratory or field and, for theoreticians, at desk, computer, and blackboard. It is rarely necessary to go outside of the domain of the university to provide the natural experiential education in these professions. Even when sociologists engage in fieldwork, they are primarily observers and recorders. They remain under the aegis of the university.

Of the professions we consider, medicine, law, and business were classified by Nathan Glazer (Schon, 1992, p. 4) as "major professions." We include, in addition to business management, the management of public affairs. The fourth profession discussed, social work, is, we believe, as "major" as any in holding together our troubled, fragmented society.

Thorne (1973, p. 122) states that "the implicit goal of law schools is to create successful lawyers, not to provide an equitable distribution of legal services. The biases of the practicing profession are reflected in the law school curricula, in the methods of teaching, and in the career models implicit in the course of training itself." While we agree with Thorne that the objectives of professional schools should include society's needs as well as "success," we question whether the schools' definition of "success" is appropriate if education does not include relationships with people from outside of the professional specialty. From the viewpoint of society, the educational objectives and practices of the schools are pertinent issues. How, and how many, students are prepared for practice are major concerns.

2
PROFESSIONALS AND PROFESSIONAL EDUCATION

PROFESSIONAL SCHOOLS

Medicine and law are two of the oldest professions. Social work is, like business management, an occupation with a history as old as that of medicine and law but which has only been considered among the professions in this century. Academic training for public administration is far from a recent development. However, there is a long break between the time when universities were established in the thirteenth century to train "the king's clerks" and the reintroduction of schools to train public officials in the nineteenth century. As early as the fourteenth century, such European universities as those at Paris, Bologna, Oxford, and Cambridge included professional schools for the clergy, the higher governmental bureaucracy, law, and medicine.

Few Americans attended professional schools before the nineteenth century. Americans seeking to enter a profession served as apprentices or helpers in recognized professions. In some professions no standards were imposed or entry limited. Thorne (1973, p. 102) commenting on professional education in the United States notes that "in law, as in medicine, it has traditionally been assumed that the training of its members is the business of the profession itself. Apprenticeships with practitioners historically preceded the opening of formal schools."

The first American professional schools were opened toward the end of the eighteenth century. These were in part modeled on the European experience, in part in recognition that it was desirable to acquire greater competencies than could be gained working for a single practicing professional, and in part in response to accreditation requirements. Most of these schools were freestanding institutions. However, even when housed with a liberal arts college, they were separate colleges. University medical schools were the earliest. Law schools were a very late nineteenth-century development. In the beginning professional schools had minimum requirements and few courses of study. For example, at the turn of the twentieth century, medical education required only three years of post–high-school study, and legal education required only two (Thorne, 1973). The baccalaureate degree in engineering has been a requirement for the profession only since 1900.

Over time, there has been a continuous increase in the time, difficulty, and cost of professional education. Most medicine and law programs now require undergraduate degrees prior to entry into the professional school, with the possibility of achieving professional status after seven years for law and eight years for medicine. While engineering still requires only the baccalaureate, there are numerous specialties, and engineering competence is rapidly outdated unless periodically enriched.

Increase in the number of schools, greater concern with the competence of practitioners, and dependence on government funding have led to a process for accrediting professional schools by associations of schools. Accreditation criteria include curriculum, academic qualifications of faculty, ratio of full-time faculty, standards for admission and completion, and library and other facilities. Since World War II, faculty research has become a major criterion. Where research and practice tend to be synonymous, as in the physical sciences, the quality of research is evidence of proficiency as a practitioner. This is not the case in the professions where there is little direct relation between research and practice.

Professional schools have higher status if they are research centers, in addition to being educational centers for practicing professionals. Both university and professional school faculties themselves tend to look down on the intellectual activities of professional education, such as teaching plumbers how to understand and use fragments of the research and theory developed by the much more highly intellectual university disciplines. Schon identifies a hierarchy of knowledge as basic science, applied science, and technical skills of day-to-day practice. He notes that "the greater one's proximity to basic science, as a rule, the higher one's academic status" (1987, p. 9). This is reinforced by studies of professional education that start with the hypothesis that professional schools should be modeled on the university graduate departments. This position has been adopted by accreditation boards and, as a consequence, by the professional schools. Herbert Simon (1976) presents perhaps the strongest argument for this position.

The selection and promotion of faculty members on the basis of their research and publications has turned most into researchers rather than teachers. Little resources are expended to improve teaching competence. While there is periodic genuflection to its importance, ability to teach is not an important criterion (Smith, 1990). Faculty members imbued with the latest research and techniques, tend to see students as empty vessels passively waiting to be filled with new knowledge.

STUDENTS

Admission to professional schools is limited to those who can afford the costs and to those for whom scholarships and stipends can be provided. Beyond this screening, admission is based in large part on applicants' grade-point average (GPA) in undergraduate school and on special national examination marks. The requirements for entry, the length and cost of education programs, and the need to forego other opportunities tend to limit entry to young well-to-do and scholarship students. The costs to the individual leads many to focus on financial benefits for recompense. This emphasis tends to be strengthened by professional socialization.

Questions have been raised about the validity of admission criteria. Using meta-analytic techniques to integrate the findings of thirty-nine research studies, Bretz (1989) found no significant relation between GPA and adult success in a number of professional fields, including business, teaching, engineering, and medicine. In a reply to Bretz, Dye and Reck (1989) reported their review of a similar set of studies. They found a modest positive relation that was strengthened if grades were limited to the last two years of college and the students' major subject. Close reading of the article indicates that the relations are very modest, just outside the range of chance. If there is a positive relation between GPA and success in professional education, as other research indicates, then Bretz's findings could imply that there is no relation between success in graduate education and subsequent success as a professional. This raises issues of criteria for admission and the relevance of some professional education.

PROFESSIONAL EDUCATION

There are significant differences between the nature of the work performed by professionals in the research-oriented natural and social sciences and by practitioners in the applied professions. The former deal, for the most part, with describing, understanding, developing, and testing theory in order to predict relations and characteristics of natural and social phenomena. The latter adapt and use the theory and techniques developed in the former for the purpose of providing services for people and organizations.

In research fields, practitioners work with things; if people are involved they are the objects of study, not the recipients of services. In service professions practitioners perform services for individuals and groups. Relationships between professionals and clients are much more interactive and intimate. Nothing in students' schooling prior to professional school prepares them to apply learning in the unstable, uncertain, ambiguous, and conflictive situations that they will face in practice. And there is little in professional education to help them. While the need is recognized, there are other needs that compete for primacy. The highest priority is educating students in the latest theory, techniques, and research.

Faculty members, in general, do not have the time, training, experience, or will to help students acquire the competencies they will need to relate to clients, fellow professionals, and others in the work venue. Consequently, graduates tend to be well equipped with theory and general knowledge but not with experiential learning.

Professional education tends to vary between learning sequences in which students first learn and apply techniques and then learn the theory of the relations and one in which the order is reversed. Early in the life of a profession, when apprenticeship is customary, the first of these approaches is dominant. As teaching becomes a specialized activity, university curricula for the professions generally provide a theoretical foundation followed by synthetic experience. In the second approach learning is primarily passive. The occasional synthetic experiential learning is not a substitute for natural experiential education. This separation between theory and experience is a major reason for the failure of much professional learning relating to interpersonal relations to transfer to practice. We see a third approach in which theory and practice are directly linked, that is, natural experiential education, as the most effective means for insuring transfer of learning. Graduate schools that evolved from schools for company personnel made efforts to integrate theory and practice from the outset (Betters-Reed, 1986).

The case method was introduced in legal education and later adopted in other professional schools as a substitute for practical experience. However, as Thorne (1973) observes, the separation between theory and practice was not decreased by the introduction of the case method of instruction at the Harvard Law School. This approach, he says, was "geared toward the principle of law rather than the details of practice" (Thorne, 1973, p. 103). The same comment can be made of the use of the case method in management and other professions.

In some professions it is not easy to provide natural experiential education. Where it is possible, it may be very difficult to schedule so as to effectively tie passive and experiential learning. There are a few cooperative education programs in law, business management (MBA), and engineering, as well as isolated cases in other professions (Brown and Wilson, 1978). Some schools employ synthetic experiential education as a substitute for experience. However, education for the professions has not changed significantly for more than fifty years. Except for medicine, the emphasis is on passive learning in a classroom setting. Where experience is part of education it tends to be either secondary or a process for learning techniques in a specialty.

CHANGE

Basic professional education should ensure general competence at an acceptable level in the entire field. However, as conditions change, knowledge increases, and better services are demanded, earlier levels of competence are not considered sufficient for effective practice. Three ways for satisfying these needs are specialization, continual lifelong learning, and introduction of new occupations. Specialization requires more than the general learning acquired in first professional education. Lifelong learning calls for an institutional means of providing the education without requiring long absences from practice. Assigning tasks between occupations involves defining the tasks and occupations and interoccupational relations. Professional schools have roles to play in all of these approaches.

The most difficult of the roles is dealing with accumulation of new tasks and assignment of tasks to other occupations. Before the nineteenth century, much of what is now the work of a physician was performed by others, such as midwives, barbers, and clerics. "The work of lawyers overlaps with that of accountants, realtors, process servers, bail bondsmen, probation officers, welfare workers, private detectives, and insurance adjusters" (Thorne, 1973, p. 115). The paralegal occupation, which has become important in the last twenty years, results from increased specialization and division of labor in legal practice. In medicine the need for support occupations has been so strong and specializations of support and complementary occupations so great that schools of allied medical professions have evolved. Social work has support occupations. There is an undergraduate program in social welfare. Individuals with this degree are admitted to the National Association of Social Workers. Persons with baccalaureate degrees in other fields, with two years of experience in social work are also admitted (Gurin and Williams, 1973, p. 207).

The dominant profession usually defines the tasks performed by the support occupations. Thus Gurin and Williams note, "a high percentage of [social work] professionals [work] in medical and psychiatric settings where the dominant profession has tended to be medicine rather than social work. . . . Professional social workers have thus been largely ancillary to either politically dominated mass service systems or medically dominated professional systems" (1973, p. 203). Interrelations among professionals and between professionals and paraprofessionals are a continuing problem area.

Whitehead (1948), referring to the fragmentation and integration issue, notes that

another great fact confronting the modern world is the discovery of the method of training professionals, who specialize in particular regions of thought and thereby progressively add to the sum of knowledge within their respective limitations of subject. In consequence of the success of this professionalising of knowledge, . . . modern professionalism in knowledge works in the opposite directions so far as the intellectual sphere is concerned. The modern chemist is likely to be weak in zoology. . . . Effective knowledge is professionalised knowledge, supported by a restricted acquaintance with useful subjects subservient to it. . . . In the modern world, the celibacy of the medieval learned class has been replaced by a celibacy of the intellectual which is divorced from the concrete contemplation of the complete facts. (p. 196)

Fragmentation has taken place. Satisfactory integration has not. This is essential as integration of services among professionals, on the one hand, and between professionals and support occupations, on the other, determine the quality and cost of professional services. Integration tends to be ignored in professional education.

In medical education the two-year internship is expected to prevent the fragmentation of several years of education in a specialty. Except for covering the general field in the first professional program, there is no education to help practitioners to integrate services.

ASSESSMENT OF PROFESSIONAL EDUCATION

"[Former Secretary of Education] Alexander said that he would be interested in suggestions for new ways to evaluate universities and colleges, including bypassing the regional accreditation bodies that now have that responsibility" (*New York Times*, November 16, 1991). Alexander was concerned with the use of "cultural diversity" standards as criteria in accrediting colleges. It would have been more to the point if he were concerned with output criteria. Such assessment as there is focuses on input criteria in terms of faculty, facilities, curriculum, and student admission standards. There is little assessment of educational activities and virtually none of output.

CONTINUING EDUCATION

A half century ago Whitehead noted that our present age differs from the past in that, "the rate of progress is such that an individual human being, of ordinary length of life, will be called upon to face novel situations which find no parallel in his past. The fixed person for the fixed duties, who in older societies was such a godsend, in the future will be a public danger" (1948, p. 196). Nowhere is this danger greater than in the services provided by professionals. Rapid changes in knowledge, tools, technology, and public demands have reached the point where many workers can be expected to engage in three or four occupations during their working lives. Most professionals do not usually change to another occupation, but they have to invest in gaining new competencies. Fowler (June 6, 1989) reports a growing concern with the failure of many professionals to continue formal education.

This concern is recognized in medicine by state requirements for continuing medical education. Lawyers attend special courses dealing with changes in the law, particularly tax law. Social work and management are not subject to as clear-cut changes in tasks and techniques; nevertheless, concerned professionals attend special courses and seminars. Individuals and organizations invest in training. Lusterman (1977) reports that 74 percent of American firms with 500 or more employees authorize employees, primarily managers and professionals, to take outside courses during working time. There is greater proliferation of postgraduate courses for engineers than for most other professionals. The National Technological University, a cooperative effort by thirty-five engineering colleges, provides postgraduate education for practicing engineers. However, continuing education for professionals is not a universal requirement. Curricula are rarely defined. And, the effectiveness of many programs is open to question.

CRITICS OF PROFESSIONAL EDUCATION

Criticism of professional education is neither new nor novel. Content of the education and the preparation of students as practitioners have been and continue to be major issues. There is agreement that education must include content derived from the best current research and learning to ensure that graduates are competent practitioners. Differences arise in assigning priorities to these two objectives. The argument for priority of content is that without appropriate content there can be no progressive practice. The learning argument is that the nature of delivery and the relationships between practitioner and client have more effect on the quality of service than mere knowledge of content. These critics claim that excessive concern with content and knowledge over learning for transfer to practice leads to counterproductive, fragmented competence and poor services.

The differences are not recent. Charlton refers to a famous physician of the sixteenth century as saying, "One had as good [sic] send a man to Oxford to learn shoemaking as practising [sic] physick" (qtd. in Hughes, 1973, p. 15). In the beginning of the twentieth century the point of attack was on the quality of the content and the competence of faculty. The recommendations focused on discontinuing use of part-time, practitioner faculty in favor of full-time, research-oriented, academic professionals. The lack of adequate research knowledge and activity on the part of the faculty was deplored. This criticism tends to appear whenever professional education moves into the university where the intellectual status of natural and social sciences is high and that of the professional schools' content is low.

Current criticism is directed toward the competence of graduates to provide effective services. Simon (1957) attempts to reconcile differences in priorities presented by "the dilemma of rigor or relevance." He proposes that synthesis should give equality to both objectives, with an edge to rigor. While only a slight moderation of the research priority, only now are some schools considering this. Schon (1992, p. 8), claims that "the crisis of confidence in professional knowledge corresponds to a similar crisis in professional education. . . . Schools are blamed for failing to teach the rudiments of effective and ethical practice. . . . Underlying . . . is a version of the rigor-or-relevance dilemma. What aspiring practitioners need most to learn, professional schools seem least able to teach."

Schon (1983) also claims that "we should start not by asking how to make better use of research-based knowledge but by asking what we can learn from a careful examination of . . . the competence by which practitioners actually handle indeterminate zones of practice" (p. 13). Introducing the concept "reflection-in-action," competence to think of relationships in the course of providing services in "indeterminate zones of practice," Schon (1983) states that "tasks of the reflective practicum are out of place in the normative curriculum of the professional schools," since the emphasis of learning in professional schools is on use of a known body of knowledge to deal with identified problems (p. 309).

While most schools recognize the need to tie theory and experience—to make learning experiential and to integrate education—the tilt is still toward rich, fragmented content. Even in schools most concerned about practice, learning to interact effectively with the people in the work venue is neglected. The division of education into distinct content modules has advantages from the viewpoint of dispensing and accumulating knowledge and technique but serious disadvantages for use in practice. Among these disadvantages are difficulty in integrating learning for service in practice, tendency to overemphasize instrumental tasks over expressive tasks, and inapplicability of experiential approaches (Hoberman and Mailick, 1992).

Smith (1990) contends that educational policy in American institutions of higher learning teaches conformity to professional dogmas and worthless research and deemphasizes teaching.

Some want schools to help students acquire wisdom, intuition, etc. Whitehead (1955) states that "the proper function of a university is the imaginative acquisition of knowledge. . . . Imagination is a contagious disease. It cannot be . . . delivered to the students by members of the faculty. It can only be communicated by a faculty whose members themselves wear their learning with imagination" (p. 101). This prescription for preparing professionals to continue to learn and to cope with new circumstances calls for a faculty of concerned, creative mentors rather than of dispensers of knowledge and technique.

Although society bears a major cost burden for their education, fewer and fewer professionals feel an obligation to make a contribution to the welfare of society or to the community—and, in particular, to the poor and underprivileged. Criticism of professional schools is that they are not effective in countering this tendency. Professional societies, not infrequently, discourage voluntary contributions. Schools have introduced courses in ethics, but their effectiveness is questionable.

One might expect that there would be public pressure to focus education on meeting society's needs. However, because society has so many needs and is so poorly informed about which needs would be served by change, society has no influence. One school of critics, mostly in the man-made field, want schools to give greater emphasis to developing socially engaged citizens and to accepting the responsibility for moral education. These critics feel that research should be directed toward resolving such social ills as poverty. According to these critics, emphasis should move from the new to designing the better, less costly, and more useful (Bok, 1990).

We conclude with a table showing the current requirements for entry into representative professions.

Table 1
Education and Certification for Professional Standing

Profession	1	2	3*	4	5	6	7	8	9
Accounting	Y	Y	N	‡	Y	N	N	Y	N
Clerical Profession	Y	Y	N	††	††	N	Y	††	††
Engineering	Y	Y	N	‡	Y	Y	N	Y	N
Law	N	Y	Y	Y	Y	N	N	†	†
Management	Y	Y	N	N	N	N	Y	†	†
Medicine	N	Y	Y	Y	Y	N	N	†	†
Social Work	Y	Y	Y	Y	Y	N	N	†	†
Teaching (Secondary)	Y	Y	N	?	N	Y	N	N	N

Y Yes   N No.

1. Special baccalaureate degree program in professional area.
2. Special advanced degree program in professional area.
3. Advanced degree necessary for recognition as a professional.
   (*It is possible to achieve professional status in virtually every field by substitution of experience and independent study for formal education. However, the requirements are usually very stiff and few meet them.)
4. Certification by government or professional organization.
5. Special experience or advanced degree necessary for certification.
6. Baccalaureate necessary and sufficient to practice as professional.
7. No degree necessary to practice as a professional.
8. Extensive use of synthetic experiential learning.
9. Extensive use of some forms of natural experiential learning.
   (†Discussed in detail in chapters dealing with specific professions.)
   (‡State certification is required to be able to "certify" to the correctness or safety of specific services, records, findings, plans, etc.)
   (††Certification and special experience set by the denomination.)

CONCLUSIONS

Fields of professional education have common characteristics. In addition to preparing students to apply in practice a specialized content area, these characteristics include both social and professional objectives, faculty tilted toward theory and research, content based on theory and research from more academic and research-oriented disciplines, an independent school within the university family, high cost of tuition, limited admission, postbaccalaureate education, and a time-consuming course of study.

The increasing complexity and specialization in professions and the increase in the number of professions have introduced numerous structural problems in providing services. The most difficult interdisciplinary issues, particularly those involving interdependent services from different professions and specializations within a profession, are not considered in the professional schools. This makes issues and related problems virtually unsolvable in practice. Frequently issues are indefinable to the satisfaction of the different stakeholders. A related criticism is that professional education does not prepare students to develop and maintain productive relationships with clients and co-workers in the performance of professional tasks.

While the underlying problem in professional education for the service professions is succinctly put as the "rigor-or-relevance" dilemma, the actuality is much more complex and involves many other issues.

3
SOME LEARNING THEORY

The brief presentation of learning theory in this chapter is designed to provide a basis for the analysis of professional education. In its details the views are those of the editors and not those of the other contributors. However, all of us discuss the need to develop and conduct more effective, experiential educational programs to prepare students to practice their professions. Discussion focuses on, but is not limited to, educational objectives and content and the learning process. Other issues include faculty, student body, environmental forces, and assessment of professional education.

From elementary school through professional school, the role of the school as seen by most faculty members is to provide opportunities for neophytes to absorb information and gain competencies from interactions with the teacher. The major educational approaches employed in academies, colleges, and universities for more than two thousand years have been primarily lecture, seminar, Socratic questioning, discussion, and reading, that is, a variety of "talk" techniques for transmission of knowledge. When professional education left the workplace and discarded the older apprenticeship approach (Smythe, 1990) to enter the professional school, this view of learning in large part superseded learning through practice. Emphasis moved from learning by doing and contemplation of activity and consequence to "pure" thought and from practice and analysis of practice under the tutelage of competent clinicians to learning theory and techniques, primarily symbolic action and abstract analysis from lectures by knowledgeable researchers.

For the purpose of analysis, we categorize learning approaches as either passive or experiential. The definitions and applications are not without ambiguity. With this caveat, we define passive learning as learning activities that do not require participants to gather data, interact with others, respond to changing circumstances, implement decisions, or deal with the consequences; and we define experiential learning as including those activities omitted in passive learning. Passive approaches include discussion, lecture, reading, case analysis, and exercises. Experiential learning includes role-playing, simulation—and, above all, real experience.

GENERAL THEORY

The theories relating to learning, motivation for learning, learning styles, and transfer of learning are redundant and occasionally contradictory, with little empirical evidence to support any. While such evidence would be useful, the issue is, for practical purposes, irrelevant. We are interested in whether the theory is useful for designing and conducting education for service professionals. A theory is useful if it helps us to understand relations and to anticipate consequences. A theory not useful in one situation may be useful in another. The terms *theory* and *model* are sometimes used interchangeably. We distinguish between them. A *model* is a specific representation of the general relations expressed in a *theory*.

That theories and models may not be "true" and still useful is troubling to many. This doubt can be dispelled by consideration of different kinds of maps for the same geographic area. No one is a "true" representation. Yet each may provide useful information. In general, theory tends to simplify complex relations by removing from consideration variables and relations considered to be of lesser concern or too ambiguous, in order to permit focusing on the variables and relations of topical interest.

Simplification can make it easier to define and understand relations among selected variables; help increase accuracy and usefulness of predictions; and, as a result, provide the basis for design and implementation of activities to reach an objective.

It has been observed that theory is the reality generally accepted in our culture. Theory is necessary for practice and learning. However, theories are dangerous if used as if they were literally true. Symbols are not real things. A theory is a figment of the imagination—representing, at best, a partial explanation. Models are a further simplification. Research, in the service disciplines, most often relates to models. Consequently, in practice based on research, it is desirable to heed Kaplan (1964): "Seek simplicity and distrust [it]" (p. 318).

SOME LEARNING THEORY

Our educational theory is derived from those of John Dewey and Kurt Lewin. Dewey (1910, 1974) saw experience as the organizing force for all learning and hypothesized that learning is most effective when it is self-directed, guided by theory and tied to experience. Experiential learning (1974) results from identifying relationships between cause and effect, between action and personal consequences of the action. Dewey emphasized learning as an integrated lifelong process rather than a set of isolated, unconnected occurrences. He postulated a three-phase learning process in which experience is followed by reflection, in order to review and generalize from the synthesis of theory and experience, and is concluded by a new generalization to be tested in practice. This leads to a new cycle of learning.

Lewin (1951) assumed that learning is a function of the person's life bank and of the learning venue. In the Lewin model, learning takes place when experience is analyzed to validate or change theory. In the process, new insight is gained. Learning comes from observation, feedback, and reflection. A five-element cycle is posited. The stages are abstraction, concrete implication, experience, observation-feedback, and reflection. Reflection leads to reinforced learned behavior and to new or higher level abstraction. Lewin hypothesized that learning requires going through the entire cycle. We assume that the cycle can start at any stage, with learning taking place at each stage. Each stage picks up from the preceding one.

We assume two principal learning sequences. The elements of the first are the need to respond to a specific situation; this triggers a life-bank search for an appropriate model to guide action; identification and adaptation of existing models and creation of new models; selection of the model to use; use of a model; and analysis and reflection of use and consequence. The sequence is concluded by incorporation of new elements of learning in the life bank. The second sequence originates from feedback from an activity or from observation of an activity. This is followed by analysis and reflection on what took place, that is, the event is compared with existing life-bank models. If no model fits, the data are organized using existing theory (in rare cases new theory may be needed). The final steps are to induct new elements—for example, theory and models that explain the observed relationships, particularly those between action and consequences—and integrate them into the life bank.

The latter model is useful for both passive and experiential learning. Learning approaches can also be usefully analyzed in the context of the

Lewin three-stage model for change: unfreeze, move (i.e., change), re-freeze. The three stages can be used to define objectives and assessment for educational programs. Little professional education is concerned with "unfreezing." This is an error. Students' life banks determine how problems are framed and attacked. Their life banks contain significant knowledge and experience regarding professional services and relation-ships with others but are not as rich as those of the faculty regarding the special theory, research, and competencies of the profession. Little in professional learning takes cognizance of the students' life banks. Most education and training focus on the "move"—that is, change—stage. The problems are defined and framed for students and the "answers" provided. It is assumed that there will be uncritical acceptance of specific techniques and approaches taught by the faculty and that tests will fix these in the students' life banks.

MOTIVATION TO LEARN

There are intrinsic and extrinsic motivators for learning. In the service professions intrinsic motivators are assumed to include the desire to change and use learning, the desire to help people, and anticipated pleasure from practice. Extrinsic motivators include expected financial benefits and status.

Skinner (1971) provides a theoretical base for the use of rewards to learn, move, and refreeze behavior. Skinner's arguments and conclusions have been strongly attacked by educational and human relations theorists such as Argyris (1964). Argyris argues that

- emphasis on reinforcement leads to conditioned responses and not to learning stemming from reflection about action and consequences;
- rewards that educators consider to be "motivators" may not motivate students to learn;
- learning motivated by a reward may not be used in practice;
- unless the expected reinforcement is provided when expected, the student may change behavior inappropriately.

Since such rewards as grades, scholarships, awards, and special recogni-tion are primary motivators in professional schools, the consequences hypothesized by Argyris may be a matter of concern.

We assume that professional students' motivation is increased if

- the learning can be used during or soon after the learning takes place,

- the learning results from integration of theory and classroom activities with clinical practice,
- the practice is in a work venue under conditions similar to those faced by practicing professionals.

INDIVIDUAL LEARNING STYLES

People learn in many ways. The same person may learn in different ways under different circumstances. In addition to the life-bank characteristic, variables affecting learning style include learning venue, approach, and content; other variables involve age (Knowles, 1980) and occupation (Kolb, 1984).

We do not believe that the differences in learning styles are direct functions of age or occupation but of related variables, content and richness of the learner's life bank. Young people respond to different motivators because there is little in their life banks to conflict with what is being taught.

Some theorists assume more detailed analytic models of learning styles that can be easily employed effectively in group educational programs. However, the possible relation between learning style and professional occupation is of interest in mentoring. Kolb (1984) defines two learning dimensions—abstract/concrete and active/reflective—and four learning styles derived from these. The following is a summary of his conclusions.

- Abstract conceptualizing and active experimenting characterizes "convergent" learners. These are common among technical and engineering occupations.
- Concrete-experience and reflective-observation types are characteristics of "divergent" learners, social workers, and personnel workers.
- Abstract conceptualization and reflective observation are "assimilation" types, common in information and research occupations.
- Concrete experience and active experimentation are "accommodating" types common in management.

We assume, along with other cognitive theorists, that motivation and ability to frame and solve problems is in part a function of the venue in which the need arises. We go further to assume that transfer of learning is a function of the relation between the learning and use venues. From this it follows that not all experiential learning is of equal value for transfer to a specific use venue.

LEARNING APPROACHES

Passive approaches can be more effective for increasing knowledge and skills that do not involve action or relationships with others. Passive learning assumes that students are motivated to acquire knowledge and to use the knowledge in practice. The basic assumption of passive professional education is that language can express reality adequately enough to motivate and guide practice. This is questionable. Much of professional education is training students to recognize recurring situations and employ standardized techniques. Acceptance of, and stress on, common answers rather than the unique characteristics of clients and service tends to make passive learning the approach of choice.

In experiential learning the student is physically engaged in a professional activity with real consequences. We assume that living through and reflecting on the action and consequences leads to more effective learning and transfer of learning to future practice. There are two types of experiential learning: synthetic and natural. Synthetic experiential learning takes place in special learning venues constructed for the purpose of providing the learning opportunity—for example, moot courts in legal education and dissection in medical education. The experience as well as the venue tends to be focused on providing learning opportunities, increasing specific competencies, giving insight into defined relationships, and providing experience in using cognitive learning in a behavioral context.

The "practicum" proposed by Schon (1992) "seeks to represent essential features of a practice to be learned while enabling students to experiment at low risk, vary the pace and focus of work, and go back to do things over when it seems useful to do so" (p. 179). He warns against "striving for realism [that] overloads students with practical constraints." However, the absence of risk and the concern with consequences makes this a form of synthetic experiential learning. Schon's caution points to a basic difference between synthetic and natural experiential learning. Schon's analysis can be used as an argument for competent mentors' helping students deal with the practical constraints rather than as an argument against using natural experiential learning.

Natural experiential learning makes use of naturally occurring situations and problems in an actual work venue. The experience may be a special or a normal work assignment. Students are subject to the totality of variables and uncertainties of that venue. Feedback is focused on real performance and is individualized. Contemporaneous self-assessment and teacher feedback provide the information for decision making, action, and reflection. Supervised casework in social work and internship in medicine are examples.

In the context of our broad definition of venue as the total, encompassing environment, learning is gained in interactions between the learner and the learning venue, from the interplay between internal (learner) and external (venue) forces. Increased competence is also gained by practice in performance and reflection before, during, and after the action.

Raw, unreflected, experience is not assumed to be transferable learning. It is insufficient for generalizing. At best, it is a basis for "common sense" learning, the knowledge that action A in situation B led to result C. This provides the motivation and competence to take action A the next time a situation B arises, if C is desired.

The critical phase in the learning cycle is transfer, the application of learning in practice. While every learning approach can be useful, we and many theorists believe that natural experiential learning is more effective than other learning for transfer of learning to the use venue.

A key variable affecting transfer of learning is "time." There are different times: time spent in acquiring the learning; time between learning and use; and, in experiential learning, the time between action and reflection upon consequences. Students who wish to become practicing professionals tend to be impatient with time spent on learning. They want learning to be efficient, concentrated, useful; and they want it to lead to increased competence in short order. Natural experiential learning is effective for all of these objectives, except acquiring learning rapidly. Natural experiential learning is a difficult approach to use when an objective is to reduce time spent on professional education. However, failure to employ experiential approaches has led to continuing basic professional education after graduation. In medicine, the traditional solution is to mandate internship and residency after graduation. In law it is a probationary period of careful supervision and assignment. Synthetic experiential learning approaches can, by focusing attention and speeding up consequences, reduce and eliminate time intervals. Passive-learning techniques ignore time conditions.

A second, possibly more intractable, problem affecting extensive use of natural experiential approaches is faculty competence and motivation. Faculty members play different and more difficult roles in experiential education than in passive learning. They have to serve as coaches, role models, and mentors. They have to assess and provide feedback on students' use of learning in a manner designed to motivate and challenge students to reflect on the use of learning and the outcome of the use. Their focus has to be on helping students to transfer learning to the work venue and to learn from experience, avoiding what Whitehead has labeled the "grooves of professional thought." The competencies for these roles are not usually considered in selection and promotion of faculty.

FEEDBACK

Feedback from use of learning is important in all learning approaches. It is critical in experiential learning. It provides information for reflection and analysis, for improving competencies, and for structuring independent study. Faculty can obtain information about the efficacy of the learning process.

Knowles (1987) advocates use of a learning contract to formalize feedback. The contract's terms structure feedback and assessing learning. The contract is a learning plan, to which the student and the instructor agree. A typical contract defines objectives; a plan to achieve these objectives; and evidence, criteria, and standards to assess achievement. The process is the basis for self-assessment and discussions with the mentor. It can be used effectively with all learning approaches. To some extent, doctoral research is a contract approach.

There are levels of feedback. At the first level, it is information about goal attainment, competence, and performance. At the second level, it is information about the validity and usefulness of the feedback process—that is, reflection—and the criteria and standards for assessment. Both of these could be used to great effect in professional education. At best, only the first is used consistently.

LIFELONG LEARNING

Unused learning can be rapidly lost. Change in theory and practice in all occupations is increasing more and more rapidly. Tasks change; and even when they don't, new technologies and conditions can make competencies obsolete a few years after graduation from professional school.

Some occupations become obsolete. This doesn't happen in the professions. Professions do not become obsolete, but professionals can. Unless professionals are attuned to change, they may find themselves performing tasks of paraprofessionals.

Many professionals are self-motivated to continue learning. However, becoming strongly motivated and competent in lifelong independent learning is difficult. Few are able, and sufficiently motivated, to design and implement plans for themselves without extensive training and external incentives.

In addition to motivation for continuing effort, professionals must add to their life banks competencies to seek, process, and integrate new learning; systematically reflect on experience; and practice deducing courses of action from general theory and inducting general theory from experience.

These are some of the competencies needed for both passive and experiential independent learning. However, acquiring these competencies is not easy. A major problem is that education is guided from first grade to passage of licensing examination. Practitioners are not encouraged by clients to engage in experiential learning. Practitioners and clients want treatment to be the same as that which in the past led to satisfactory results. For independent experiential learning, practitioners must be willing to try a new treatment and reflect on the consequences in order to assess whether this is superior to past results. Continued learning tends to be passive. Practitioners are not researchers by schooling, by their own instincts, by clients' wishes, and by society's rules. Reasonably successful behavior is changed reluctantly. This is not conducive to independent experiential learning. The research point of view could be most valuable; natural experiential learning is a form of operational research. However, research methodology is rarely taught with the objective of helping students acquire lifelong learning skills. Where continued learning is mandated, it tends to be passive. Frequently it is through reading and self-administered tests. While faculty members agree that continued learning is highly desirable, few schools are active in developing and conducting programs. Professional societies provide some learning opportunities.

RESEARCH ON LEARNING

There is research literature relating to assessment of primary and secondary education and on the effect of training programs. We found no significant empirical studies of the effectiveness of professional education. Berryman (1987) questions the utility and effectiveness of school education for practice. She states that the research literature relating to issues of education, training, and employment does not support assumptions of positive correlations between educational processes and objectives. Our search leads us to question the value of the research and assessment literature for professional education.

It is not easy to determine exactly what is gained from professional education that is used in practice. It is difficult to assess education and relate it to practice without well-defined objectives and reliable and valid processes for gathering and analyzing the data. Research involving matched control and experimental groups is not feasible. Consequently, our support for assumptions about the value of an educational approach depends on case experience and reflection. Each of the contributors has had extensive experience in the use of experiential natural education.

4
FOUR PROFESSIONS

SOME COMMONALITIES AND DIFFERENCES

The four professions selected for analysis—medicine, law, social work, and management—fall into the categories man-made, soft, and service. The performance of practitioners depends to a great degree on the quality of interpersonal relationships. Practitioners have a continuing responsibility to individual clients as well as to society. To a greater extent than members of other professions, members of these professions have to contend with ambiguity, uncertainty, uniqueness, absence of universal rules, and incommensurable and multidimensional value systems. It is not effective in these professions to base decisions on universal, consistent sets of objectives and principles.

Each has roots in a research-oriented discipline. Medicine in part depends on knowledge developed in the "natural" sciences of biology and chemistry. Law is based on jurisprudence, history, and a form of logic. Social work stems from religion, psychology, and social psychology. Management in the private sector stems from economics and social psychology. In the public sector political science served as the primary base. However, it now draws on a number of fields, including the same disciplines as business management.

Perhaps the major commonality is the growth in the number of graduates from professional schools. For example, the number of M.D. degrees granted increased from 5,612 in 1949–1950 to 15,115 in 1989–1990, an increase of 169 percent; and the number of law degrees increased from 8,262 in 1955–1956 to 36,437 in 1989–1990, an increase of 341 percent. The increase in the number of Master of Business Administration (M.B.A.) degrees has in some periods been even greater. Social work and public administration degrees have had periods of rapid increase and periods of no increase. However, in all professions the number of degrees granted have been far in excess of the increase in the population. The greatest absolute and percentage increase has been in women with professional degrees. The number in medicine has increased in the same period from 584 to 5,138, 780 percent. In law, the number went from 288 to 15,378, an increase of 5,240 percent! While the number of schools also increased—medicine from 72 to 124, 72 percent; law from 131 to 182, 39 percent—it in no way compares with the number of graduates (National Center for Educational Statistics, 1993a, p. 88). The increased burden on facility members and education is obvious.

In most states, licenses are required for the practice of medicine, law, and social work. There are powerful professional associations in law and medicine and an influential association in social work. These associations exercise significant influence on standards for education and entry to the profession. Management differs. No license is required, and there is no strong association or fixed standards. The professional societies have minor influence in the public sector and less in the private sector.

The four professions differ in their use of natural experiential education. In medicine, there is extensive use of clinical education. However, the venue differs from that in which most will practice. The learning is in a hospital, many patients are poor and dependent, and almost all have serious ailments. Experiential education is used on a voluntary basis in legal education. There are a variety of venues. However, most provide service to persons who have difficulty in gaining access to legal representation. In social work, natural experiential education is the primary approach. Graduates not infrequently go to work for the agencies that provided the learning experience. There is little natural experiential education in management curricula in the United States.

While there are distinct specialties in each of these professions, only two provide specialized education. There is special undergraduate management education in such areas as accounting, marketing, and finance. In medicine there is an elaborate program in graduate medical education. There is some specialization in the second year of social work education.

MEDICINE

"The University of Salerno in Italy, the earliest of European universities, was devoted to medicine" (Whitehead, 1955, p. 96). Schools of medicine were among the first professional schools in every country. Very early the medical schools were research as well as educational centers. This may be one reason for their prestige.

American medical education has had three phases. During the colonial period the treatment site was the primary educational venue. There was greater dependence on schools in the nineteenth century. A few states had licensing laws. There were few requirements for entry to study. Courses of study were short, and "many entered practice without having completed the formal training period" (Thorne, 1973, p. 20). Even in the latter half of the century entry to many medical schools did not require preliminary education. The American Medical Association was a force for increasing requirements for entry to schools and for licensing to practice.

In the post–World War I period discontent with medical education led to the 1922 Flexner study. The recommendations were widely adopted and provide the basis of current medical education.

Despite its high status, medical practitioners throughout history have admitted to uncertainty in practice. Thomas (1987) states that we do not know enough; and faced by many illnesses that we do not understand, we are unable to do much beyond trying to make the right diagnosis.

LEGAL EDUCATION

American legal education prior to the middle of the nineteenth century was a form of apprenticeship in which students "read for the law" under a practicing lawyer. As the practice became more demanding and the number of lawyers increased and more British legal texts became available, "lecture" schools associated with "master" practitioners arose to provide more theory-based education to complement on-the-job learning.

Stronger academically oriented schools drove the "practitioner schools out of business." The schools' educational approach consisted mostly of independent reading, lectures, discussion, and examinations. Dissatisfaction with the passivity of the approach led to some change. The formal case study and the moot court were introduced and widely copied. Clerkship after graduation and prior to admission to the bar was provided. While medical education has been to a great extent standardized, in law there are differences between approaches of the "national" and "practitioner" schools. The former emphasize theory and philosophy of law and appellate decisions. The latter emphasize the practice of local law. Since the 1970s there has been interest in clinical education. By 1976, almost 90 percent of the law schools in the United States approved by the American Bar Association provided some aspects of voluntary clinical programs (Gartner, 1976).

There are "cram" schools in many professions to prepare graduates to pass state licensing examinations. But in none are they as widely employed as in the law. Thorne (1973) notes that "the cram course, a marginal and highly expedient enterprise, has long filled the gap between law school training and the content of state bar examinations" (p. 142).

SOCIAL WORK

Social work is a young profession. Recognition as a profession leading to formal professional education dates to the post–World War I period. Neither the field nor the required professional competencies are well defined. In large part this results from rapidly changing social, political, and economic conditions that determine social work's goals, programs, and technology, as well as from efforts to enlarge the domain of the profession.

Income, status, and independence of practitioners affect recruitment. Because most practitioners are employed by either government or non-profit agencies, salaries tend to be among the lowest of professions. Social service policies are set, for the most part, by employers, thus limiting practitioners' independence. Since the status of service professionals is a function of perceived income and status of clients, status of social workers is low. Fortunately for society, most social work candidates are highly motivated by strong social service drives. This tends to negate the disadvantages of the profession. Social work is the only profession in which natural experiential education is the primary learning approach in professional schools.

MANAGEMENT

Graduate programs in business administration developed in schools with baccalaureate programs in such specialty areas as accounting, marketing, and finance. The curriculum for the M.B.A. degree adds material from economics, statistics, and social psychology. Education for the public service has a long history. "In England, at Cambridge, in the year 1316, a college was founded for the special purpose of providing 'clerks for the King's service' " (Whitehead, 1955, p. 96). However, the Master of Public Administration (M.P.A.) degree is a twentieth-century development. At the outset, the M.P.A. was based on political science with courses in practitioner areas such as personnel administration. The content now is closer to that in the schools of business administration. There is difference in the status of the degrees. The M.B.A. is seen as superior to the M.P.A. In part this stems from the higher status and salaries of business management.

Except for a few programs that use cooperative-education programs in such areas as financial analysis and cost accounting, business and public administration education employ little natural experiential education (Brown and Wilson, 1978). For educational purposes, the few programs for practicing managers do not seem to make significant use of students' current experience.

5
ISSUES

Issues relating to professional education fall roughly into a dozen or so categories. Some have been indicated in the preceding chapters. Some are of great importance. Others are marginal. Issues are not of the same importance in every profession. Consequently, the issues discussed will vary according to profession. However, each author will consider the question, How well does professional education help students acquire the competencies needed to practice the profession? Although all the categories listed below are important, we have chosen to focus on two crucial elements that the educational approach employed and the content of the education.

Other categories of issues that are discussed are

- objectives of the professional school
- the nature of the profession and its status
- specialization
- paraprofessionals
- school administration
- faculty members
- students
- certification

- interpersonal relationships
- environmental forces
- assessment of professional education

EDUCATIONAL APPROACHES

We identify three educational approaches: passive learning, synthetic experiential learning, and natural experiential learning. In addition, relationships between the learning and use venues are considered. The importance of this relationship is emphasized by critics of professional education in every field. Thus, Thorne (1973) quotes with evident approval the statement by Eliot Freidson that "education is a less important variable than work environment. There is some very persuasive evidence that 'socialization' does not explain some important elements of professional performance half so well as does the organization of the immediate work environment" (p. 99).

What approaches should be used in professional education? Passive learning is most efficient and effective for the acquisition of knowledge; synthetic experiential learning, for gaining technical competencies; natural experiential learning, for transition of learning to practice.

To what extent should education be "holistic" and to what extent "modular," with well-defined courses in each discipline? The holistic approach is usually more effective for transfer to practice. The modular approach is more effective for the recruitment of outstanding faculty members in important specialities and for the transfer of knowledge and technical learning.

How are the objectives of the transmission and transfer of learning to be balanced in the learning approaches?

CONTENT OF PROFESSIONAL EDUCATION

Content is what the student is expected to learn by attending the professional school. How should content be determined? Are there useful models, criteria, and standards? Should the emphasis be on research findings and the conduct of research or on preparation for professional practice? Should focus be on general or specialized competencies? Should the content be based on the competency of students? What content should be left to postgraduate education and experience?

OBJECTIVES

There are many populations that have a stake in the nature and quality of professional education. These populations include the society that supports professional education, the faculty members of the school, the students, the members of the profession, the providers of related services, the university, and above all the population served by the profession. Each of these populations has different objectives. How do these relate to the objectives of professional education and practitioners? Is the primary objective helping students to acquire competency in providing needed services to special populations or to all populations in need of services, or helping students to contribute to improving techniques and adding to knowledge derived from systematic, scientific research, or helping students to obtain entrance to a restricted occupation?

Universities have traditionally been, and are expected to be, research centers. How does the objective of preparing practitioners relate to the research activity? What are the priorities? This is a major point of controversy. How does it affect education for practitioners?

THE PROFESSION

The nature and status of a profession and its perceived importance for the people served and for society as a whole influence the willingness of society to invest in education for the professional and affect the ability of schools to recruit students and faculty members and obtain financial and other support. How, in turn, do education and research activities of professional schools affect the status of the profession? How do activities of practitioners and professional organizations affect education? What is the role of the schools in advancing the status of the profession and inculcating and policing "proper professional practice and behavior"?

SPECIALIZATION

As information and technologies increase and demands for services grow, it becomes very difficult for professionals to be expert in every task performed in their field. One consequence is specialization, that is, becoming expert in a distinct area, with defined tasks requiring special knowledge and technologies for satisfactory services. Specialization is a characteristic of every profession. How should specialization be defined? Should it be a role of the professional schools? Is preparing specialists a responsibility of professional schools? How should preparing specialists affect professional education and practice?

PARAPROFESSIONAL OCCUPATIONS

Growth in a profession involves not only developing new tasks, knowledge, and technologies, but also involves routinizing older tasks and separating competencies needed to perform tasks into the simpler and more complex and difficult. Another aspect of specialization is the assembling of sets of the more routine and simple competencies as well as those that must be performed under direct supervision, in order to create a new, lower level occupation. This is a continuing process. The new occupations have been classified as paraprofessional. Sometime the tasks assigned to a paraprofessional occupation increase in complexity and difficulty until that occupation becomes its own profession. One example is nursing. What should the role of the professional school for the parent profession be in defining the role of paraprofessionals and in educating them?

ADMINISTRATION OF PROFESSIONAL SCHOOLS

Universities are in a general way responsible for setting objectives, helping to obtain the necessary input, and monitoring college outputs. How do these activities affect education? How can college administration help improve the quality of education and the competency of graduates?

Administrators and faculty members maintain relationships with their counterparts in other branches of the university. Should there be an ongoing, systematic interchange of knowledge and faculty members that would make a university more than a collection of colleges? Would fostering such relationships be a proper role for the professional school?

THE FACULTY

The faculty is more than a professional elite, it is the repository of knowledge, technology, and tradition. But it is also—and of equal importance—the role model for good professional behavior. It is responsible for developing and selecting its own successors. What should be the criteria for selection of faculty members? What should the powers and responsibilities of faculty members be?

STUDENTS

What is the relation between selection criteria for entry and those for determining educational content and standards? Does selection pick the candidates who are most likely to become competent practitioners or who may help advance learning and technology? What is the effect on professional education of admission criteria that emphasize undergraduate performance, equality for minorities and women, potential to contribute to society, and ability to pay for education? Should professional schools influence undergraduate education?

CERTIFICATION AS A PROFESSIONAL

Professional societies have to a large extent been able to control the governmental certification process, including criteria and standards. How do their influence and the certification process affect professional education? What role should professional schools play in certification? Should they prepare students to pass certification tests? Should the ability of graduates to be certified be a measure of a school's education? There are efforts to develop examinations leading to national certification of some professionals (Ravitch, 1990). Is this desirable, and what would the effect be?

Continuing education and periodic testing for competency is a requirement in some professions in many states. What should the role of the schools be? Should these schools be required for all professions? How would this affect professional education?

INTERPERSONAL RELATIONSHIPS

Every service profession involves developing and maintaining effective relationships with the people served; working with consultants and specialists in their own profession, with persons in other professions, and with nonprofessionals; supervising paraprofessionals; and serving as team members and "case managers" who coordinate the activities of others. A profession that is dominant in one setting may be support in another. Sometimes the same person may be in these two roles. These relationships call for knowledge of the objectives and domains of others, sensitivity to their values and possible value conflicts, and the ability to resolve conflict and deal with uncertainty and ambiguity. Critics of professional schools claim that they do not address these concerns realistically or effectively. Schon (1992) doubts whether schools, in their normal classroom, teacher/student approach can help students acquire the competencies. Is it a responsibility of the schools? Could they help students learn? How could trying to provide the learning affect professional education?

ENVIRONMENTAL FORCES

The forces in the environment determine a system's input and the acceptance of its output. These forces influence the resources available, the nature of the student body and faculty, which graduates are accepted as qualified professionals, and even which school will continue as a viable institution. Practitioners also have to know and be able to deal with forces in the environment where they will practice. Are schools responsive to these forces? How should the environment affect professional education?

ASSESSMENT OF PROFESSIONAL EDUCATION

There have been many assessments of professional education. Some assessments—for example, the Flexner study on medical education—have had a radical effect on the nature of education for a profession. However, there are no significant empirical evaluations of professional education in any area. There are many technical reasons, not lack of interest, for this. Are reliable and valid empirical evaluations possible? How important are reliable, valid assessments? What kind of assessments are needed?

These are some of the major issues that should be addressed in any analysis of professional education that is directed toward making education a more efficient and effective instrument for the advancement of our society. This collection does not pretend to be definitive in any sense. It is an effort by knowledgeable, experienced, concerned educators to point to some directions for study and to present some tentative answers.

Part Two

SECTION II: MEDICAL EDUCATION

Robert H. Ebert

6

HISTORICAL PERSPECTIVES

Colonial America adopted much of English culture and manners, but it did not duplicate the rigid guild system of English medicine. William Byrd, a prominent landowner and official in colonial Virginia, writing in 1728, explained the reason as follows: "The New Proprietor [of New Jersey] inveigled many over by this tempting Account of the Country: that it was a Place free from those 3 Scourges of Mankind, Priests, Lawyers and Physicians. Nor did they tell a word of Lye, for the People were too poor to maintain these Learned Gentlemen" (Boorstin, 1958, p. 229). The citizens of colonial America were fortunate that this was so, for the draconian measures, such as bloodletting and purging, used to treat everything from stroke to childbirth fever (a severe streptococcal infection) killed more patients than were saved.

As a consequence, medicine in this country evolved in a highly informal and uniquely American way (Boorstin, 1958, pp. 209–39). Anyone could practice medicine. It was common on a plantation for the wife of the owner to become the unofficial physician to the family and those who worked on the plantation. Some lay persons became purveyors of herbal concoctions and other nostrums, while others became expert in a procedure, such as bonesetting or midwifery.

The Reverend Cotton Mather became interested in medicine as a branch of natural history and in his studies learned of the efficacy of "inoculation" as a protection against smallpox. Inoculation with the serum from a smallpox lesion taken from a patient with a mild illness was first discovered to protect against smallpox by physicians in India as early as the fifth century, but it was not until the early eighteenth century that the method was introduced in the Western world. There was a serious smallpox epidemic in Boston in 1721. At the onset Cotton Mather persuaded Dr. Boylston to inoculate against the disease. Despite considerable opposition from others in the medical profession, Boylston proceeded with inoculation, and many lives were saved. Mather even did a crude statistical study to prove the point.

Those few who were trained to be physicians were educated in an apprenticeship system. A young man at an early age would become the apprentice of an established physician and would do everything from household chores to assisting the physician on his rounds to the houses of his patients. Much of what the apprentice learned was experiential; and as the apprentice learned, he was given more and more responsibility. He was also tutored by his mentor in what little theory of medicine existed and was given books to read on anatomy and therapeutics. Some who had finished apprenticeship and could afford to do so traveled to Europe to complete their studies.

The colonial physician, except for one trained in Europe, was a true general practitioner, expected to do everything from bonesetting to caring for infectious disease. He delivered babies, did what little surgery was possible without anethesia, and comforted the dying patient. He made little money and was often paid in kind.

Not until the latter part of the eighteenth century was there any university education for the physician in this country. In 1765 the College of Philadelphia (renamed the University of Pennsylvania) established a professorship in the theory and practice of medicine. A similar department was formed at King's College (now Columbia University) in 1768; and in 1783 Harvard College established a chair in the theory and practice of physic.

These fledgling university departments, all of which became medical schools, did not, however, become the paradigm for American medical education. During the nineteenth century the proprietary schools dominated medical education in sheer numbers. Some had tenuous university connections that had little meaning except to attract students. The first proprietary school was established in Baltimore in 1810. It was described by Flexner (1910) as the "so-called medical department of the so-called University of Maryland" (p. 5). It is ironic that Baltimore, the future site of Johns Hopkins and Flexner's ideal medical school, should also be the home of the first proprietary school, a type of institution despised by Flexner. During the next 100 years, over 400 proprietary schools were founded in the United States, only a fraction of which survived until 1910 (Flexner, 1925).

Proprietary schools were shockingly bad. They were commercial enterprises, pure and simple, owned by one or more physicians who did the teaching and collected the fees. The teaching was often done in a proprietary hospital by lecture and occasional demonstrations. Learning was entirely passive and inferior to the apprenticeship system, which, at the very least, provided some hands-on experience. The only prerequisites for admission were the ability to read and write and pay the fees. As a rule, the course of study lasted two years with the second year often a repetition of the first. When the products of these schools began to practice medicine, it truly was "practice" for the first time. One of the benefits that the proprietary physicians derived from their method of teaching was referral of difficult medical problems from those whom they had taught.

Perhaps it is not surprising that proprietary schools should become so dominant during the nineteenth century. They were, after all, a kind of institutionalization of America's informal and unregulated practice of medicine. By midcentury the number of university-based medical schools had increased. But, even here clinical professors were usually successful practitioners. They were autonomous and had only loose university connections. Surgery came into its own after the successful introduction of surgical anesthesia in the 1840s. The practice of surgery came to dominate medical practice in those hospitals used for teaching, since there was so little else that could be done therapeutically. The principles of asepsis described by Semmelweis and antisepsis by Lister in the midnineteenth century were accepted much more slowly than anesthesia. Hospitals remained dangerous places to be cared for until the latter part of the century. Until then it was better to be cared for at home or in a small proprietary hospital because of the danger of infection.

Two systems of medical education grew side by side—one was influenced by the flowering of medical science in Europe as more and more faculty members spent some time studying in the great European clinics; the other was more influenced by one or another medical sect. Paul Starr (1982) has described the battle for turf among the various medical sects, including the homeopaths, the eclectics, the osteopaths, the physiomedicals, and the allopaths. The battle was finally joined in the latter part of the nineteenth century, when allopathic medicine, the purveyor of scientific medicine, became the undisputed mainstream American medicine. After that the other medical sects gradually lost their appeal to the public and either disappeared or became so influenced by medical science that they lost their individuality.

By the end of the nineteenth century there had been substantial improvement in the teaching of medicine in the university-based medical schools. In Boston, New York, Philadelphia, Cleveland, and Chicago, medical centers flourished. Scientific medicine was endorsed with enthusiasm by both the medical profession and the public. But it was in Baltimore that the paradigm of medical education for the next century was proclaimed with the founding of Johns Hopkins University in 1876, Johns Hopkins Hospital in 1889, and Johns Hopkins Medical School in 1893. The munificence of the Baltimore merchant, Johns Hopkins, made this possible. In this well-endowed new university and hospital, uninfluenced by entrenched physicians, it was possible to create an entirely new environment for the teaching of medical students. A stunning medical faculty was recruited, headed by men such as Osler, Welch, and Halsted, all with international reputations. Without question, by the start of the twentieth century, Johns Hopkins had become, almost overnight, the leading medical school in the nation.

The American Medical Association (AMA), founded in 1847, had a difficult time establishing itself as anything more than the advocate of allopathic medicine, one among other medical sects. By the end of the century, however, the AMA's leadership came from among the leaders of American medicine, recognized here and abroad. In 1903 the AMA's Council on Medical Education was founded (Starr, 1982). Its permanent members were distinguished professors, including Councilman from Harvard, Vaughn from the University of Michigan, Frazier from the University of Pennsylvania, Bevan from Rush Medical College (Chicago), and Witherspoon from Vanderbilt. The council immediately called for the reform of medical education to be initiated by closing the worst of the proprietary schools. However, it discovered that it could not proceed as aggressively as it would have liked, since many of the rank and file members of the AMA were graduates of these same schools.

The stage was set, however, for the next step in a drama that was to culminate in the famous Bulletin No. 4 of the Carnegie Foundation, published in 1910, the so-called Flexner Report (Flexner, 1910). Members of the Council on Medical Education found a willing ally in Henry S. Prichett, who had resigned as president of the Massachusetts Institute of Technology to become the president of the Carnegie Foundation. Prichett had decided that a study needed to be done on the status of the American university. He was easily persuaded that a good place to start would be with medical education. To the surprise of some, Prichett chose Abraham Flexner to do the job. Abraham Flexner's brother Simon, president of the

Rockefeller Institute, a physician and distinguished scientist, would have seemed a more logical choice. But, it was Abraham the schoolmaster who was recommended as the ideal person by those who knew him, including President Eliot of Harvard.

Abraham Flexner was a graduate of Johns Hopkins University, a classics scholar who became the headmaster of a private preparatory school in Louisville, Kentucky. Graduates of his school who went to Harvard College did well. It was in this way that Flexner came to the attention of President Eliot. They became good friends, and Eliot often advised Flexner as to his future career. Although Eliot had great respect for Flexner's quality of mind, Eliot felt that it could be expanded by a trip abroad. He advised Flexner to take a sabbatical in Europe. Flexner accepted the advice. In the course of his visits to European universities, he observed the high level of German academic medicine with its university base. He was persuaded that medical education must have its home in the university and that clinical medicine should be taught in a university hospital.

Shortly after his return from Europe, Flexner was approached by Prichett and asked to review the status of American medical education. Abraham Flexner at first demurred, thinking that he was being confused with his brother Simon; but he warmed to the idea when he realized this was a serious offer.

Unlike the commissions that have reviewed medical education in the recent past, Flexner worked without a committee or large staff. He personally visited all 155 medical schools in the United States and Canada and wrote a brief critique on each, which included comments about the quality of the faculty, the adequacy of the facilities, the university affiliation (if any), and an overall impression of the quality of the medical education provided. When Flexner's report was published in 1910, it created a sensation because of its devastating attack on the nation's medical schools. Flexner called for the closing of all proprietary schools. Even prestigious medical schools, Harvard among them, did not go unscathed. Hopkins and Michigan were among the very few that were praised.

Probably no other report, public or private, has had such a profound effect on professional education as the one written by Abraham Flexner. One by one the proprietary schools closed; new state licensing laws were written, often with specific educational requirements. Even university-based medical schools adopted many of the recommended reforms.

Not everyone was happy. Flexner's life was even threatened. But the day was won. The practice of medicine would never again be casual or informal. As a consequence of the more rigorous educational requirements for entry into the medical profession, an important step was taken toward increasing the prestige of the practicing physician. With greater prestige came increased financial reward.

Since Flexner has had a profound influence on medical education in this country during much of this century, a brief description of his educational philosophy is in order. As a former schoolmaster, it is not surprising that his thinking about the reform of medical education was based to a large degree on his theories of preprofessional education. He was an admirer of John Dewey; and in the small volume *A Modern College and a Modern School* (1923), Flexner elaborated on a philosophy of education similar to Dewey's (1938).

Flexner rejected the idea that certain subjects "trained the mind" and believed that schooling should be practical. People learn best by observing and doing rather than by participating in passive teaching exercises. But experiential learning is more than experience. It must include learning to analyze and understand what has been experienced. In Flexner's view, the purpose of education at all levels was to prepare the individual for life. If a person planned to enter a profession, college should provide the educational background for that profession. The student planning to enter medical school should take courses in biology, physics, and chemistry. The prospective student of law should have a background in political science, economics and ethics. In Flexner's opinion, general education was too protracted in the United States as compared with other developed countries, delaying unnecessarily entrance into a professional school or the beginning of a business career.

Flexner's view of medical education was entirely derived from his general philosophy of education. It should be active, with little reliance on lectures. Flexner (1910) stated: "On the pedogogic side, modern medicine, like all scientific teaching, is characterized by activity. The student no longer merely watches, listens, memorizes; he *does*. His own activities in the laboratory and in the clinic are the main factors in his instruction and discipline" (p. 53).

He viewed research and teaching as inseparable because the investigator and the scientifically trained physician use the same approach to problem solving. The investigator constructs a hypothesis and tests it in the laboratory. The clinician makes a tentative diagnosis based on medical history and a physical examination, and the clinician tests the diagnosis by laboratory procedures—and, if necessary, by using a therapeutic trail.

The student should acquire a strong background in the laboratory sciences—anatomy, physiology (including the nascent science biochemistry), bacteriology, pathology, and pharmacology. These sciences should be taught in such a way as to make clear their relevance to clinical medicine. The major environment for clinical teaching should be the in-patient service, where the student assumes a supervised responsibility for the diagnosis and treatment of "his patients"—in other words, real life experience with real patients.

Flexner was of the opinion that the medical school should be an integral part of the university; in this way the education of medical students would be truly academic. He also believed that a proper medical school should have a university hospital. Whether or not the university hospital was owned and operated by the university was less important than the hospital's mission. (The university did not own Johns Hopkins Hospital.) It was his view that the primary missions of a university hospital were to teach and do research. The care of patients was vital to the fulfillment of these two missions but was entirely secondary. To fulfill these primary missions, the staff should be salaried and full time.

In 1910 very few physicians even in the best schools extended their training beyond a year of internship. Graduate medical education was of no concern to Flexner. He believed that a year of internship in a community hospital was a good preparation for practice. Internships should be unrelated to the university hopsital except for a small handful of gifted students destined for academic medicine.

Higher educational standards resulted in considerable attrition among the American medical schools that existed in 1910, and those that survived supported reform. But there were problems. By the mid-1920s medical educators complained that medical schools were being over-regulated to the detriment of medical student education. Partly as a consequence of the Flexner Report, partly because organized medicine wanted reform, state licensure boards began to define in detail what the preparation for medicine should be and what should be included in the medical school curriculum. Further regulation came from the Council on Medical Education of the AMA and from the Association of American Medical Colleges (AAMC). What was missing was a set of general principles to guide the regulators.

Responding to these complaints, the AAMC in1924 appointed a Commission on Medical Education charged with developing appropriate educational guidelines. The members of the commission were drawn from among the most distinguished university educators in the United States and Canada, including five past or present university presidents (President Lowell of Harvard chaired the commission). Both the AMA and the AAMC were represented. A full-time staff was funded by contributions from medical schools in the United States and Canada, the AMA, the

Rockefeller Foundation, the Carnegie Corporation, and the Josiah Macy, Jr. Foundation. Interim reports were made; and in 1932 a final report, *Commission on Medical Education* (1932), was published in book form. The recommendations are of particular interest because so many have been echoed in the reports of successor commissions to the present day.

The overarching principle enunciated by the commission was that medical education should be individualized to the extent feasible. It should not be a lockstep progression through a set of required courses, but should seek ways to encourage students to become self-learners, since medical school graduates would, of necessity, have to continue their education on their own for the remainder of their professional lives. Here are some of the criticisms of medical education in the immediate post-Flexner era and some of the recommendations:

- The rapid advance in scientific knowledge has resulted in an overcrowded curriculum, which in turn encourages rote memorization rather than understanding.

- Laboratory exercises in the basic sciences intended to encourage learning by doing have too often become so concerned with technical minutia that the true purpose of the experiments is obscured. The suggestions are made to do fewer experiments, to have more demonstrations by both student groups and instructors, and to spend more time synthesizing what can be learned from experimental findings.

- There should be fewer lectures, more small group teaching, and more time for independent study.

- Professors who teach on the in-patient services too often assign students to the care of patients who are very sick or have rare diseases.

- Out-patient teaching is an essential part of the education of the student, since ambulatory care more accurately reflects how physicians will spend most of their professional time. Most out-patient teaching is done by junior faculty or busy local practitioners with little interest in teaching. The commission recommended that senior clinical faculty teach in the out-patient department.

- Too little emphasis is given to the social and economic aspects of illness. Students must learn how the patient's environment can influence the outcome of medical care.

- Specialized knowledge encourages students to think of illness in terms of deranged organ systems. Students must learn to treat patients, not diseases.

- Thirty-five percent of medical graduates become specialists—often self-styled. There needs to be better accreditation of specialists in order to protect the public.

Few could argue with the wisdom of the criticisms and recommendations of the commission, yet very little happened to change the pattern of medical education between 1932 and 1946. The curriculum remained crowded. Students continued to memorize too much. There were too many lectures and too few small-group opportunities to learn. Teaching on the hospital wards more often than not reflected the clinical interests of the faculty rather than the needs of students. Out-patient teaching was looked down upon by both faculty members and students, and assignment to teach in the out-patient department was considered as exile to Siberia by any faculty members other than the most junior. Clearly, there were problems with both synthetic experiential learning in the laboratory as well as with natural experiential learning on the wards and in the out-patient department. Both types of experiential learning suffered from a lack of clear definition of educational goals.

During the 1920s and 1930s, there were changes in the character of the student body as proprietary schools closed. Students were better educated—a minimum of two years of college were required for admission to medical schools—and there was a preponderance of white middle-class males. Enrollment of women fell to 8 percent and remained at that level for decades. Full-time faculties were small compared to today's standards. Full-time clinical faculty members were all expected to teach, do research, and care for patients. The number of residents in the specialties of medicine was small, and most students took only one year of internship after graduation. Surgery was a hospital-based specialty, but it was common in the medical specialties to train in the private office of a well-known specialist.

Despite its defects, American medical education had come of age during the first half of the twentieth century; and by the end of World War II, it was prepared for another great transformation.

7

MEDICAL EDUCATION,
1946–1970

Scientists in Western Europe led the medical advances during the nineteenth century and the first part of the twentieth century (Major, 1954). They established the principles of organ physiology, pathology, bacteriology, and immunology that formed the early basis of modern medicine. An understanding of the etiology of infectious diseases was the essential first step toward prevention—and, eventually, treatment—of some of the worst killers of mankind. Uncontaminated drinking water and vaccination did much to control epidemic infections. Ehrlich's search for a "magic bullet" in the form of a chemical to destroy the spirochete that caused syphilis was only partially successful. But the principle of chemotherapy led to the discovery of agents capable of curing pneumonia and tuberculosis. Subsequently, the discovery that a common mold, penicillin notatum, could produce a powerful agent, penicillin, capable of killing a variety of pathogenic bacteria, led to a search for other potent antibotics.

All of this happened before and during World War II. The war was a turning point in the nation's commitment to biomedical research (Ebert, 1986). Much of what has happened to medical education and medical practice is a consequence of government decisions made at the end of World War II. The mobilization of the scientific community to build an atom bomb was used as an example of what could be done quickly if the financial resources were made available and if the scientific community was mobilized. It was reasoned by analogy that similar great advances could be made in finding the causes and cures for such major killers as cancer and heart disease. Two fateful decisions were made that have affected both medical education and medical practice. The first decision was to expand the National Institutes of Health (NIH), using a categorical disease approach. The second decision was to fund most extramural research in the nation's medical schools and universities reather than in research institutes. The first decision encouraged a disease-oriented approach to illness that tended to diminish the importance of the individual's response to illness and to further foster the view that good health is defined as the absence of disease. The second decision tied the funding of medical education to research funding for the quarter century following World War II.

The immediate post–World War II period was a time of great excitement, ferment, and change. There was a general mood of optimism in the nation; medical education shared that mood. Suddenly, there was the vision of enough money to support both new research laboratories and the young people to help man them. It was the beginning of the golden era of NIH support.

Another dramatic change occurred that was to affect the practice of medicine for the remainder of the century. Young physicians drafted into the military after internship, as well as physicians who had been in general practice, discovered that properly credentialed specialists did very well in the service. They were given higher rank, higher pay, and were assigned to better positions. The lesson was quickly learned. On discharge from military service, many physicians who had been in general practice—or had intended to enter general practice if they had not been drafted—decided to become specialists. They signed up for residency training in record numbers. Thus began a new era during which almost all medical-school graduates expected to continue clinical training for an additional three to seven years. Graduate medical education (GME) became a more important teaching activity for clinical faculty than the education of medical students.

The NIH not only provided money for research grants, it also provided liberal training grants in the subspecialties of medicine. The avowed purpose of such training grants was to prepare a new generation of clinical investigators, but it was understood that many trainees would become subspecialist practitioners. That was acceptable since those who governed the NIH believed there was a shortage of well-trained subspecialists. The best of the trainees were recruited as full-time salaried faculty. There began to be a shift in the balance between full-time and part-time faculty.

In the immediate postwar period heads of clinical departments continued to honor the tradition that full-time faculty members should teach, do research, and care for patients. Further, it was expected that a medical subspecialist should be able to teach general internal medicine. Similarly, an academic surgeon was expected to be a general surgeon first and a subspecialist second. However, the increasing complexity of subspecialty practice made this progressively more difficult. As a consequence, subspecialists discovered that they were more comfortable with teaching residents and fellows about their specialties than teaching general medicine, general surgery, or general pediatrics to medical students.

A significant shift in loyalty occurred during this period of rapidly rising research support of the nation's medical schools. Both basic science and clinical faculty members who were supported in large part on research grants felt that they owed their primary allegiance to the NIH, not to the university. They came to resent demands on their time for teaching or committee work since that was not what they were being paid to do. This was a particular problem in large research-based medical schools. Such attitudes were understandable, since faculty members receiving salary support solely or in part from the NIH were aware that the medical school did not have the "hard money" to support its entire faculty.

Despite the hazards to the teaching environment as a consequence of heavy dependence on "soft money" there was considerable interest in curriculum reform during the period 1946–1970. A new generation of academic leaders emerged in the nation's medical schools during this period, many of whom saw the need for change in the way in which medical students were educated. The impetus for reform began when deans and department chairmen occupied more dominant positions, and subspecialties were not as powerful as they were to become. The most dramatic example of reform occurred at Western Reserve University—subsequently Case Western Reserve after the merger of two neighboring universities, Case and Western Reserve. Dean Joseph Wearn saw the need for change in his medical school but was unable to implement reform until he had the opportunity, as a consequence of retirements, to replace all of the heads of the major basic science and clinical departments (Ebert, 1986). He chose only those who shared his zeal for revolutionary change. Planning began in the late 1940s, led by Professor Hale Ham, who was recruited for the job from Harvard Medical School. Wearn and Ham made a formidable team. Wearn recruited the academic leadership and raised the money from The Commonwealth Fund to launch the reform. Ham mobilized the faculty to plan the new curriculum and with remarkable skill guided a totally democratic approach to change. Both junior and senior faculty were engaged, so that when the first class began the new curriculum in 1952 no faculty member could say he or she had not been consulted. It was a masterful implementation of a strategic plan originally conceived by Wearn and his new department heads.

The new curriculum was based on these important principles:

- There should be an early introduction to patients and an emphasis on a holistic approach to care that takes into account the interaction between individuals and their environment. The choice of pregnancy as the first natural experiential approach to learning medicine was deliberate, since pregnancy and birth are normal events. This was thought to be consistent with teaching the normal function of the human body before considering the various ways in which it becomes deranged as a consequence of disease.

- There should be small group discussions of both biomedical science and patient care. Frequent meetings with faculty preceptors helped students cope with their feelings about assuming the physician role for the first time.

- There should be teaching by subject committee rather than by discipline. In other words, members of departments of physiology, anatomy, biochemistry, and internal medicine would teach jointly a subject, such as the normal kidney, but would not teach separate courses in biochemistry, physiology, etc.

- Exposure to patients would increase progressively throughout the four years and would stress continuity of care.

- Each student should be provided with a multidisciplinary laboratory, the purpose being to stress the importance of an integrated approach to biomedical knowledge.

- Students were to be treated with dignity as trusted colleagues. This was a deliberate effort to exorcise an environment of fear fostered by the previous authoritarian department chairmen.

The Western Reserve experiment in medical education received world-wide attention from medical educators. So many visitors wished to see for themselves this bold reform that a special office had to be created to manage the visits. Did it succeed? Certainly it attracted excellent faculty interested in education, and the quality of the student body improved. Students liked the curriculum, did well on National Board Examinations, and placed well in the competition for the best residencies. Parts of the curriculum were adopted by other medical schools, but none replicated the entire curriculum. Many schools, however, experimented with an earlier introduction to patients than had been traditional. Did it foster better experiential learning? The answer is a qualified yes.

The Family Clinic provided an introduction to patients in the first year. Each student was assigned to a pregnant woman early in her pregnancy and was expected to follow the woman through her pregnancy and her child after birth. The Family Clinic was administered by the Department of Pediatrics and had some enthusiastic mentors, including Dr. Benjamin Spock. The students enjoyed this early experience with patients but were often uncertain about their role, having no clinical skills. As a consequence, they performed more as social workers than as physicians. They learned about the socioeconomic problems of the poor, since most women in the program were so-called "public patients" (later, Medicaid patients). But the degree to which this influenced future understanding is more difficult to evaluate. Certainly it did not influence the choice of a specialty. The proportion of students from Case Western Reserve choosing a career in general medicine, general pediatrics, and family medicine reflects the national average.

There were two types of ambulatory-care experiences. One was a so-called continuity clinic in which students continued to follow patients seen in family clinic as well as selected patients whom they had cared for during in-patient clerkships. The latter group of patients were chosen to demonstrate the importance of continuity of care for the chronically ill. The other ambulatory-care experience was in the so-called group clinic. Here students worked up new patients and discussed diagnosis and therapy with assigned instructors. Experiential learning in this clinic was directed more to the biomedical than to the social aspects of disease and was not much different than similar clinic experience in other medical schools.

The family clinic and continuity clinic were popular with students early in their clinical experience. Both clinics attempted to emphasize the importance of the individual, but interest waned as students spent more time on in-patient services. Specialized, high-technology medicine can be enormously seductive, and interest in disease tends to displace interest in the individual during this phase of experiential learning. Attempts were made to structure in-patient experience in a way that would take into consideration all aspects of illness—social as well as biomedical—but with limited success. Of all the changes in the Case Western Reserve curriculum, the modifications of in-patient teaching were the least innovative.

Two divergent forces were at work in the nation's medical schools during this period of curriculum change. One was the force of research-based, technology-dominated specialized medical care. This was the strong force and was centered in the major teaching hospitals. The weak force was community oriented, centered in departments of community medicine, family medicine, preventive medicine, or divisions of general medicine and general pediatrics. Valiant efforts were made to encourage experiential learning in community clinics and in clinics oriented toward concern for the individual with as much attention paid to the societal as to the biomedical aspects of illness. But the weak force had difficulty in competing with the strong force for the hearts and minds of medical students. Briefly, during the social ferment of the late 1960s and early 1970s, there was heightened interest among medical students in the "community," but ultimately "big medicine" won out.

Part of the problem was money. Community-oriented medicine did not share in the NIH bonanza. University hospitals did. They grew in size and complexity as full-time staffs expanded and as new diagnostic and therapeutic technologies were introduced. Federal funds were made available for expansion of hospital research and teaching space. Many universities with medical schools and other health professions schools developed new organizational arrangements in order to manage this growing research, teaching, and patient-care establishment. Consortia were created, called Academic Medical Centers (AMCs) or Academic Health Centers (AHCs). Each of these included a medical school, one or more health professions school (such as nursing or dental medicine), at least one major teaching hospital, as well as other more loosely affiliated hospitals. These consortia were usually presided over by a vice-president or vice-chancellor, but the real power resided in the head of the university hospital who had the largest budget.

Nineteen seventy marked the end of the Golden Era of the NIH. Those who had come of age in academia after the end of World War II had come to assume that ever increasing NIH support would continue indefinitely. The 1970s brought a rude awakening. Medical school deans, professors, and junior faculty learned that the federal government was under no obligation to support medical education using research dollars. But as we shall see in the next chapter, one addiction was replaced with another. While research dollars declined as a percent of medical school support, faculty practice-plan income rose. Academic medical centers were saved financially, but at a cost.

Another change heralded the end of an era. Complaints from their constituents about difficulties in finding doctors, particularly in rural areas, caused members of Congress to wonder why there was a shortage of physicians in view of the amount of money being spent by the nation's medical schools. The Senate Labor and Welfare Committee decided that there was a shortage of 80,000 physicians, and in 1968 the first of a series of medical manpower acts was passed in an effort to increase the number of practicing physicians.

8
1970 TO THE PRESENT

In 1963 the Health Professions Educational Assistance Act (P.L. 88–129) was passed by Congress. It provided funding for medical school construction and rehabilitation as well as for loans to medical students. This was the first of a series of bills passed by Congress in the 1960s and 1970s designed to provide direct aid for medical education and the only piece of legislation that did not deal specifically with a putative shortage of physicians. The Health Manpower Act of 1968 (P.L. 90–490) and the Comprehensive Health Manpower Training Act of 1971 (P.L. 92–157) both provided financial incentives to medical schools for increasing medical school enrollment. Congress was aware that the most pressing need was for more primary care physicians. Additional legislation provided federal funding for the creation of new medical schools, particularly those that would educate more generalists. The Family Practice Act of 1970 (P.L. 91–486) provided support for departments of family practice offering residency training. This was necessary since the financing of residency training is hospital based and does not support extensive use of family practice clinics or off-site facilities for training. In 1976 Congress passed the Health Professions Assistance Act (P.L. 94–484), which tied capitation payments through 1980 to the proportion of graduates entering the primary care specialties. But the effectiveness of this effort to legislate the mix of specialists being trained became moot when Congress decided to discontinue all capitation on the assumption that further increase in medical school enrollment was unnecessary.

MEDICAL SCHOOL RESPONSE

Medical schools and academic medical centers had long since lost any qualms about government influencing academic policy. Additional money was always welcome, particularly if NIH support was likely to decline. The number of medical school graduates nearly tripled from 1960 to 1961 and from 1979 to 1980, rising from 5,275 to 15,135. During the same period the number of medical schools increased from 86 to 126 (Ebert and Brown, 1983). Naturally medical school administrators were disappointed when capitation was discontinued; but a far more important source of revenue was exploited, as we shall see a little later in this chapter.

New medical schools declared a special commitment to training more primary care physicians. Those that were state supported included primary care in their mission statements. For example, the Ohio State law that chartered the Northeastern Ohio Universities College of Medicine (NEOUCOM) in 1973 states: "The principal goal of the College shall be to graduate physicians oriented to practice medicine at the community level, especially family physicians" (NEOUCOM, 1993). The mission statement of the college says: "The mission of NEOUCOM is to graduate well-qualified physicians able to pursue any specialty of medicine at the community level, especially primary care" (Campbell, 1991). This was a somewhat watered-down, yet positive, commitment to primary care.

Increase in the enrollment in U.S. medical schools was accompanied by an even larger percentage increase in faculty (Ebert, 1983). From 1960 to 1980 there was a 198 percent increase in enrollment, a 224 percent increase in preclinical faculty (4,023 to 13,039), and a 408 percent increase in full-time clinical faculty (7,201 to 36,566). Obviously, there were reasons other than increased enrollment for the large percentage of increase in full-time clinical faculty.

Medical schools continued to experiment with different approaches to medical student education. Interactive computer-assisted instruction came into wide use. McMaster Medical College in Canada pioneered in problem-based learning, the purpose of which was to correlate basic science knowledge with clinical medicine (Norman, 1992). Problem-based learning begins with the statement of a clinical problem. A small group of students, usually with an instructor, then attempts through reasoning and use of the literature to elucidate the basic disease mechanisms involved. There is feedback at the end of the exercise, so that the group discovers how well it has done.

Patel, Groen, and Norman (1991) designed an experimental study to determine if there was a difference in reasoning between students enrolled at McMaster in a problem-based learning curriculum (PBLC) and students in a conventional curriculum (CC) at McGill. Beginning, intermediate, and advanced students from each school were given a standardized test designed to determine the way in which students used basic science knowledge to explain the signs and symptoms of a specific disease process. Both groups of students were given access to the same basic science and clinical texts. It was found that PBLC students used more backward-directed (deductive) reasoning, whereas CC students used predominantly forward (inductive) reasoning. PBLC students made more elaborations than CC students and also made more mistakes. Even beginning PBLC students used deductive reasoning, a fact attributed to early instruction in the method of reasoning used in the McMaster curriculum.

How effective is problem-based learning? In a recent critical review of the pertinent literature, investigators at McMaster (Norman and Schmidt, 1992) noted that sixty schools worldwide have adopted this approach despite a paucity of evidence as to its superiority over more traditional learning. Based on the evidence they conclude the following: There is no evidence that problem solving, independent of content, can be enhanced by problem-based learning. On the positive side, the knowledge acquired may be less than in a traditional curriculum in the short term, but retention is greater. There is evidence that problem-based learning stimulates interest in a subject, encouraging more use of reference material. It is inferred that this may encourage self-directed learning later in life. There is some evidence, though not conclusive, that students in a problem-based curriculum have a greater ability to correlate basic science concepts with clinical problems than do students in a more traditional curriculum.

An important innovation has been the use of standardized patients for synthetic experiential learning (Stillman et al., 1983). Standardized patients may be real patients or simulated patients using actors, students, or others. A real patient is "standardized" to give a true history in response to appropriate questioning, but not to volunteer information. Such a standardized patient may also be asked to judge the skill of the person taking the history or performing a physical examination. This is not very different from what was done in the past with the learning of history taking and physical diagnosis. It was common to ask patients with prominent signs and symptoms of disease to return annually to be examined by new cohorts of second-year medical students. Simulated patients are trained to give histories of illness in response to appropriate questions by students. The patients are "standardized" in the sense that they have been programmed to describe symptoms of specific diseases. Simulated patients are also used for learning how to do complete or partial physical examinations.

Stillman et al. (1990) surveyed 136 medical schools in the United States and Canada and found that 70 percent used standardized patients in one form or another. Here is the score:

- Breast and pelvic examination   84 schools
- Examination of the male genito-urinary tract   45 schools
- Interviewing skills   62 schools
- History content   57 schools
- Patient education and counseling   39 schools
- Complete physical examination (PE)   33 schools
- Segments of PE   48 schools
- Brief history and PE   46 schools

The training of standardized patients is of the greatest importance, since the success of the model depends on the skill of role-playing. Stillman believes that sharing of training resources among medical schools would permit greater use of this form of synthetic experiential learning.

It is not difficult to understand why this approach to learning the basics of clinical medicine is important. In the past, history taking and physical diagnosis was done on the wards of teaching hospitals. Instructors were assigned small groups of students and, with the help of the housestaff, identified patients suitable for examination by students. Greater concern for patient rights, sicker in-patients, and shorter hospital stays have made it increasingly difficult to use this time-honored approach to instruction in physical diagnosis. Further, the use of standardized patients for acquiring interviewing skills allows much more effective interaction between instructor and students, as well as among students, than was possible with the traditional approach. The same is true for acquiring skill in physical examination. The use of this form of synthetic experiential learning provides an additional bonus. It permits a penetrating critique of how the behavior of the physician doing a patient interview and physical examination can affect the doctor-patient relationship. Many medical school graduates who have not been exposed to this type of learning have reported that no instructors had ever watched them take a history or do a complete physical examination.

DID FEDERAL MANPOWER LEGISLATION ATTAIN ITS GOALS?

The primary goal was to increase the number of practicing physicians, and that was accomplished. But the effort to increase the proportion of primary care physicians in the physician manpower pool failed completely. There were secondary goals with mixed results. One was to improve the geographic distribution of physicians. This was successful to the extent of increasing the number of subspecialists practicing in small cities and large towns. It was unsuccessful in correcting the physician shortage in rural America and inner cities. The greatest disappointment was that the legislation did nothing to correct the imbalance among the medical specialties. The assumption had been made that a substantial increase in the number of medical school graduates would provide a self-correcting mechanism for the imbalance. It was reasoned that an oversupply of subspecialists would result in intense competition with loss of income, making the practice of primary care more attractive. This reasoning failed to take into account a medical care system with a method of payment that created an almost insatiable demand for subspecialist care. It also failed to realize that many subspecialists also provide some primary care.

IMBALANCE AMONG THE SPECIALTIES

Why have U.S. medical schools failed to meet their commitment to educate more primary care physicians? The reasons are complex, but two stand out. First, medical schools control the education of medical students, but do not have any direct control of residency training. Second, the dominance of primary teaching hospitals in academic medical centers has accentuated the importance of nonuniversity functions—such as patient care, hugely profitable faculty practice plans, and the training of residents and fellows—to the detriment of strictly medical school educational responsibilities.

The reader will recall that Flexner considered the internship a nonmedical school experience. The 1932 report of the Commission on Medical Education stressed the need for coordination of the various phases of medical education, including internship and specialty training, but did not suggest that medical schools should have direct responsibility for graduate medical education. As the system evolved, specialty boards and residency review committees controlled by organized medicine set the standards and oversaw the credentialing of specialists. Thus, all graduate medical education remains outside the jurisdiction of the medical school and the university, despite the admonitions of medical educators in various reports and commissions (Coggeshall, 1965). This means that medical schools have no authority to coordinate the education of medical students and residents, nor do they have the power to influence the educational content of residency training. Since the length of residency and fellowship training lasts for three to seven years, the medical school controls a smaller fraction of the formal clinical education of the physician than extra-university agencies.

The irony of this situation is that most residency training occurs in university hospitals or hospitals affiliated with academic medical centers. And the heads of clinical departments in academic health centers have direct responsibility for the education of both medical students and residents. But they wear two hats. As university professors they are accountable to the medical school for the education of medical students. As heads of hospital departments they are accountable to outside agencies for the education of residents and fellows. The confusion of roles is compounded by the involvement of residents in the education of medical students.

Skeptical readers will shake their heads in disbelief. If department heads have responsibility for both medical student education and graduate medical examination (GME), what is the problem? Surely, medical schools could gain control of residency training if they really wanted to. Medical school deans and university presidents have the ultimate power of academic appointment. They appoint department heads, so presumably deans and presidents could replace these clinical chiefs. If medical school and university administrators truly believed that academic control of residency training could improve the educational quality of the experience, why not insist on university control? Why not bring to bear the intellectual resources of universities and medical schools in order to examine the most appropriate mix of generalists and specialists to meet the nation's needs? Why not restructure training programs to meet those needs?

In theory all of these questions are reasonable, but they ignore a basic reality—who pays the clinical faculty. Clinical departments generate most of the money to pay their faculty through clinical practice plans and research grants. Very little comes from deans' offices. In fact, the flow is often in the reverse direction—from clinical departments to deans. And most heads of clinical departments prefer the present separation of authority.

Even medical schools founded with the mission of educating more primary care physicians have little influence on the career choices of their graduates. For example, the Northeastern Ohio Universities College of

Medicine designed an accelerated program intended to train more primary care physicians. After two years in one of the three cooperating universities, students transferred to the medical school in order to be educated in an environment intended to encourage an interest in primary care. It was believed that clinical education provided in community teaching hospitals, staffed by family physicians as well as specialists, would provide that environment. But the graduates of the program have not behaved any differently than graduates of other medical schools. The majority have chosen subspecialty training and practice. What was forgotten was that subspecialty practice is well represented in large community hospitals.

It is not only the power of the purse that prevents medical school deans and university presidents from trying to influence graduate medical education. Universities and medical schools like to have faculty stars who attract outside funding and who bring prestige to their institutions. The stars today are the subspecialists, not the generalists. Deans are products of the system and tend to accept what exists. There is little likelihood that reform will be initiated by medical schools.

As noted earlier, university hospitals dominate academic medical centers. After 1970 increased competition for NIH funding resulted in a frantic search for other sources of funding. Lucrative faculty practice plans provided the answer. High-tech subspecialty practice was the most financially rewarding, and much of the expansion of full-time clinical faculty noted earlier was directed toward this end. Faculty subspecialty practice replaced the NIH as the major source of funding for academic medical centers.

The importance of this dependence on subspecialty practice is the educational environment that it creates. Not only are most clinical instructors subspecialists, but subspecialty practice is seen as glamorous and financially rewarding. Experiential learning in such settings does nothing to encourage a desire to become a generalist. Even residents in internal medicine and pediatrics who entered training intending to become generalists are often seduced by the lure of the subspecialties.

There is an ongoing debate about the appropriate learning experience for the generalist, well summarized by Moore (1992). Specialists and subspecialists express the view that caring for very sick patients prepares the physician for the care of patients with less serious illnesses. They discount the idea that the generalist needs any special skills apart from an understanding of disease. The generalists argue that special skills are needed. Not only should generalists be well prepared to care for common diseases—such as hypertension, diabetes, and the usual infectious diseases—but they should also have additional skills. They need to understand their patients as individuals with individual needs, likes, and preferences. They must be skilled interviewers and counselors. They must know the attributes and limitations of the subspecialists whom they employ as consultants. They must know the limitations of labatory tests and how to manage medical resources. Generalists need to know about the community in which they practice, including special community problems. They must be attentive to the importance of preventive measures, which may vary according to age group. And, above all, they must orchestrate the total care of their patients. Those are not skills that are honed on the busy in-patient services of major teaching hospitals.

Finally, there is an imbalance between generalists and subspecialists because of the way in which our society's reward system works. We require medical students to incur large debts to pay tuition if their families lack the necessary resources. We are willing to pay far more for expensive procedures than for a physician's time in the examining room. We demand immediate access to our generalist physicians (if we have them) but are willing to wait to see subspecialists. If we have health insurance, we are shielded from the excessive charges often made for procedures performed by subspecialists—for example, a charge of $7,000 for the removal of a bunion by an upstate New York surgeon. This exorbitant figure was arrived at by "unbundling" charges—meaning to break down charges into component parts. H. F. Pizer, in the *Boston Globe* (1992, p. 14), wrote that it's as though charges for a cup of coffee were a dollar for the coffee, $1.50 for the cream, 75 cents for the sugar and $2.00 for the use of the cup and saucer.

Who can blame the medical school graduate with an $80,000 debt who chooses a career as a subspecialist rather than as a generalist! He can pay the costs of his medical education with greater ease because he will have a higher income, he can work fewer hours if he wishes, and he will have greater prestige in the profession. Society offers him no special incentives to become a generalist, so why not take the easier route? It condones $7,000 for the removal of a bunion, but is unwilling to pay a fraction of that amount for the time a generalist must take to do a complete examination.

9

CRITIQUE AND ANALYSIS: THE FAILURES OF AMERICAN MEDICINE AND THE NATION'S MEDICAL SCHOOLS

At the beginning of the twentieth century, university-based medical schools were poised to participate in the great advances in the science and technology of medicine. The results have been spectacular. Hypertension can be treated effectively with drugs, reducing the risk of heart disease and stroke. Thrombolysis, during acute attacks of myocardial infarction using clot-dissolving substances, has saved many lives, as has coronary bypass surgery. Individuals with crippling osteoarthritis of the hip can walk painlessly again after hip replacement. Kidneys can be transplanted, and patients waiting for a suitable transplant can be kept alive and functioning with renal dialysis. Forms of cancer once uniformly fatal can now be treated with chemotherapy and irradiation. And the list goes on. These are some of the very real accomplishments of medical science and subspecialty medicine.

Success, however, has been accompanied by an array of problems. Our health care system was not prepared to deal with the costs associated with these rapid advances in medical technology. Medicare and Medicaid fuel the federal deficit; corporate America believes that the continuing escalation of medical care costs could make American industry noncompetitive in international markets. The working public worries that loss of jobs means loss of health insurance. An estimated 35 million individuals who are uninsured are terrified of the financial consequences of serious illness. A working family without health insurance could lose all it possesses.

The magnitude of the problems associated with the way in which this country provides and pays for health care is the subject of national debate.

Change is inevitable. We cannot much longer sustain a rate of inflation of health care costs that continuously exceeds the rate of increase of this country's Gross National Product (GNP). There is no great mystery about the causes of this crisis. There are three: (1) the cost of new technology, (2) an oversupply of subspecialists and technologies, and (3) payment mechanisms that encourage excess demand. Let us consider each of these causes separately.

There are two kinds of therapeutic advances. One is curative and has the potential of saving money. The treatment of streptococcal infection with penicillin is an example, for eradication of streptococcal infection prevents rheumatic fever. Rheumatic fever is frequently associated with serious heart disease, which is expensive to treat. The other kind of therapeutic advance—and the more common one—alleviates but does not cure. Coronary artery bypass surgery alleviates the symptoms associated with coronary artery disease and even prolongs life. But it does not alter the underlying process. One consequence of a treatment that improves the quality of life for some is a large increase in the cost of health care for all. There are many such examples.

Some of the most dramatic advances in medical technology have been diagnostic. Almost invariably they add to the cost of medical care. The big-ticket items, such as magnetic resonance imaging (MRI) or position emission tomography (PET) are particularly expensive. But even such routine procedures as cardiac catheterization add enormously to the cost of medical care.

Thus, we pay a substantial price for the great advances in biomedical research. The solution, however, is not putting a brake on scientific discovery. Other developed nations enjoy the fruits of scientific discovery without our costs. The issue is the prudent use of new technologies. Do we use them wisely? The answer to that question is addressed in a consideration of the other two causes of inflation of medical care costs: (1) an oversupply of subspecialists and technologies and (2) an excess demand for specialty service.

Elsewhere in the text we have noted that our educational system is designed in such a way as to encourage the training of subspecialists. Subspecialists are expert because they have the knowledge and skill to use the latest—and, frequently, the most expensive—technologies available to medicine. It is important to remember that the vast majority of these subspecialists have not contributed to the development of new diagnostic and therapeutic measures. But they certainly have increased the demand for the hardware. In a letter to the *New England Journal of Medicine*, a California physician (Morgan, 1993) has noted that there are forty-one

MRI centers in Orange County, California, with a population of 2.4 million, while Canada, with a population of 27 million, has only twenty-two MRI centers. Seventeen of the MRI centers in Orange County are independently owned—with physicians as investors in most of them. It is common for investor-physicians to refer their patients to the facilities in which they invest. There are significant differences between the Canadian and U.S. health care systems. Canada does not have investor-owned diagnostic facilities, nor does it have a payment system that encourages unnecessary use of expensive technologies. In Canada the ratio of subspecialists to primary care physicians is about 50:50; in the United States it is closer to 70:30.

Subspecialty practice is not confined to major teaching hospitals. Every large community hospital has its share of subspecialists. Because we also have an excess of hospital beds, there is competition for patients among hospitals in communities other than those that serve the poor. One way to meet the competition is to offer the latest in all of the available diagnostic and therapeutic technologies. Thus, we have a system of care that encourages a profligate supply of specialty services in both teaching and nonteaching hospitals.

An oversupply of subspecialists and technologies would not in themselves cause inflation of medical care costs if it were not for the way in which we pay for care. Fee-for-service medicine, freedom of choice of a physician, and indemnity insurance that pays for the costs of care have been the hallmarks of our system of care. Organized medicine endorses and defends each of these principles. Unfortunately, they are principles that encourage a demand for services that fuels the supply side. A fee-for-service system does not encourage economy in the utilization of technology on the part of the physician. Freedom of choice of a physician has been interpreted by the patient as freedom to self-refer to a variety of specialists. Indemnity insurance shields the patient from the excessive costs of many medical technologies. One of the reasons for the outcry about the excessive cost for prescription drugs is that it is one of the few costs most patients bear directly.

HEALTH CARE REFORM

The ultimate solution to the crisis in our health care system is impossible to predict. But two issue must be addressed: (1) excessive cost and (2) what to do about the uninsured. It is important to note that the majority of the uninsured are employed. There are two major payers of health insurance—government (federal and state) and employers. Most Americans receive health insurance provided as a fringe benefit by employers. Since the benefit is not taxed, labor unions have bargained for more and more insurance coverage with as much vigor as the higher wages. The more complete the insurance coverage, the more expensive it becomes. Many small employers feel that they are unable to provide health insurance and remain profitable.

Health insurance in the United States originated in the private sector. In the 1930s boards and managers of nongovernmental hospitals worried about reimbursement and devised a plan to insure against the cost of hospitalization. The regionally based insurance plan that they created in the mid-1930s was called Blue Cross. Blue Cross did not cover the cost of physician services provided in hospitals. To insure against these costs another organization was created called Blue Shield. Together, these organizations came to be known as Blue Cross/Blue Shield. Both were not-for-profit organizations and were originally intended to insure against the costs of hospital care. Other expenses were out of pocket. Gradually benefits were extended to office visits, referral to specialists, and to all medically approved diagnostic and therapeutic procedures. Health insurance became a huge business that attracted the major private insurers. Blue Cross/Blue Shield was designed as an insurance plan based on "community rating." That meant that all individuals and families in a community received coverage for the same premium. Some private insurers found it more profitable to rate on a group basis. Thus, insurance for a group of college students was far less expensive than for a group of middle-aged employees.

In the mid-1960s Congress passed legislation that created Medicare and Medicaid. Medicare entitled individuals 65 years of age and older to a set of defined benefits. Medicaid was an insurance program for the poor, the cost of which was shared by federal and state governments. Organized medicine was vehemently opposed to Medicare, fearing that the federal government would interfere with the practice of medicine. The wording of the final legislation was written to reassure the physician lobby that government would not interfere with the freedom of choice of a physician, fee for service, and "reasonable and customary fees." At the time, no one anticipated the enormous effect that these entitlement programs would have on the federal budget.

Despite efforts such as prospective payment of hospitals by government, the cost of care continues to escalate, although at a slower rate. It is self-evident that whatever plan is devised to provide insurance for those currently uninsured will increase the cost of health care. Thus, any final solution to our health care crisis must provide ways to control costs.

How can that be done? Only by curtailing both the supply and demand sides of the equation. On the supply side that means eliminating unnecessary hospitals beds; paying for new technologies based on need, not demand; and correcting the imbalance between subspecialist and generalist physicians. On the demand side it means controlling referral to subspecialists.

These are not easy goals to achieve, but there are ways. Managed care is one such way. Perhaps the best example of managed care is the staff or group model Health Maintenance Organization (HMO). In the staff model, physicians are salaried by the HMO. In the group model, a group of physicians bargains with the HMO to provide care at a certain price. In both models care is prepaid. That means that for a defined premium all necessary care is provided at whatever cost to the provider. Clearly it is to the advantage of the provider to use resources prudently. One way to do this is to have each member of a managed care plan choose a primary care physician within the plan. That physician will provide most of the care required, referring to subspecialists only when medically necessary. In successful HMOs at least 50 percent of the physicians providing care are primary care physicians. There is also an incentive to provide preventive services.

There are other ways to control costs. One is called global budgeting. This means budgeting a certain amount of money for health care each year. To do so successfully, one must have a single payer, such as government. Health care that is paid for by a combination of private and public payers does not lend itself to global budgeting. Another way to control cost is to ration. In a sense, we ration now based on ability to pay. It would be more equitable to define a minimum set of benefits available to everyone. But the phrase, "rationing of health care," has ethical connotations. Further, it offends our sense of worth. If we are the wealthiest nation in the world, why must we ration anything?

REFORM OF MEDICAL EDUCATION

Reform of our health care system is inevitable, unless we wish to bankrupt the nation. How we educate physicians must be responsive to the kinds of reforms likely to be made. Academic medicine is justified in taking credit for many of the remarkable advances that have been made in medical science. But it must also share in the blame for a medical care system out of control. Academic medical centers have provided the model for high-tech medicine in community hospitals. They have compounded the problem by training an excess of subspecialists and failing to educate a sufficient number of primary care physicians. They have become so financially dependent on high-priced, fee-for-service, subspecialty practice that they lack incentive to change. In summary, academic health centers are a part of the problem. As presently constituted, they certainly are not the solution. There is as urgent a need today to reexamine how we educate physicians as there was at the beginning of the century.

The reexamination should begin with a consideration of how medical schools choose medical students. There will always be a need for medical scientists, but it is a mistake to assume that proficiency in science should be the prime qualification for medical school admission. It is time for admissions committees to think about the different roles future physicians will play. A few will become academic physicians and scientists. The majority will enter practice either as subspecialists or as primary care physicians. The qualities one is seeking in these two types of practitioners are not identical. Both should possess a reasonably high level of intelligence. Both should possess high moral and ethical standards. But primary care physicians must truly enjoy interacting with people. That is not something learned in medical school. It must be identified as a character trait at the time of medical school admission. Usually it is evident from the kinds of extracurricular activities that students have enjoyed. It could be argued that all physicians, including subspecialists, would be better doctors if they were genuinely caring individuals. True, but it is less important for a subspecialist in a technique-oriented field. To be effective for a lifetime of practice, primary care physicians should be more interested in the individuals whom they are caring for than in the diseases that their patients present them with. The science of medicine is knowing how to use effectively the necessary tools with which to diagnose and treat disease. The art of medicine is understanding that each person is an individual who will respond to illness in a unique way. One of the fascinations of medical practice is to observe how differently individual patients cope with illness. Primary care physicians have a unique opportunity to do so since they know their patients. They also know the difference between curing and healing. It is possible to cure a disease and still have a sick patient.

If we are to correct the imbalance among the various branches of medicine, the nation's medical schools should choose at least half of each entering class based on suitability for primary care. It would be a disservice to medicine if the most prestigious medical schools opted out of this obligation, using the excuse that their primary purpose is to train medical scientists and leaders of academic medicine. Since a relatively small proportion of medical students are suitable candidates for productive careers as medical scientists, that obligation can be easily met. But more important is the opportunity for these elite schools to choose some of the best and brightest to provide the academic leadership in primary care. If primary care is to assume a position of importance in the hierarchy of academic medicine, such leadership is essential. Over the past half century medical education has evolved in ways that have emphasized the central role of the subspecialist rather than the generalist in our medical care system. This has happened because the tertiary care teaching hospital is the principal educational environment. It is an environment that recognizes the importance of primary care physicians as a useful source of referrals, but an environment that is disinterested in their education. Flexner viewed the teaching hospital as an extension of the medical school and university. Instead, the medical school has become so financially dependent on the nonacademic activities of its clinical faculty that it has become little more than an academic appendage of the teaching hospital. This is because the university hospital is at present the dominant partner in the academic medical center in which the medical school operates. Partly as a consequence, the medical school is increasingly isolated from its university home. Clearly, any reform of medical education designed to meet the needs of a changing medical care system must reexamine the present configuration of so-called academic health centers. Perhaps it is time for the university to reassert its educational leadership in the education of the physician.

A reexamination of the interface between the last two years of college and the first one or two years of medical school might be a place to start (Ebert, 1981). So-called general education does not occupy four years of college. Almost all students specialize in some area of knowledge during the last two years. For those students who know that they wish to become physicians and have the necessary intellectual and personal qualifications, would it not be reasonable to integrate those three or four years, perhaps with some saving of time. There could be different tracks for those students with strong science interests and aptitudes and those with interests in a more socially oriented curriculum. Such an integration could eliminate some of the redundancy in the teaching of molecular and cell biology. Time would be available to give greater emphasis to the societal aspects of medicine. Would this require students enrolled in colleges without medical schools to transfer to other universities once accepted by the medical schools in those universities? Not necessarily. It would be possible, for example, for a college in one university and a medical school in another to plan jointly a curriculum for a student admitted to medical school while still enrolled in college. The argument is made that the four college years are sacrosanct and should not be professionalized. Yet much of the time spent in college may be spent preparing for a professional career. Engineering is an example. Furthermore, the high cost of medical education and frightening student indebtedness demand some reconsideration of the time element. Shortening the time spent at the university level does not necessarily impair educational quality. In fact, it may improve it.

The most significant changes that have been made in medical education over the past forty years involve the first two years of medical school. Early exposure to patients, pathophysiology taught by an interdisciplinary faculty, the use of standardized patients to teach physical diagnosis and history taking, and problem solving as a way of making learning more interactive are all approaches that have improved the learning experience for medical students. The same cannot be said for the clinical years in medical school and beyond.

A rethinking of clinical education is essential, beginning with the appropriate relation between medical school and graduate phases of clinical education. The two must be integrated and planned as a continuum. In particular, there must be a reconsideration of the education of the primary care physician. To be an effective family physician, general internist, or general pediatrician requires much more than a brief exposure to every medical specialty in a hospital setting. Special skills are needed—skills that subspecialists may or may not possess. By the third year of medical school, the majority of medical students know what direction their careers will take. Even today, students have decided by the end of the third year. It is then that they begin to visit the residency programs to which they wish to apply. There are three broad categories of choice: (1) subspecialty practice, (2) primary care, and (3) medical science. Each requires a separate track.

Let us consider first the educational needs of primary care physicians. To whichever of the medical specialties they wish to belong, they have certain needs in common. They must learn to listen for what is said and for what is not said. They must be sensitive to the different ways in which patients and families respond to illness as a consequence of cultural and social differences. They must learn how to talk to patients in ways that encourage understanding. This means avoiding medical jargon. It means choosing the right time to talk about serious matters. Little is accomplished by first telling a patient he or she has cancer, then discussing options for treatment. The shock of the diagnosis prevents the patient from thinking of anything else. Therapeutic choice is better talked about at another time—unless, of course, the patient asks. Primary care physicians need to project empathetic understanding without becoming emotionally involved. In particular, they must learn not to appear judgmental. To do so will almost certainly interfere with a productive interchange between doctor and patient. Effective diagnosis and treatment are often dependent on the ease with which patients and physicians can discuss matters. Patients must always feel that they have choices, but not choices forced on them by the abdication of responsibility by their physicians.

Primary care physicians must learn to be excellent diagnosticians. Managed care systems, to be effective, must rely on primary care physicians who have diagnostic acumen and who don't use consultants to avoid making difficult decisions. In many ways primary care physicians must be better diagnosticians than subspecialists, for they must cover a broader field. Not too long ago this was expected of the general internist and general pediatrician. They were the consultants to general practitioners and surgeons. Today their job is more difficult. They must be equally skilled in diagnosis while making prudent use of diagnostic technologies. They must learn when the services of a subspecialist consultant are required. An important consequence for the education of primary care physicians is that they need, for effective transfer of learning to practice from natural experiential education, patient populations and treatment venues that are different from those that are satisfactory for subspecialty and research students.

A better education program could be planned for family physician, general internist, and general pediatrician if it were planned as a continuum between medical school and residency. For this to be accomplished, the medical school must be responsible for educational-content continuum. It must ensure that the uniquenes of the individual patient is not forgotten because of preoccupation with disease. It must reinforce an understanding of the socioeconomic aspects of health and illness. And the medical school must be certain that the principles of prevention are not forgotten during the later clinical years.

The reader might ask, "Why not educate all physicians in this way? Aren't we talking about universally useful skills?" To a degree we are. But these skills are less important for the subspecialist or medical scientist. In general, the technical training of subspecialists is of a high order. But none of the specialties—such as surgery, internal medicine, or pediatrics—is simply the sum of its subspecialties. Each has a particular philosophy and approach to medicine that must be learned. There needs to be a resurgence of emphasis on each broad specialty in the education of its subspecialists. This is less apparent in the fields of psychiatry and obstetrics and gynecology, possibly because they are less technology driven.

Competition for funding among medical scientists is intense. Physicians seeking outside research funding have little chance of success unless they are well trained in both medicine and science. M.D.–Ph.D. programs have been particularly successful in training some highly skilled medical scientists. Academic medicine will continue to value research accomplishment, as it should. Primary care has had difficulty establishing itself as an academic discipline because it has a weak research base. This can be remedied by using the same approach that has been used by many medical subspecialties: Employ the research method of other disciplines. Just as hematology has used the tools of molecular biology, primary care can use the methodologies of epidemiology, biostatistics, and the social sciences.

As noted earlier, the configuration of academic health centers is not appropriate for the education of primary care physicians. Radical health care reform could make these centers obsolete. Few academic health centers have good facilities for ambulatory care teaching except in the subspecialties. To meet the nation's manpower needs, medical schools must either create new teaching settings or must affiliate with organizations, such as HMOs, that provide primary care environments. The Harvard Community Health Plan (HCHP), founded over twenty years ago with teaching and research as a part of its mission, is such a setting. It has over 540,000 members, a staff of dedicated physicians, both generalists and specialists, and a long-standing commitment to teaching. Harvard's new Department of Ambulatory Care and Prevention has its headquarters at HCHP.

Over the latter half of this century, the practice of medicine has been largely shaped by how we pay for medical care and by how we educate physicians. Both have encouraged the profligate use of resources. Change in how we pay is beginning. Change in how we educate cannot be far off. One can only hope that the medical school as part of the university will reassert its moral leadership and reshape the education of physicians so as to meet the public's needs rather than its desires. The public may desire unlimited access to "high-tech" medical care at no cost to the consumer. But someone has to pay, and ultimately the public pays, directly or indirectly. The medical profession shares in the responsibility of ensuring that all of our citizens have easy access to necessary care of high quality. But the profession also shares responsibility for the prudent use of medical resources. The education of every physician should include discussion and understanding of these obligations.

SECTION III: LEGAL EDUCATION

Frederick M. Hart and J. Michael Norwood

10

THE ORIGINS OF LAW SCHOOL EDUCATION

In the United States, attorneys are considered officers of the court, and primary control of the legal profession is placed in the hands of the judicial branch of government. Generally, the state supreme courts control admissions to the bar and attorney discipline for state courts. The federal courts exercise authority over who is granted a license to practice in their courts. Authority over the profession is, to some degree, delegated by the courts to bar associations. Legislators enact some laws regulating the legal profession. Consequently, the profession is basically self-governing. It is through this mechanism of self-governance that educational requirements for admission to the bar have been established.

Bar admission rules vary among the states and have been modified throughout the nation's history. The most significant change occurred during the 1920s when the American Bar Association (ABA) established standards for law schools. Its Section on Legal Education and Admissions to the Bar was granted the power to administer these standards through an accreditation process (Stevens, 1983).

Before the establishment of ABA-approved law schools and their acceptance by the courts as providing the most prominent means of educational preparation for entry into the profession, common methods of preparatory training for legal practice included apprenticeship or graduation from a proprietary law school. Proprietary law schools, while providing a systemized means of legal study, maintained the practical orientation of law office training (see ABA, *Special Committee for a Study of Legal Education, Law Schools and Professional Education*, 1980). For a period of time after lawyers became a reform target of Jacksonian Democracy in 1828 for being a part of a politically powerful aristocracy, virtually anyone of "good moral character," regardless of education or training in the law, could become a lawyer (see ABA, *Special Committee for a Study of Legal Education, Law Schools and Professional Education*, 1980).

After the 1920s, ABA-approved law schools soon came to dominate preparatory legal education. As of 1992, all fifty states permitted initial applications for admission to the bar from graduates of ABA-approved law schools; only eight states permitted applicants who had completed prescribed law office study; a total of seventeen states also permitted applicants who had completed schooling requirements other than gradua-tion from an ABA-approved law school or law office study (Conference on Legal Education in the 1980s, 1981).

The ABA was established in 1878 as a national lawyers' group. The new ABA proposed that students learn the principles of law in school, then apply them for at least a year in an office, and, finally, pass a public examination by impartial examiners appointed by the courts. The ABA proposal was only a recommendation since each state determined its own requirements for admission.

At the end of the nineteenth century, although there were still few formal requirements for becoming a lawyer, many states concerned about stan-dards for entry into the legal profession began to require a formal period of study or apprenticeship and a written bar exam. In 1889, the ABA called for the establishment of an organization of law schools. In 1890, the American Association of Law Schools (AALS) was created and adopted a minimum standard for its members. This was the first step toward the eventual adoption of accreditation standards by the ABA. The initial ABA standards required that "every candidate for the bar be a graduate of a law school, which required two years of prior college education, a minimum of three years study of law, an adequate library and a sufficient full time faculty." After World War II, in response to a significant increase of student attendance at law school, there developed a new movement for higher standards of competency for lawyers in order to help protect the public. It was at this point that many law schools became postbaccalaureate profes-sional schools requiring a prior college degree for acceptance.

ORIGINS OF THE DOMINANCE OF THE CASE-STUDY METHOD

The genesis of modern ABA-approved law schools can be traced to the middle of the nineteenth century. In 1840, there were nine university-affiliated law schools with 345 students. These law schools were at the undergraduate level and often did not require a prior high school diploma. It was believed that affiliation of a private or proprietary law school with a college or university would improve education and enable it to confer a degree. The rise of the modern law school truly began in 1870 when Christopher Columbus Langdell was appointed Dean of the Harvard Law School. Langdell introduced the case method of study as the exclusive technique necessary for educating lawyers. He rejected the role of experiential clinical or practical training provided in apprenticeships or by proprietary schools. By the early twentieth century, Harvard's case method of study became the leading model for the modern law school (Seligmen, 1978). Since the 1960s there has been a resurgence of alternative teaching methodologies, such as the problem method, computer-aided instruction, and clinical education, simulation, demonstration. The case method of study retains great cachet with legal educators and remains a vital teaching technique employed in law schools.

The case method of study consists of detailed analysis of appellate decisions primarily in the context of doctrinal logic. Langdell believed that law was a science consisting of certain principles or doctrines, that "to be able to apply them [the principles and doctrines] with constant facility and certainty to the ever-tangled skein of human affairs is what constitutes a true lawyer," and that "the shortest and the best, if not the only way of mastering the doctrine effectually is by studying the cases in which it is embodied." The theory espoused by Langdell was that the legal system was composed of a logically consistent set of principles that could be best derived through the empirical study of appellate cases and that these principles could then be objectively applied to each new case as it occurred (Langdell, 1980).

In the classroom, the case method consists of a professor and a large number of students analyzing logically related appellate case opinions in order to discern the legal principle or set of principles articulated by the courts and in order to identify the relevant facts to which the principle or principles are applied. Ultimately the "correctness" of the judicial decisions are justified or destroyed based on the logical applicability of the appropriate legal principles to the relevant case facts. The public-policy desirability of the legal principles as applied to the relevant facts of the cases under study or as applied to a set of hypothetical new facts dreamed up by the professor may also be examined to further test the "correctness" of the opinions. Frequently, the class consists of a series of questions posed by the professor. Students responding to the questions are challenged to defend their answers with reasoned arguments. Finally, students are tested on their mastery of the cases studied by means of a blind-graded essay examination in which the students are asked to apply the legal principles derived from the cases to a new set of facts and to justify their conclusions.

The case method of study proved to be a powerful tool for instructing students in legal reasoning and in understanding the legal system. Students learn to read cases and statutes analytically and to identify the legal principles necessary to determine the outcome of a dispute. They synthesize, organize, and reconcile seemingly disparate and self-contradictory legal principles and sort out critical relevant facts from those with little or no bearing on a logical application of appropriate legal principles. They learn to apply the principles derived from the cases and statutes to new sets of facts in a soundly reasoned way, distinguishing principles that may apply to one set of facts from those that should be employed in a different situation. The most common justification for the case method of study is that the end result is that students learn to "think like lawyers" (see Weaver, 1991). Assuming study by means of the case method alone is adequate to prepare lawyers for the profession, as Langdell believed, it has the added attraction, to university business officers, of appearing highly cost effective. Arguably, it can be successfully employed, as Langdell did, in classes with a large number of students and can be adopted by schools with high student-to-faculty ratios. The only "laboratory" expense on which it is dependent is a well-stocked library.

BREAKING THE LIMITS OF THE CASE METHOD OF STUDY IN LAW SCHOOLS

Since the introduction of the case method of study at Harvard, shortcomings of the method have been criticized by both legal educators and practicing lawyers. The following are the major criticisms of the case method of study.

- It postulates a strictly adversarial model of legal systems resulting in training students principally—and too narrowly—as litigators rather than as problem solvers armed with a broad understanding of dispute-resolution techniques and of the role of law and lawyers in a diverse society.
- While teaching students to "think like lawyers," it falls short of adequately instructing students in the full range of fundamental lawyering skills—such as interviewing, counseling, fact investigation, trial practice, and negotiation—necessary to practice law competently.

- It fails to adequately inculcate students with a deeply felt sense of professional responsibility (ethics), the shared values of the legal profession, and the overarching justice mission of law and lawyers.
- Confining the study of law to appellate cases unnecessarily limits the formulation of valid legal theory by failing to fully correlate it with important knowledge developed by the social sciences that may be vital to a complete understanding of legal principles, legal systems, and lawyers' work.

Since the late 1960s, critics of law schools' heavy reliance on the case method have become increasingly determined, resolute, and influential, resulting in the augmentation of curricula at most law schools by courses employing serveral alternative teaching methods. This was the first major effort to reform legal education since the widespread acceptance of ABA-approved law schools as the primary avenue to entry into the profession. It was led by a group of loosely associated law professors centered at Harvard, Columbia, and Yale and became known as the American Legal Realists movement. The movement's proponents attacked the Langdellian notion that law is an exact science based on the objective (value-free) application of legal rules. They argued that law should be viewed as it actually operated. American legal scholarship became reoriented toward process rather than substance. The Realists movement occasioned great intellectual ferment among law faculty at prestigious law schools and resulted in lasting and significant reforms in the way in which these faculty taught.[1] In a common attempt to integrate law and social sciences, new editions of law books came out with "Cases and Materials on X" rather than "Cases on X." The reliance of legal study exclusively on an examination of appellate cases was broken. Seminars in which students explored the law from many perspectives beyond the application of case rules were introduced. A few schools added social scientists to their faculties.[2]

THE RISE OF THE CLINICAL EDUCATION
MOVEMENT

Perhaps the most radical proposal to reform legal education coming from a member of the American Legal Realist movement was advanced by Jerome Frank. He attacked Langdell's assumption that the case method of study was both practical and within the German scientific tradition. Frank maintained that under the Langdellian model, law schools were too unrelated to practice. In a speech to the ABA Section on Legal Education in 1933, Frank stated: "The Law student should learn, while in school, the art of legal practice. And to that end, the law schools should boldly, not slyly and evasively, repudiate the false dogmas of Langdell. They must decide not to exclude, as did Langdell—but to include—the methods of learning law by work in the lawyer's office and attendance at the proceedings of the courts of justice" (Stevens, 1983, 156–57).

In an article published in the June 1933 issue of the *University of Pennsylvania Law Review*, Frank suggested four basic components of his proposal to reform legal education. First, he proposed that "a considerable proportion of law teachers in any law school should be men with not less than five to ten years of varied experience in the actual practice of law" (Frank, 1933, pp. 414–18). Second, he suggested that the study of cases should be retained but augmented to include "reading and analysis of *complete records of cases*—beginning with the filing of the first papers, through the trial in the trial court and to and through the upper courts." Third, he urged that "*law students should be given the opportunity to see legal operations*. Their study of cases should be supplemented by frequent visits, accompanied by law teachers, to both trial and appellate courts." Finally, drawing upon the medical school model, he stressed that legal education could greatly benefit from the establishment of a legal clinic or dispensary in each law school. These clinics would be staffed by full-time faculty who had varied practice experience who could be assisted by graduate and undergraduate students and by leading members of the bar. The professional work done in the clinics "would include virtually every kind of service rendered by law offices." Frank asserted that through their education in the law school clinics, "students would learn to observe the true relation between the contents of upper court opinions and the work of the practicing lawyers and the courts." Frank elucidated this statement by writing that

the student would be made to see, among other things, the human side of the administration of justice, including the following:

(a) How juries decide cases . . .

(b) The uncertain character of the "facts" of a case . . .

(c) How legal rights often turn on the faulty memory of witnesses, the bias of witnesses, the perjury of witnesses.

(d) The effects of fatigue, alertness, political pull, graft, laziness, conscientiousness, patience, impatience, prejudice and open-mindedness of judges. How legal rights may vary with the judge who tries the case and with that judge's varying and often unpredictable reactions to various kinds of cases and diverse kinds of witnesses.

(e) The methods used in negotiating contracts and settlements of controversies.

(f) The nature of draftsmanship . . . (Frank, 1933, p. 418)

These elements of Frank's "clinical lawyer-school" are an early cursory outline of the clinical teaching method, its purpose and content. Serious scholarship aimed at refining this crude beginning was not undertaken until after expansive experimentation with the clinical method began in the late 1960s and early 1970s.

During the late 1960s and early 1970s, several forces converged to provide a strong catalyst for change in law school education.

First, during the 1960s and early 1970s, many young student activists engaged in an intense reexamination of societal values, traditions, and institutions, including higher education and law schools. Students demanded that law school curricula become more "relevant" by addressing significant social problems, such as poverty, environmental degradation, and the rights of women, children, and other historically underrepresented and disadvantaged groups. Further, students exhorted law schools to recognize that their responsibility extended beyond theorizing on these massive problems in the classroom. They urged the schools to become direct participants in solving social problems by taking actions that could serve to reform the profession and that could promote change in American society at large. The student action agenda included such items as reforming student admissions and faculty hiring practices so that the demographics of the legal profession would become more representative of the population at large; the student agenda also encouraged (through course credits and other incentives) both students and faculty to work on actual legal problems in areas of great need.

Second, "Watergate," in which a number of high level government lawyers participated in illegal and unethical practices, caused an erosion of public confidence and respect for the legal profession and caused the profession to examine the role of ethics in the study and practice of law. In 1974, the ABA amended its accreditation standards to include required instruction in professional responsibility.[3]

Third, in 1973 a notable and widely publicized critique of lawyer competence was delivered by the Chief Justice of the Supreme Court, Warren Burger (1973). His scathing report on the performance of trial lawyers in federal courts called for improved preparation before lawyers could assume responsibility for handling a trial. Burger pointed to legal education as a cause of inadequate advocacy: "Law schools fail to inculcate sufficiently the necessity of high standards of professional ethics, manners and etiquette as things basic to the lawyer's function. With few exceptions, law schools also fail to provide adequate and systematic programs by which students may focus on the elementary skills of advocacy" (p. 7).

During this time, law schools and universities enjoyed a period of prosperity that provided the funds to expand facilities and faculty in order to accommodate the swelling student enrollments of "baby boomers." The growth in law school budgets owing to expanding student enrollment coincided with the formation of the Council on Legal Education for Professional Responsibility, which provided additional funds and incentives to encourage law schools to experiment with clinical education.

The robust clinical legal education movement that emerged in the late 1960s and early 1970s embraced many of the objectives of student activists, persons concerned with the state of professional ethics and competence, and faculty wishing to experiment with new teaching techniques. Clinics have responded to activist concerns that law schools assume a meaningful role in the solution of significant social problems. They have provided a vehicle through which law schools directly contribute to the shared responsibility of lawyers, as guardians of justice, to deliver quality legal services to all segments of American society, including the poor, those accused of committing crimes, and others with limited access to lawyers by reason of race, ethnicity, health, lifestyle, or mental condition. Topics covered in clinical courses have included welfare law, family law, consumer law, criminal law and procedure, prisoners' rights, housing law, employment rights, and other subjects "relevant" to concerns for "social justice." American law students, working under the supervision of qualified lawyers and professors, have represented needy clients in the real world of law practice. This has helped to fill the gap in access to justice, and, in their formative law school years, sensitized lawyers to the fundamental professional responsibility of providing legal counsel to all.

The clinical movement has also responded to concerns for improving lawyer competence and professional ethics. Because the focus within the movement has been on providing legal services for people in need, clinics have helped to develop the "human" skills required for competent legal services. These skills can only be learned in the context of the real world of lawyers representing clients. Other learning associated with clinical education has included client interviewing and counseling, case evaluation and planning, fact investigation and discovery, negotiation and other forms of alternative dispute resolution, legal writing and research, and trial and appellant advocacy. Because clinics engage students in the actual practice of law, many of the moral and ethical dilemmas that confront lawyers have frequently become the subject of student learning. In-depth exploration of these issues in clinical classes has been common.

COUNCIL ON LEGAL EDUCATION FOR
PROFESSIONAL RESPONSIBILITY (CLEPR)

The key advocate in the movement to expand and enhance clinical education in law schools during the formative years in the 1960s and 1970s was William Pincus, who served as president of the Council on Legal Education for Professional Responsibility, Inc. (CLEPR) from 1968 to 1980. Pincus's interest in clinical education began in 1958 when he was working for the Ford Foundation and saw a link between legal education and the efforts of the National Legal Aid Association to provide needed legal services to poor people. He "believed that both legal education and legal aid stood to gain by a clinical connection that would roughly parallel that between medical education and teaching hospitals and clinics" (Pincus, 1980, pp. 21–25). He gained the support of Emery Brownell, executive director of the National Legal Aid Association (later to become the National Legal Aid and Defender Association, or NLADA), leadership in the American Bar Association, and a few law school faculty members. The Ford Foundation provided a grant of $800,000 to be spent over seven years to establish the Council on Legal Clinics (CLC) of the National Legal Aid and Defender Association.

"CLC was dedicated and concerned about the social conditions of the poor and the working classes. It wanted direct exposure for law students to the miseries that overwhelmed others and lay behind the legal situations of individuals against whom the law seems to operate" (Pincus, 1980, p. 25). The CLC faced many difficulties in pursuit of its goals. The legal aid offices in which students were to do their clinical work were generally in disgraceful condition, poorly equipped, and staffed by woefully underpaid and overworked employees. Many members of law school faculties labeled legal aid work as nonintellectual, repetitive, and boring. Few were prepared by temperament or training to engage in "hands on" clinical teaching. They preferred traditional classroom learning and discerned little intrinsic value in extra-classroom activities except as these contributed to empirical research or provided observations to be used in furtherance of classroom discussions. In general, it was far too easy for law school faculty to ignore the legal needs of the underprivileged and disregard a rich teaching methodology. CLC pursued its goals by funding small grants, supporting films and publications (including teaching materials) and organizing conferences. Through the efforts of the CLC, law schools started to consider alternatives to strictly classroom teaching.

When CLC's funding was to be renewed by the Ford Foundation in 1965, enough progress had been made in establishing the viability of

clinical education in law schools for the Association of American Law
Schools (AALS) to agree to take over the operation of the CLC program.
A $950,000 grant was made by the Ford Foundation to the AALS. The
NLADA, recognizing the advantages of having the program continue
under educational sponsorship, turned over administration of the program
to the educators. The NLADA retained its representation on the successor
council. The AALS, to avoid appearing to choose between factions supporting or opposing any particular form of clinical education, decided to
rename the program Council on Education in Professional Responsibility
(COEPR).

In 1967, Professor Howard Sachs, who served as project director for
both CLC and COEPR, resigned to become dean at the University of
Connecticut. The search for his successor occasioned COEPR to seek
substantially increased funding to more effectively encourage and support
clinical experiments in law schools. In response, the Ford Foundation, in
the spring of 1968, authorized the creation and funding of the Council on
Legal Education for Professional Responsibility (CLEPR) for an initial
five-year period with a promise of support for another five-year period. At
that time, Pincus left the Ford Foundation staff to become president of
CLEPR because, according to Pincus (1980), "I was confident that, with
10 years and good financial support from Ford, we could make a construc-
tive impact on legal education" (p. 27).

During its ten years' existence, CLEPR, under Pincus's leadership,
succeeded in making clinical education an important part of the curriculum at virtually every law school in the country. CLEPR carried on
its work through persuasion, conferences, publications, and substantial
seed-money grants to schools that demonstrated commitment to quality
clinical programs (partly by matching CLEPR's grant money with the
clinical-program funds). Largely through the efforts of CLEPR, many
talented, energetic, and committed professors, clinicians, and students
employing the clinical method of learning significantly advanced the
study of law, legal institutions, and the work of lawyers, especially as
these have related to the promotion of a just society.

NOTES

1. Standard 502 of the ABA's *Standards for Approval of Law Schools* states in part:

(a) The educational requirements for admission as a degree candidate is either a
bachelor's degree from a qualified institution, or a successful completion of
three-quarters of work acceptable for a bachelor's degree at a qualified institution.
In the latter case, not more than ten percent of the credits necessary for admission

may be in courses without substantial intellectual content, and the pre-legal average on all subjects undertaken and in addition, on all courses with substantial intellectual content, whether passed or failed must at least equal that required for graduation from the institution attended.

2. Broadening the study of law beyond appellant case analysis opened legal education and scholarship to important explorations of theoretical thinking about law, including feminist jurisprudence, critical legal studies, law and economics, and critical race theory. These constructs for understanding the application of law in the context of social interests have mostly been taught in classroom settings that do not involve experiential learning. However, the incorporation of these constructs in clinical teaching is not uncommon.

3. In the ABA's *Standards for Approval of Law Schools*, Standard 302 (a)(iv) states that "the law school shall: require of all candidates for the first professional degree, (to have) instruction in the duties and responsibilities of the legal profession and its members, including the ABA Model Code of Professional Responsibility, are all covered. Each law school is encouraged to involve members of the bench and bar in such instruction."

11
KEY PARAMETERS OF THE CLINICAL METHOD OF STUDY

One of the CLEPR's final grants in 1977, in the amount of $150,000, funded the work of the AALS–ABA Committee on Guidelines for Clinical Legal Education. The committee's published guidelines, project-director's notes, and consultants' reports, consisting of 268 pages of analysis, reveal the scope and depth of work carried on by many legal educators in advancing the state of clinical education in American law schools during the CLEPR years. The committee identified and discussed seven principal issues relating to the contributions of clinical training in meeting the challenge of preparing law students for the legal profession:

1. Why should law schools devote time to clinical education as compared with traditional studies?
2. What contribution can clinical legal education make to the development of a lawyer?
3. What special contribution to professional responsibility can clinical education make?
4. What should be the status of individuals who teach clinical courses?
5. What are the relative strengths and weaknesses of simulation and live cases?
6. What are the relative strengths and weaknesses of field placements and law school–operated clinics?
7. How are law schools to pay for clinical education? (Association of American Law Schools, 1980, p. 9)

These questions remain central to the continuing debates about the efficacy and extent of the use of clinical teaching methods in the nation's law schools. They provide a useful framework for exploring recent developments in the field. For the purpose of this exploration of experiential education in law schools, these seven questions can be restated as four: (1) What is the purpose and content of clinical legal education? (2) What are the characteristics of clinical teachers? (3) What are the characteristics of the diverse clinical teaching methods? (4) Where do law schools find the resources required to fund clinical programs?

THE PURPOSE AND CONTENT OF THE CLINICAL METHOD

The purpose and content of clinical legal education is difficult to elucidate with a high degree of specificity because clinical education is not a law subject at all; it is a teaching methodology or technique (Speigel, 1987). In 1991, the AALS's Committee on the Future of the In-House Clinic (1991) defined "clinical legal education" as

first and foremost a method of teaching. Among the principal aspects of that method are that students are confronted with problem situations of the sort that confront lawyers in practice; the students deal with the problem in role; the students are required to interact with others in attempts to identify and solve the problem; and perhaps most critically, the student performance is subjected to intensive critical review.

In 1992, the ABA's *Report of the Task Force on Law Schools and the Profession* gave a similar, though somewhat broader, description of the "clinical method of instruction" when listing the elements of effective skills teaching:

Effective teaching of [lawyering] skills and values ordinarily involves these components:

1) Development of concepts and theories underlying the skills and values being taught;

2) Opportunity for students to perform lawyering tasks with appropriate feedback;

3) Reflective evaluation of the students' performance by a qualified assessor.

Because one of the central elements of the methodology, the "opportunity for students to perform lawyering tasks with appropriate feedback" can be accomplished in the context of any work that lawyers perform—such as drafting wills, giving legal advice to corporate boards, lobbying a legislator, or delivering a closing argument: virtually any law subject or lawyering skill can be taught using the clinical method. Acknowledging that clinical education is a methodology and not a subject, its purpose and content becomes an open question. The clinical method is rich with potentiality, and legal educators continue to experiment with its many possibilities.

In its 1991 *Final Report on the Future of the In-House Clinic*, the AALS Section on Clinical Legal Education listed nine educational goals: (1) developing modes of planning and analysis; (2) providing professional skills instruction; (3) teaching means of learning from experience; (4) instructing students in professional responsibility; (5) exposing students to the demands of acting in a role; (6) providing opportunities for collaborative learning; (7) fostering a professional commitment to service in the public interest, (8) providing a context for the examination of particular doctrinal areas of the law, and (9) critiquing lawyers and the legal system. The broad sweep of possibilities suggested by this list adds emphasis to the potentiality of clinical education. Nevertheless, most of the items on the AALS list can be reconceptualized to fall under the broad umbrella of "skills" education. Planning and analysis, learning from experience, accepting professional responsibility and acting accordingly, collaborating, and analyzing law in context at a more abstract level are all "skills." It is with "skills" education that the clinical method of instruction has become most closely associated.

As discussed earlier in this chapter, one of the driving justifications for the clinical movement has been the urge to better prepare lawyers to be competent practitioners. During the past two decades extensive research has been devoted to examining the skills and values that a lawyer should possess in order to represent a client competently. Much of this work has been done by clinical teachers, and the clinical method has been used extensively to teach those lawyering skills.[1] In addition to those listed, other skills include legal reasoning and analysis; case evaluation and planning; client interviewing and counseling; negotiation and other forms of alternative dispute resolution; legal drafting; pretrial, trial, and appellant advocacy; problem solving; fact investigation, and recognizing and solving ethical dilemmas. Indeed, because the clinical movement has become so closely associated with skills education, many legal educators consider clinical methodology and skills education synonymous.

The close association of clinical education with "skills" education is reflected in the work of several recently constituted ABA committees and task forces that were commissioned to prepare reports on the issues faced by the legal profession concerning the raising of the levels of competence, professional responsibility, and morality throughout the profession. At least three of these reports have directly addressed the law schools' role in improving competence and standards of professional responsibility in the profession.[2] All three have noted the need to increase and improve education in fundamental lawyering skills, including interviewing, counseling, negotiation, trial advocacy, practice management, writing, research, and problem solving, and have referred to clinical teaching methods as an effective means of developing these skills.[3] These reports also concluded that although law schools play an important role in providing skills training, becoming and remaining a competent lawyer is an ongoing process that begins before entry into law school and continues throughout one's professional career. Thus prelaw preparation, law school, the bar examination process, mentoring, peer review, and continuing legal education all play important roles in the development of a competent lawyer.

THE SERVICE AND JUSTICE MISSIONS OF CLINICAL LEGAL EDUCATION

During the early years of the clinical movement, strong assertions were made by CLEPR[4] and other parties that law schools that implement or expand clinical programs should design their programs with a view to providing legal services to needy clients.[5] These arguments came from activist students,[6] activist faculty,[7] and some of the agencies that provided funds to help establish clinical programs.[8] Indeed, many clinics relied on grants and contracts from state and federal agencies, sources that frequently included a service commitment as a condition of the grant or contract.[9]

Of course, a natural tension exists in "live-client" clinics regarding whether to allocate available resources to service or to the education of students. CLEPR and other parties argued that this tension was easily reconcilable so long as control over the appropriate balance between service and education was in the hands of the students' faculty supervisors.[10] Those favoring an evenly balanced reconciliation of the tension between service and education asserted that law schools' acceptance of shared responsibility with the profession for providing direct services to clients disadvantaged in access to justice had significant intrinsic as well as educational value. One sample explication of the educational value of clinical education in a service setting came in 1969 from John Ferren, then the Director of the Harvard Legal Services Program:

As lawyers try to fashion a more just society, they must take suitable account of those human situations which put the greatest strain on our society and cause the legal process to function at its worst. Riots, rent strikes, and the chaos of destitute families are all manifestations of oppression and alienation which no lawyer can hope to deal with unless he himself can understand and feel what reconciliation is needed. This means that lawyers must have broader capabilities in human relations than our law schools have attempted to nourish in the past. The only way for students to grow in this respect is through fieldwork, that is, personal involvement with the application of law at its lowest and roughest levels. There is no better way to learn how people are actually affected by and feel about the institutions and laws by which they are governed. And equally important, there is no better way for students to learn how they will have to relate to persons they undertake to help.

More as a response to assertions that law schools could make a major contribution to fulfilling the vast need for legal services to the poor (either through volume or quality of services delivered) than as a rejection of the educational validity of engaging law students in an examination of the nature and function of law as it is manifested in the most disaffected segments of society, most law school and clinical faculties accepted the position articulated by Gary Bellow[11] and Earl Johnson in an article published in 1971:

It is questionable whether service to the unrepresented, despite the enormous need, can be a major function of clinical programs. It is, of course, true that there are incidental services performed to clients in a clinical setting. Certainly, the provision of such services to the poor, who have no alternatives to the service provided, poses special problems of accountability and resource allocation which have not yet been fully recognized. Nevertheless, the need for a work load sufficiently limited to encourage reflection and analysis by the student, the time required to effectively teach in a clinical setting, and the continued turnover of students each semester makes service to clients, even in legal aid clinics, a marginal benefit of such programs at best. A service orientation by clinical programs can too easily become a rationale for permitting law teaching to slip into vocational, how-to-do-it instruction. Where the courthouse is, or how a legal form is to be filled out, can be learned without the commitment of resources, time, or energies that are part of most clinical undertakings. (pp. 670–71)

The debate about the importance of the role of service in clinical programs was seemingly settled in 1980 when the marginalization of the service component of clinical education received the official approval of the ABA and the AALS. That year, the Committee on Guidelines for Clinical Legal Education, established in 1977, under the joint sponsorship of the AALS and the ABA (1980) stated in its *Guidelines for Clinical Legal Education* under the heading "Educational Purpose": "The primary purpose of clinical legal studies is to further the educational goals of the law school, rather than to provide service. Law school clinical legal studies may introduce law students to client representation in the context of adversary proceedings and the counseling of clients in the ordering of their personal, business, professional, and public responsibilities."

Wide acceptance of the position that service to needy clients has only a marginal role in clinical programs affects curricular planning by law schools in several ways. There are at least four ways in which the law schools' interests appear to be served: (1) there is an alleviation of pressures from students, the profession, and the public that law schools devote a portion of their resources to the mission of broadening access to justice; (2) law schools gain freedom to allocate their clinical resources in pursuit of educational goals unfettered by the context of addressing problems associated with unequal distribution of wealth and power; (3) law schools gain freedom to choose from a diverse variety of clinical teaching methods other than those centered on the representation of needy clients (methodologies often included under the general heading "clinical" include simulation or role-playing, planning courses, and placement of law students to work as externs in a variety of legal settings outside of the law school, such as working with judges, government lawyers, legal aid lawyers, and private practitioners); (4) by remaining on the sidelines of the potentially volatile issues that arise when distribution of wealth, power, and justice becomes an important focal point of legal education, law schools can maintain a pretense of political neutrality.[12]

There are other ways in which the hidden messages contained in the conventional belief that service in the mission of broadening access to justice is of marginal concern to law schools and their clinical programs are potentiality harmful to the interests of law schools, the profession, and society. These hidden messages include the following: (1) service in the interest of access to justice is peripheral to the practice of law for which students prepare; (2) lawyers have little ability or responsibility to increase justice in society; (3) lawyers' work is disassociated from human relations; (4) lawyers' opportunities and abilities to contribute to the betterment of their communities are limited.

Notwithstanding the pronouncement of the ABA and AALS in the *Guidelines for Clinical Legal Education* (1980) and the oft-repeated conventional wisdom that service in the cause of access to justice is of marginal importance to clinical education,[13] forceful advocates in favor of retaining a meaningful service component in clinical education persist. Those favoring a service component stress the importance of engaging students in this work, not because law school clinics are capable of making a meaningful contribution to broadening access to justice as far as meeting the volume of need is concerned, but because doing so is an essential element of education in professional values,[14] concepts of social justice, and lawyers' roles as agents of justice in the communities in which they live and work.[15] They further argue that valuable research leading to the advancement of social justice is bolstered through active engagement by legal educators and law students in the great issues concerning the nature and purpose of law and lawyers' work.[16] These issues include the impact of race, gender, class, power, and wealth on justice in society. Concern that law schools participate in public service has also led to the establishment of a growing number of pro bono projects that engage students and faculty in volunteer public service work.[17]

THE VARIETY OF CLINICAL METHODS

Four different modes of the clinical method are found in curricula. These include, in-house, "live-client" clinics, extern placements, simulations, and problem courses.

An in-house "live-client" clinic engages students in the representation of actual clients with real problems. Students in these clinics are expected to assume responsibility for taking whatever actions are necessary to handle the clients' cases, including interviewing, counseling, drafting necessary documents, and appearing in court, if necessary. The students' work is conducted under the watchful supervision of an experienced lawyer who holds an academic appointment. In-house is a term of art used by legal educators to refer to a "live-client" clinic that is usually housed within the law school (the law school building) and operated by law school personnel.

In an extern clinic students are placed outside the law school to gain practical experience in a variety of settings. Many externship placements are with governmental agencies, judges, public defender offices, legal aid offices, and private practitioners. Students usually are given less responsibility for acting on the real problems handled by the personnel at their placement, and supervision of the work is primarily assigned to the placement office, with back-up guidance from the law school faculty. There is usually little emphasis in extern placements on critical reflection on the students' performance of tasks or on the nature of law and the legal profession.

In the simulation mode of clinical instruction, students use artificial scenarios or situational scripts to replicate an experience they may encounter in practice. Students may perform the role of (1) lawyers, (2) witnesses facing examination by lawyers in trials or depositions, (3) clients, (4) judges, or (5) other persons likely to be found in the context of a circumstance involving legal work. The students' performance of the assigned tasks is subjected to critical review by a qualified assessor. This mode of training has proved very adaptable to training students in litigation skills, including pretrial, trial, and appellant practice, and enjoys great popularity with both students and faculty.

In the problem method of instruction, students are given a "problem." The problem is meant to be reasonably complex, involving several legal issues requiring the application of statutes, regulations, and cases to resolve. The problem may be formed in the context of legal circumstances, such as legislation, negotiation, drafting, litigation, or planning. The student is asked to approach the problem from a specified role, such as a judge, advisor, planner, legislator, or law clerk. The problem is distributed in advance to give the students the opportunity to engage in in-depth, well-organized, legal analysis. Inquiry into the students' analyses of the problems becomes the focus of class discussion. The assigned cases, statutes, regulations, and other materials become tools for helping solve the problems. This method can be distinguished from simulation in at least two ways. First, in the problem method, students engage in role assumption for the purposes of discussing their analysis rather than executing the actions or assuming the role based on analysis of the problem. Second, the critical review is primarily focused on the quality of the students' analysis rather than their performance of a lawyering task.[18]

Legal educators are faced with deciding which modes of clinical education are best suited for specified purposes. Each mode has its own strengths and weaknesses.

In-house clinics are generally viewed as providing the most suitable learning environment for promoting critical reflection about the students' work, the role of lawyers in society, and the nature of law as it relates to society's needs. Students enter into collaborative relationships with faculty, and share the common goal of solving client problems. Because real people are affected by the students' work, motivation to perform well is high on the part of the students and the faculty supervisors. The problems presented to the students to solve are often rich in complexity of facts and human relationships leading to many valuable learning opportunities. However, the support personnel and infrastructure needed to support a fully operational law office required by in-house clinics and the low student-to-faculty ratios needed to ensure educational quality make in-house relatively more expensive to operate than any other mode of clinical education. The variety of educational experiences present in an in-house clinic, and the often unpredictable, uncontrollable, and haphazard way in which educational opportunities arise often leads to a lack of uniformity in the experiences of the students.[19]

Extern placements provide opportunities for students to work in offices outside of the law school in a diversity of settings and are relatively inexpensive to operate.[20] However, there is usually less careful attention paid by the law school to the selection of the students' supervisors. The supervisors are not professional educators and are not paid by the law school to create a high quality educational experience for the students. The law school has less control over the students' experience and takes less responsibility for it. Students in placement programs are also usually given less direct professional responsibility for handling the legal matters encountered in the office.[21]

Simulation offers the advantage of control by the instructor. The inherent uncertainty and complexity of real situations confronting lawyers can be greatly simplified, students can be interrupted during a simulation exercise for course corrections and immediate feedback, potential harm to real clients is limited, skills can be isolated and developed in an orderly fashion, and, although students' faculty rations must remain relatively low, the cost of a simulation program is less than live-client clinics. On the other hand, because simulations are contrived and controlled situations, they lack the factual complexity and uncertainty of real life motivation and emotional involvement in the process is reduced, and the collaborative relationship between the instructor and student is more difficult to form.

The problem method of clinical education is similar to simulation in that it has the advantage of manageability, control by faculty, and relatively low cost. However this mode of the clinical method is even more abstract in application than simulation and is usually restricted in focus to legal analysis or reasoning skills, although drafting skills occasionally come into play.

The number of law school courses utilizing one or more of these modes of clinical instruction has risen steadily during the last two decades. In its 1992 *Report of the Task Force on Law Schools and the Profession*, summarizing data from its own survey and other available surveys, the ABA noted this growth:

Data on skills courses are available for three distinct modes of instruction—clinics, externships, and simulations—plus a catch-all "other" category. One can trace the growth in simulation and "other" skills course offerings by comparing data gathered for 1974–75 with data for 1984–86 and with data for 1990. Such a comparison shows that in 1974–75, 109 schools reported 834 courses. A decade later, in 1984–86, a survey of 164 schools showed 1576 courses, an increase of 25.7% per school. A survey of 119 schools in 1990 found 1763 courses, a further increase of 54.1% per school over the 1984–86 figures. (pp. 237–38)

Nevertheless, the ABA task force further reported that the data from its survey also revealed that the majority of students are exposed to only four or fewer courses utilizing one or more modes of clinical education. The ABA survey (1992) found that "when classes of first year 'introduction to lawyering' (29% of students enroll), first year and advanced legal writing and research (85% of students enroll), trial advocacy (58% of students enroll) and moot court (41% of students enroll) were removed from the list, the majority of graduating students had only one (32%) or no (28%) additional exposures to professional skills instruction" (p. 240).

The above results show that the majority of law students have been exposed to the simulation mode of clinical instruction, but only a minority have experienced in-house, live-client clinics. Other recent surveys reveal that in-house programs are available to only 30 percent of law students at schools where live-client clinics are offered (McDiarmid, 1990). This emphasis on simulation over the modes of instruction is most frequently attributed to the high cost of in-house programs in comparison to courses employing simulation (Kramer, 1989).

THE LAW TEACHERS EMPLOYING THE CLINICAL METHOD

Because of its close association with the mission of preparing law students to practice law competently, because students learning through the clinical method perform lawyering tasks that are then critically evaluated, and because in-house clinics and externships place students in actual practice settings, law schools have been keen to employ experienced practicing lawyers and judges as instructors. Many of these instructors are employed on a part-time basis as adjuncts and the like. The survey data from the ABA's *Report of the Task Force on Law Schools and the Profession* (1992) reveals that for all law school courses employing the clinical method, 37 percent of the instructors were part time (p. 241).

Employing part-time instructors in law school clinical courses offers the advantages of moderating cost and drawing on the special expertise of well-respected practitioners and judges. However, these part-time instructors are primarily concerned with the pressing matters associated with their full-time professional careers. Full-time clinical instructors bring an important commitment to teaching, availability and sensitivity to students, knowledge of the growing literature of clinical scholarship, an ability to contribute to that scholarship, and an interest in reflection on issues of educational theory—all of which cannot be replicated by part-time instructors.

In order to take advantage of developments in clinical education, law schools must pay careful attention to the mix of committed full-time clinical teachers and part-time instructors. Commenting on the importance of maintaining an appropriate mix of full-time and part-time instructors, the ABA's *Report of the Task Force on Law Schools and the Profession* (1992) recommended that primary responsibility for clinical instruction be assigned to permanent full-time faculty and that part-time instructors be provided with guidance, structure, supervision and evaluation by the full-time teachers (p. 245).

Clinical education, similar to legal practice, is interdisciplinary, and experts from other disciplines continue to make valuable contributions to clinical teaching (Watson, 1968). Experts involved in clinical instruction include psychologists and psychiatrists, communications specialists, sociologists and social workers, physicians, economists, and others. Most of these experts contribute on a volunteer (guest-speaker or consultant) basis. A growing awareness of the need to form interdisciplinary teams to address community and individual problems will likely result in a trend in the new community-oriented clinics to increasingly engage experts from other disciplines in clinical teaching in law schools.[22]

In addition to the issues raised by the heavy use of part-time instructors in clinical teaching, no overview of the history of experiential education is complete without noting the struggle faced by clinical teachers for status and power. From the beginnings of the clinical movement in law schools, many clinical faculty have been treated differently from other faculty as far as law school governance, job security, and pay are concerned (McDiarmid, 1990, p. 245). In an article analyzing the results of a survey of law schools conducted by the ABA in 1987, Marjorie McDiarmid (1990) has described in detail the status differentials between clinical and other faculty, and has reported that "when clinicians describe the major challenges facing their educational efforts, they uniformly rank the attitude of the other faculty as their major difficulty. . . . Objective measures of clinician status tend to support this view in that they demonstrate that clinicians are frequently accorded a status less than that accorded other members of the faculty" (p. 246).

The source of this disparity in status may be attributable to several factors. Many live-client clinics were introduced into law schools as "experiments" in legal education. They were funded, in part, by short-term grants and contracts. The clinicians staffing the clinics were hired primarily because of their commitments to teaching and public interest work rather than demonstrated ability and interest in traditional legal scholarship (Barnhizer, 1990). Issues surround the time, resources, desire, and ability to produce scholarship in an appropriate form and, published in an acceptable forum, have fueled much of the debate about status. Distrust of the clinicians and a recognition that clinicians were "different" has led many governing faculty to marginalize clinicians by limiting their status.

Limiting faculty status for clinical teachers affects the stability, influence, and respectability of clinical programs generally. In order to help correct the debilitating effect of gross status differentials between clinical and other faculty, the ABA, in 1984, adapted accreditation Standard 405(e):

The law school should afford to full-time faculty members whose primary responsibilities are in its professional skills program a form of security of position reasonably similar to tenure and perquisites reasonably similar to those provided other full-time faculty members. . . . The law school should require these faculty members to meet standards and obligations reasonably similar to those required of full-time faculty members. ("Standards for Approval of Law Schools," 1992)

The ABA continues to monitor the implementation of Standard 405(e), but its full effect on the status question remains unanswered.

THE COST OF CLINICAL EDUCATION

As stated earlier in this chapter, the clinical method generally requires lower student-to-faculty ratios and often requires more of a support structure (equipped law office, videotape facilities, staff support) than what has been traditionally employed in supporting the case method of study. Consequently, clinical education is viewed as being more costly than "traditional" legal education.

Cost has been viewed as a serious obstacle to continued growth of clinical education. Finding the resources to support it has been a challenge faced by law schools from the beginning of the clinical movement. CLEPR and the extraordinary growth of law schools provided sources of new money in the early years of the clinical movement. Based on annual questionnaires submitted by law schools to the ABA, in the 1991–1992 school year total expenditures on clinical programs was $58.228 million, and 68.4 percent of the cost of clinical programs is funded through the law school or university budgets. Grants from various sources support approximately 22.3 percent of the remainder of the cost (*Task Force on Law Schools*, 1992).

The leading source of grants (8.6% of the total 1991–1992 expenditures) was the Law School Clinical Experience Program of the U.S. Department of Education, Title IX of the Higher Education Act. The Law School Clinical Experience Program, through the efforts of Senator Wayne Morse, was authorized in 1968 (University of Chicago, 1970, pp. 40–41). However it was not funded until years later. For 1993, the program was authorized for slightly over $7 million. Under the program, the secretary of education funds applications that "(a) provide legal experience in the preparation and trial of actual cases, including administrative cases and the settlement of controversies outside the courtroom; and (b) provide service to persons who have difficulty in gaining access to legal representation" (U.S. Department of Education, 1992, p. 8). Awards can be for up to three years and generally range in size from $40,000 to $250,000 per year. Matching funds from law school budgets are required. According to the ABA's *Report of the Task Force on Law Schools and the Profession* (1992), sixty-five law schools reported receiving Title IX grants in 1991–1992. During its existence the Law School Clinical Experience Program has fostered many innovations in in-house, live-client clinical programs. Nevertheless, funding remains a serious constraint and constant challenge for clinical programs.

SPECULATION ON THE FUTURE OF CLINICAL EDUCATION

In the coming decade, attention to professional skills education will continue to grow; the diversity within the ranks of students and faculty will continue to increase; the use of technology in legal education and law practice will continue to expand; professional status issues will intensify between various categories of faculty (including traditional, clinical, and adjunct instructors; writing instructors; interdisciplinary instructors; and librarians); and issues relating to the moral and ethical responsibilities of the legal profession will continue to demand increased attention. At the same time, law school enrollments will level off and funding for law school education will become increasing tight. All of these forces will resonate in clinical education. If serious funding shortages can be overcome and if clinicians anticipate and welcome the unavoidable changes in the nature of the legal profession that are coming, predictions are favorable for future growth and continued innovation in clinical education.

NOTES

1. Clinics have made, and continue to make, an invaluable contribution to the entire legal education enterprise. They are a key component in the development and advancement of skills and values throughout the profession. Their role in the curricular mix of courses is vital. Much of the reserach leading to the advancement of knowledge about lawyering, the legal profession, and its institutions is found in the work of clinicians; and many clinicians are recognized to be among the most dedicated and talented teachers in law schools. Clinics provide students with the opportunity to integrate, in an actual practice setting, all of the fundamental lawyering skills. In clinical courses, students sharpen their understanding of professional responsibility and deepen their appreciation for their own values as well as those of the profession as a whole. See ABA, *Standards for Approval of Law Schools and Interpretations*, 1992–1993.

2. See ABA, *Report and Recommendations of the Task Force on Lawyer Competency* (1979), *Final Report and Recommendations of the Task Force on Professional Competence* (1983), and *Report of the Task Force on Law Schools and the Profession* (1992).

3. Ironically, one of the early battlegrounds for the clinical movement was to convince the courts to adopt "student practice rules" to allow supervised law students to represent clients. The courts' concern that the public be protected from incompetent law students serving as counsel have all but been eliminated; now virtually every jurisdiction in which a law school is located has adopted a "student practice rule."

4. According to the CLEPR newsletter of May 1972, "CLEPR has had two major objectives in promoting clinical work: the improvement of the education of law students and increasing the delivery of legal services to the poor."

5. "Law schools, along with colleges generally, are faced with student demands for greater personal and institutional involvement in contemporary social problems, and for a curriculum which not only provides outlets for these interests, but also responds to the students general antipathy to uniformity of approach, impersonal analysis, and competition and sanction as the primary determinants of the law schools' incentive structure. Such concerns have found immediate expression in proposals for clinical education in the law, particularly when the primary models involved legal clinics providing services to indigent clients. Either as a cause or an effect, these types of programs have received most of CLEPR's financial support" (Bellow and Johnson, 1971). "The objectives served by clinical education fall in four categories: skills training, provision of legal service, education about society, and the development of professional responsibility" (Kitch, 1970).

6. "A well run clinical program can offer an area for the realistic implementation of some of a student's activist values and for the exercise of altruistic and equalitarian motivations" (Stone, 1971).

7. To a large degree, the clinical faculty who staffed law schools' clinics in the early years were drawn from a pool of lawyers who believed in the utility of the law in

advancing social justice, and the pursuit of correcting injustice through the activity of representing those clients for whom the quality of social justice was the most questionable. . . . [T]he initial clinical faculty came to law schools primarily from legal services and civil rights offices, public defender programs, and other public interest positions" (Barnhizer, 1990).

8. See the panel discussion of financing student clinical programs reproduced in *Clinical Education and the Law School of the Future* (Chicago: University of Chicago Press, 1970).

9. For example, the Law School Clinical Experience Program of the United States Department of Education, which has provided substantial grants to support law school clinical programs since the late 1970s, gives absolute funding priority to applications that "provide services to persons who have difficulty in gaining access to legal representation" (U.S. Department of Education, 1992).

10. See McGee (1969) and the CLEPR newsletter of May, 1972.

11. Gary Bellow is widely recognized as one of the most respected spokespersons for the clinical movement. He is coauthor of a seminal text on clinical legal education. See Bellow and Mouton, *Lawyering Process*, 1978.

12. After describing U.S. society as flawed by poverty, racism, inhumanity, and injustice, and after describing the extraordinary commitment of lawyers to maintaining public order, often at the expense of positive social change, Charles Silberman, a noted commentator on social and educational problems, stated: "I am not calling for the politicalization of the law school or of the university. On the contrary, I am, in a sense, calling for the de-politicalization. The point is that the law school . . . is already politicalized through its commitment to the status quo" (CLEPR, Newsletter, August 1971).

13. In an article responding to the AALS's *Final Report on the Future of the In-House Clinic* (1991), Stephen Befort (1991), the director of Civil Clinics at the University of Minnesota, noted that of the nine goals listed for live-client clinics, the public service component ranked seventh, and he concluded: "The lower ranking of this service goal, at the number seven position, puts to rest the old service versus education debate."

14. The ABA's *Report of the Task Force on Law Schools and the Profession* (1992) listed four fundamental values of the legal profession. Among them was "Striving to Promote Justice, Fairness, and Morality." Under this heading were the following values: "Promoting Justice, Fairness, and Morality in One's Own Daily Practice; Contributing to the Profession's Fulfillment of its Responsibility to Ensure Adequate Legal Services are Provided to Those Who Cannot Afford to Pay for Them, and Contributing to the Profession's Fulfillment of Its Responsibility to Enhance the Capacity of the Law and Legal Institutions to Do Justice."

15. The Interuniversity Poverty Law Consortium was founded in 1989, with the aid of a grant from the Ford Foundation. Initial funding supported three projects located at Harvard, University of Wisconsin, and UCLA. By 1992 more than thirty law schools were members of the consortium. In the introduction to a symposium highlighting the consortium's activities, G. Lessard (1992) stated that the "consortium's members engage in collective and decentralized efforts directed toward two goals. First, to increase law school scholarship, teaching, and understanding of poverty law and the relationship between law and poverty. Second to link this scholarship, teaching, and understanding with advocacy on behalf of poor, disadvantaged, and marginalized persons and organizations that promote their interests."

16. See ABA, *Pro Bono in Law Schools* (1991).

17. For a more complete discussion of use of the problem method, see M. Moskovitz, "Beyond the Case Method," *Journal of Legal Education* 42 (March 1993): 241.

18. For a recent analysis of the comparative strengths of in-house clinics, extern placements, and simulation, see G. Laser, "Educating for Professional Competence in the Twenty-first Century," *Chicago-Kent Law Review* 69 (1993): 243.

19. For a strong defense of the educational value of externships, see S. Maher, "The Praise of Folly," *Nebraska Law Review* 69 (1990): 537.

20. Responding to concerns about the educational value of extern placements, the ABA adopted an accreditation standard to assure educational quality. Since 1979, there have been six interpretations of the standard. See ABA, *Standards for Approval of Law Schools and Interpretations*, 1992.

21. The University of New Mexico School of Law has initiated an in-house clinical course entitled "Institute for Access to Justice." Partially funded by a federal grant, experts from diverse disciplines will be employed as part-time consultants to the clinic.

22. See Robert Stein, "The Future of Legal Education," *Minnesota Law Review* (February 1992).

SECTION IV: SOCIAL WORK EDUCATION

Elaine Marshack

12
SOCIAL WELFARE

American social work education has been, to a marked extent, a function of our society's philosophy and practice of helping disadvantaged groups survive and advance. Thus, more than in the other professions discussed, it is appropriate to begin with a brief history of social philosophy and practice in the United States.

HISTORY OF SOCIAL WORK IN THE UNITED STATES

The eighteenth-century colonists in the new world modeled provisions for their elderly, sick, poor, and others in need of social assistance on England's poor laws and welfare practices. The Elizabethan Poor Law of 1601 had charged local governments with the care of the poor and stipulated local taxation to support relief given outside of residential institutions. Public welfare in the United States began similarly "as agencies mandated by state law but established, financed, and managed by officials of local government" (Leiby, 1987, p. 759). By the time of the American Revolution, public relief was one of the largest expenditures of developing municipalities. A distinctive contribution to American charity was made by religious groups, which established many of the institutional services for needy groups, ranging from almshouses for the elderly to programs for country boys seeking their fortunes in the cities (Leiby, 1987, p. 757).

In the early nineteenth century, a time of expansion and opportunity, there was growing intolerance of dependency. Poverty was blamed on the poor themselves. The public increasingly identified the poor and dependent members of society with crime, violence, and social disorder. Increasing efforts were made to move the poor off welfare roles by enforced work and the use of poorhouses. This harsh morality replaced the relatively benevolent and humanitarian attitudes of the colonials toward the poor. Social Darwinism, later in the century, gave respectability to this view. In the late nineteenth century, continued immigration and industrial growth, low wages, seasonal variations in labor, and business depressions contributed to marked increases in pauperism and dependency.

Later in the century, municipal governments abandoned the role of helping the poor. Business and professional groups then began to establish charity organization societies "for reasons ranging from benevolence to social control" (Wenocur and Reisch, 1989, p. 25). At this point two major objectives of social work began to be defined. The first was to rehabilitate the poor and eliminate poverty. The second was to mobilize members of neighborhoods to solve their shared problems. Late in the century, the Panic and Depression of 1893 stimulated efforts to develop scientific principles for practice (Lloyd, 1987). The advocates of "scientific philanthropy" played a major role in the development of professional social work and the education of professional social workers by shifting emphasis from theology and social theory to the aims and methods of service (Leiby, 1987, p. 765). Mary Richmond exemplified this view by use of a medical, or disease, model to diagnose individuals' problems in social functioning and to develop plans for helping individuals "work out their own programs" (Brieland, 1987, p. 740).

Charity organization societies had developed earlier in the century as conduits for both social giving and social control (Reynolds, 1942). Volunteers known as "friendly visitors" had the job of "uplifting" the poor and providing role models (Berman-Rossi, 1981). The training provided for the friendly visitors was a forerunner for professional education.

Settlement houses, of which Hull House and the Henry Street Settlement are among the best known, were intended to achieve the second objective. These forerunners of community centers began to be established in the 1880s. They emphasized community participation and informal education rather than charity and correction (Leiby, 1987, p. 763). Poverty and social problems were seen as resulting from political and economic conditions rather than from individual deficiencies. "The settlements created an institutionalized form of self-help for the urban poor, attempting to meet concrete needs and to socialize the poor into the new industrial order" (Wenocur and Reisch, 1989, p. 38).

THE SOCIAL WORK PROFESSION

These two points of view, provision of social services and efforts to achieve social change, provide dynamic tension in social work practice and education. Social workers are a bridge in society between the needy and those who control the resources for meeting these needs. At times of expansion, society views social work as a vehicle for its benevolence and optimism. But "in times of contrived shortage, . . . when self-aggrandizement, bias, and punitiveness are ascendant, the values and practitioners of social work become unwelcome reflections on societal priorities and injustices," forcing social workers to make "difficult choices about the extent to which they serve as arms of the institutional structures or advocates of the excluded" (Hopps and Pinderhughes, 1987, p. 353).

Only the United States among industrialized nations has a dual system of social welfare that distinguishes private provisions for those who qualify through employment from public services for those who do not (Rosen, 1987, p. 51). The social work profession and publicly regulated social agencies developed, in part, to enhance equity in access to services and to counter the abuses of early profit-making agencies (Lubove, 1965; Barker, 1987). Although social work has evolved into a central helping profession, its status as a profession has been challenged from its earliest history (see, e.g., Flexner, 1915; Greenwood, 1957; Wilensky and Lebeaux, 1965; Hall, 1968; Etzioni, 1969; Toren, 1972). Social workers' continuing commitment to address the wide range of social problems that confront society's vulnerable populations contributes to difficulty in defining social work's specific body of knowledge and in exercising domain consensus (Hopps and Pinderhughes, 1987, p. 360). Since the emergence of a large number of paraprofessionals from the antipoverty programs of the 1960s, social work's traditional hegemony has been challenged by new categories of personnel labeled human-service workers (Khinduka, 1987, p. 682).

Most social workers are employed within organizational structures, including public welfare systems, hospitals, schools, courts, and other agencies addressing special problems or populations. These social workers are expected to be accountable to both clients and service organizations. A crucial recognition is that social work does not control most of the organizations that employ social workers (Gurin and Williams, 1973, p. 202). There always is the potential for conflicts in values and preferred modes of service between social work staff and program administrators. When such conflicts cannot be satisfactorily resolved, social workers might feel ineffective and might become demoralized. An example of an arena for conflict is the health care system where funding frequently dictates length of inpatient hospital stays. In carrying out discharge planning, social workers may lack time to fully assess psychosocial needs and identify appropriate resources, especially for clients with multiple social problems such as the frail elderly or those whose medical problems are associated with substance abuse or mental illness.

Social work is viewed in some settings, such as hospitals and schools, as an ancillary rather than as a primary service. This often leads to the primary service profession's attempting to set conditions for social work practice and, in time of fiscal constraint, making social workers especially vulnerable to cutbacks and to downgrading of qualifications. On the other hand, social workers may become providers of choice when their services overlap with more costly services provided by other professions, as has occurred in many mental health counseling programs (Goleman, 1985).

Social work is strongly dependent on societal sanctions for support of its activities. While the National Association of Social Workers (NASW) does not control access to practice and can only monitor the behavior of those who voluntarily submit to its sanctions, it has spearheaded successful efforts to obtain regulation of social work practice by registration, certification, or licensing in all fifty states, Puerto Rico, and the Virgin Islands. This has facilitated social workers' participation in third-party payments from insurers, a crucial issue for both independent practitioners and agencies providing social services to clients eligible for Medicare and other governmental benefits.

Although social work has traditionally been practiced in organizational settings, private practice has become an increasingly significant alternative. The numbers of NASW members who practice primarily on a private basis or secondarily in addition to agency practice increased from 10.9 percent in 1982 to 57.7 percent in 1991 (Gibelman and Schervish, 1993, p. 136). Of the 57.7 percent, 15 percent defined private practice as their primary social work activity. While the private practice of social work has been controversial throughout the profession's history, the implications of its growth for the profession and for the delivery of social services warrants further examination. NASW in recent decades has defined standards for private practice and established certificate programs for advanced credentials, but clinical social work societies have also developed outside the professional association to advance the cause of private practice.

SOCIAL WORK EDUCATION

Social work education encompasses baccalaureate, master's, and doctoral degree programs. Postmaster's courses are also offered by many schools. Baccalaureate education is intended to prepare graduates for beginning or generalist professional practice. Bachelor of Social Work (B.S.W.) graduates are able to waive foundation requirements for many Master of Social Work (M.S.W.) programs and enter with advanced standing. The focus of M.S.W. programs is on preparation for advanced or specialist practice. The doctorate in social work prepares candidates for teaching, research, and, increasingly, administration of social services. Less common is a doctorate in advanced clinical practice.

Social work shares with other professions a history of apprenticeship training for its service providers. Courses were first developed to prepare the friendly visitors and paid agents of the charity organizations to carry out organizational roles. Through review of their practice in group meetings and individual conferences, decisions were reached about "what could and should be done to improve the conditions of the needy and influence behavior in socially desirable directions" (George, 1982, pp. 37–38). This early emphasis on supervised practice and reflection on the experience rather than acquisition and application of a well-defined body of theory strongly influenced social work education.

Charity organization workers' efforts to enrich preparation for practice beyond inservice training led to the establishment in New York of a six-week summer school in 1898. The first university-based school was at the University of Chicago in 1907. By 1910, the New York School of Philanthropy, now the Columbia University School of Social Work, had become a two-year program. By 1923, there were thirteen university-connected schools of social work. The number of schools has greatly increased in response to professional needs of social-service programs and agencies. Many programs developed out of casework agencies. In Chicago, social work education developed from the work of the settlement houses. Deriving from its origin in social agencies, early social work education consisted of a dynamic interplay between classroom and experiential learning.

Movement toward development of a professional educational association began in 1919 with the establishment of the Association of Training Schools for Professional Social Work. This became the American Association of Schools of Social Work in 1927. Standards were first suggested for "an organized curriculum, responsible administrative leadership, and university affiliation" in 1924 (Lloyd, 1987, p. 696).

In 1939 the American Association of Schools of Social Work required that members be based in institutions affiliated with the Association of American Universities. This essentially placed professional education on a graduate level and eliminated from membership undergraduate and one-year master's programs. Disaffiliated groups formed a new organization, the National Association of Schools of Social Administration, in 1942.

After a decade of dissension between these two organizations and their promulgation of conflicting educational standards, the 1950s witnessed movement toward professional consolidation (Brieland, 1987, p. 747). A landmark study in 1951, *Social Work Education in the United States*, known as the Hollis-Taylor Report, led to the creation a year later of the Council of Social Work Education (CSWE), the only national organization currently overseeing social work education. With a membership drawn from universities, the professional associations, and practice agencies, the CSWE serves as the accrediting body for social work programs. The Hollis-Taylor Report also recommended that an undergraduate-graduate continuum be established that would be responsive to the need for both basic and specialized preparation of workers (Hollis and Taylor, 1951).

In 1955 seven professional social work associations, each representing a particular field or method of practice, formed the NASW. Members of the sponsoring groups were (grand)parented in; membership now requires an M.S.W. or B.S.W. degree. The movement toward unity also led to formation of an NASW Commission on Practice in 1958, directed to define the basic elements of social work practice. Despite NASW's attempts to bridge the wide diversity of social work practice, there was little consistency in curricula among schools of social work. The thirteen-volume curriculum (Boehm) study in 1959 refocused attention from a predominant focus on casework to the full range of social work practice methods. These methods included group work, community organization, administration, and research. It also attempted to identify and define more specific educational objectives.

In the early 1960s the profession made further attempts to deal with its difficulties in "achieving a holistic and integrated model of social work practice" (Gurin and Williams, quoted in Hughes, 1973, p. 241) by moving toward a generalist model of graduate social work education. This model discouraged undergraduate professional education and advocated a social science base for graduate social work education. However, the social revolution of the late 1960s and early 1970s resulted in a rapid expansion in human service programs and opportunities for baccalaureate level workers in order to provide services to such underserved populations as the chronically mentally ill, the frail elderly, substance abusers, and victims of violence. A task force of the Department of Health, Education, and Welfare recommended in 1965 that social work education be rapidly expanded at both the graduate and undergraduate levels. In response to rising tuition costs, there was a concurrent movement on the undergraduate level to foster vocational and professional programs.

All of these factors contributed to the hotly debated decision by NASW in 1970 to admit to membership graduates of social work baccalaureate programs. The CSWE soon received authority to accredit undergraduate social work programs, stipulating that preparation for entry level generalist practice be their chief objective. Consistent with recognition of an undergraduate major, many master's programs admit B.S.W. graduates to advanced, second-year standing. By 1990 there were 366 baccalaureate social work programs and 99 M.S.W. programs (33,315 baccalaureate and 27,420 M.S.W. students) (Spaulding, 1991, pp. 22, 24). (Data were submitted by schools with 84.9 percent of the baccalaureate and 97 percent of the master's programs.)

Rapid growth in doctoral education roughly paralleled the expanding need for educators in M.S.W. and B.S.W. programs during the 1960s and early 1970s. In 1990, 247 doctoral degrees were awarded. There were 1,792 students in 48 doctoral programs (Spaulding, 1991, p. 36). The proportion of men among doctoral recipients was double that for M.S.W. graduates (35 percent compared to 17.4 percent). Ethnic minorities were also more highly represented among doctoral graduates than among master's (25.5 percent compared to 18 percent).

After rapid expansion of social work education in the 1960s and early 1970s, applications to M.S.W. programs declined between 1979 and 1983 during a period of retrenchment in social programs and rising educational costs. Part-time and work-study alternatives were developed by many M.S.W. programs to recruit candidates to the profession. By 1990, 36 percent of M.S.W. students were enrolled in part-time programs, making this route a significant alternative to the traditional two-year program (Spaulding, 1991, p. 27). The CSWE continues to require at least one year in residence.

Classes for part-time students are often scheduled in evenings and on weekends to accommodate full-time employment. Field practica may be similarly arranged. A potential pitfall is that students miss participation in daytime meetings and opportunities for professional interaction. Despite concerns that educational effectiveness might be compromised by part-time education, studies have not found substantial differences in class or field performance between part-time and full-time students (Seltzer and Wayne, 1985).

Since 1984, a liberal arts perspective has been a prerequisite for both baccalaureate and graduate education. Undergraduates typically follow a course of two years of liberal arts studies followed by two years of a social work major. The master's program involves approximately sixty credits of study most frequently offered in a two-year curriculum. The first year focuses on core content; the second, on specialization.

A comparable expectation for broad-based practicum experiences characterizes both undergraduate and graduate programs. The undergraduate goal of preparation for entry-level generalist practice leads to more generic assignments in the practicum with emphasis on concrete and supportive tasks and limited autonomy for the student. At the master's level, students carry out more specialized, skilled professional activities with increased autonomy and initiatives in the learning process.

13
CONTENT AND LEARNING APPROACHES

CONTENT

The early schools tended to organize around the specific practice tracks that were developing in the first decades of the twentieth century. Family casework and child welfare emerged from the charity-organization tradition. This tradition placed primary emphasis on assessing and developing plans to meet the needs of individuals in their environments (Brieland, 1987, p. 742). The need for new content areas arose as social workers started providing services for new populations including economically stable individuals who presented psychiatric and other social problems. Psychiatric principles strongly influenced casework directed toward prevention and rehabilitation services in mental health and child guidance. Medical social work was initiated by a physician to address psychosocial conditions that contributed to illness or impeded its treatment. School social work addressed the psychosocial needs of children that affected learning.

Since preparation for these individual tracks of practice tended to be specialized, mobility from one to another was limited and the issue of whether social work was generic or specific came increasingly to the fore (Brieland, 1987, p. 743). In identifying eight generic aspects of casework in the late 1920s, the Milford Conference succeeded in unifying the casework area by finding "a politics and a language for affirming the whole" (Wenocur and Reisch, 1989, p. 137).

The 1960s and 1970s witnessed an increasing schism between direct practice with clients and social administration or social policy, leading to renewed efforts at cohesiveness by the professional establishment (Gurin and Williams, 1973, p. 210). Subsequent curriculum policies have reflected the dual intent of ensuring a common base of knowledge for all students while allowing opportunities for specialization.

Both baccalaurate and master's programs provide access to professional practice, but the relationship and continuity between the two is still being clarified. According to the 1992 Curriculum Policy Statement of the CSWE, the two levels of education "differ from each other in their depth, breadth, and specificity of knowledge and skill that students are expected to synthesize and apply in practice" (CSWE, 1992, p. 3). Both must provide a foundation curriculum encompassing social welfare policy and services, human behavior and the social environment, social work practice, research, and field practicum within the framework of the common body of knowledge, values, and skills. The master's level must also include specialized content for advanced practice that can be organized by practice methods or roles (e.g., casework or community organization), fields of practice (e.g., child welfare or mental health), population groups (e.g., the elderly or African Americans), or social problems (e.g., substance abuse or poverty).

LEARNING APPROACH

As a consequence of its evolution from training for work in social agencies, early social work education was a limited form of natural experiential learning based on work experience in these agencies. While the emphasis on practice as an integral part of the educational process remained, there was an early movement away from agency domination toward "a vision of social work education as a professional discipline in which teaching . . . became subject to university objectives for professional education and . . . standards for scholarship and research" (Kendall, 1959, p. 3). As sponsorship of social work education moved increasingly to universities, the role of social agencies in the educational process shifted to one of collaboration (Carlton, 1985, p. 5). The educational approach changed from one in which class teaching was seen as "an academic extension of and support to experience in the field . . . to a conception . . . in which field and class experiences were seen as mutually interacting and supportive" (Finestone, 1967, p. 25). This is closer to the ideal form of natural experiential learning.

The opportunity to apply classroom learning in social agency settings has always been considered an essential component of the social work educational experience, but it wasn't until 1932 that the practicum, or "field work," was formally designated as a basic element of the curriculum. In the adoption of a minimum one-year curriculum plan at that time, both class and field instruction were required (Skolnick, 1985, p. 4). The adoption of the minimum curriculum in 1932 also established the provision that "not more than one-third or less than one-quarter of the total credits of a school might be in field work" (Bruno, 1944, p. 160). The proportions of class and field credits remain generally the same.

In work-study programs (for which preprofessional experience may be a requisite), enrollees carry both student and employee roles in social service programs. A 1987 survey found that 9 percent of students enrolled in sixty-three respondent M.S.W. programs were using their employment sites as practicum settings (Black, 1989, p. 2). A major issue is assurance of an educational focus in the practicum with supports from both school and agency for a shift in the employee's role to student/learner.

In contrast to most professions, social work has consistently assumed that "students can and should carry professional responsibility for service from an early point in the educational process" (Kendall, 1959, p. 3). This controversial position asserts that practice throughout the educational process enhances students' motivation for providing social work services and facilitates their integration of theory. It is predicated upon an assumption of (1) reflection on experience based on theory taught in both class and field and (2) consistent educational guidance to guard against students' sole reliance on their beginning skills to deal with complex human problems. Practice is also seen as fostering students' development of concepts and principles derived from theory for the purpose of guiding their ongoing social work activity.

Most commonly students in social work begin the field practicum within a few weeks of entering the program. In 1984 the CSWE established minimum numbers of practicum hours, 900 for the M.S.W. degree and 400 for the baccalaureate degree. The predominant M.S.W. structural arrangement is for students to practice in field agencies concurrently with classroom courses for two or three days a week. Most M.S.W. students have placements in different social service agencies during each of two years. In some schools, blocks of classroom teaching alternate with blocks of field practice, allowing primary focus on one component of learning at a time and the possibility of a wider geographic distribution of practicum agencies.

The organizations in which social work students practice mirror the wide diversity of social service programs in the country. Most are under public and voluntary auspices; placement of students in profit-making services occurs but may be seen as conflicting with the profession's emphasis on services to the most disadvantaged. Social work is practiced and taught in such varied services as child welfare, programs for substance abusers, health facilities, income maintenance, schools, correctional facilities, programs for victims of abuse and violence, employee assistance programs, community centers, and counseling agencies.

A primary relationship between a field instructor and student has characterized the field practicum in social work from the beginning. An apprentice model in which "learning by doing under the concerned and vigilant appraisal of the supervisor" (Wijnberg and Schwartz, 1977, p. 108) had carried over from social work's preprofessional history and predominated into the 1920s. Some characteristics of this model survive in current field instruction.

A field instructor is usually an experienced M.S.W. who is an employee of the agency in which a student is placed by the school for the practicum (field work). If social workers are not available for this role, social work program faculty are charged to "assume additional responsibility to assure that a social work focus is maintained in instruction as well as in planning and evaluating the students' field experience" (CSWE, 1984, pp. 47, 57). An exploratory comparison of groups of social work and nonsocial work field instructors found that the importance placed on the development of social work values was the greatest area of difference between the two (Strom, 1991, p. 193). Since values play a crucial role in informing practice, the failure to emphasize this curriculum component may be a serious lack in field teaching by nonsocial workers (Rohrer, Smith, and Peterson, 1992).

Most social work programs provide at least an orientation to an educational role for new field instructors, and many mandate attendance at seminars addressing such content as orientation and engagement of students, development of assignments and learning contracts, educational theory and its application in assessment of learning styles and needs, evaluation of student performance, administration of student assignments, use of student recording for teaching, socialization of students to the profession, and termination (Abramson and Fortune, 1990, pp. 274–75).

A field instructor is expected to meet regularly with a student in individual conferences, usually weekly for one to two hours. Students are generally required to submit written documentation of their practice for review by field instructors. The detailed process recording of each client contact that had earlier formed the basis for the educational process is now supplemented by use of formats specific to a student's major practice focus and learning needs.

In addition to detailed or summarized accounts of interviews or group meetings, student recording of practice might include logs, minutes, records of service, or works-in-progress such as grant or program proposals. Taping or direct observation of student performance may also be done. Evaluations of student performance prepared by field instructors are generally mandated at the end of each semester.

Assignments for student practice are drawn from the social work program in which the student is placed. It is expected that assignments will be graduated in relation to a student's ability and readiness. However, complexity of a practice situation cannot always be anticipated at the outset. Students may begin by observing the practice of agency social workers or by coparticipating with them. As students assume primary responsibility for practice, field instructors often use synthetic and natural experiential approaches, including role-playing, practice simulation, anticipatory planning, and discussion of a partial "blueprint."

Initial teaching is likely to be heavily didactic and supportive in order to provide information, direction, and affirmation for students' beginning efforts. As students develop an experiential base, the typical teaching process focuses on retrieval of a practice activity, reflection on its effectiveness or effect, a search for the professional knowledge base that informs the situation, and selection of appropriate responses or actions (Bogo and Vayda, 1987). Over time, field instructors increasingly direct their teaching to observed patterns in students' practice that are indicative of the students' specific strengths and needs. Generally, teaching moves toward increased efforts to encourage a student's reflectiveness as a basis for arriving at practice decisions. While this framework may be broadly applicable, it does not address wide variations in field teaching content and methodology. Tutorial teaching provides the opportunity for a high degree of individualization but also varies in quality and consistency.

As psychiatry developed during the 1920s, attention in social work practice shifted to understanding the individual who was being helped, often to the minimization of the social context (George, 1982, p. 41). A counterpart approach in education assumed that "to facilitate growth and change for the client, a social work student must experience a personal growth process" (Bogo and Vayda, 1987, p. 21). While this approach held sway in some social work programs, most advocated separation of the educational process from provision of treatment to a student. In instances when patterned responses of a student were found to impede effectiveness in practice, it was considered sufficient for a field instructor to identify these responses and expect a student to deal with them outside of the learning relationship or, if the responses remained pervasively intrusive in the learning process, to leave the program.

As role-systems theory and educational approaches for adult learning were developed, emphasis shifted to a view of the teaching-learning process as a series of transactions in which both field instructor and student contribute and grow. With an emphasis on reciprocity, the basis for the relationship is likely to shift from psychological coercion to shared recognition of the field instructor's expertise (Wijnberg and Schwartz, 1977, p. 109).

There has also been movement away from reliance on a single teaching relationship impelled by both the changing nature of practice and concepts of adult learning. The increasing diversity and complexity of social work activities and the expectation that students have broad-based practice opportunities have contributed to placements that involve concurrent practice in more than one program area or modality of practice. There is also recognition that reliance on a single teaching relationship might "foster inordinate dependency, infantilize students" or "encourage organizational docility and discourage risk taking" (Marshack and Glassman, quoted in Schneck, Grossman, and Glassman, 1990, p. 86; Germain and Gitterman, 1980, p. 299).

Studies of the learning styles of both B.S.W. and M.S.W. students suggest a predominant preference for concrete experience over abstract conceptualization (Papell, 1980; Kruzich, Friesen, and Van Soest, 1986). Practice opportunities might, therefore, be crucial in providing an experiential base for theory building.

Social work theory is neither static nor timeless but rooted in the living context of social problems, the clients who experience them, and the programs developed to address them. The knowledge base of social work draws predominantly on psychological, sociological, organizational, and social policy theories to explain the basis and context of client behavior, the nature of social problems, interactions between clients and social workers, and the societal and organizational context for practice. The finding that social workers tend to be guided in their practice by general approaches to clients rather than by explicit use of theory (Coccozzelli and Constable, 1985; Carew, 1979) might suggest that the educational process has not labeled content by its theoretical origins, presents practice principles drawn from a range of theories, or is applied by its students without attribution.

While class instruction emphasizes frameworks for practice, the one-to-one relationship in the practicum provides a unique opportunity for field instructors to help students reflect on their experience, draw on informing principles, and generate hypotheses as a basis for future action; however, school and field do not move in lockstep. They may be teaching different interventive approaches to emerging social problems, sometimes leaving students to grapple with discrepant perspectives.

14
FACULTY AND STUDENTS

Social work education is dependent on factors other than the content and educational approach. Faculty and student issues are discussed in this chapter.

FACULTY

School-based faculty were first drawn from the body of experienced providers. Until the 1960s, the terminal degree for most faculty was an M.S.W., but academic hiring in recent years has favored doctoral graduates. Although most faculty have practiced social work, some have had little experience or might not practice after joining a faculty. A question is sometimes raised about whether such faculty can address the "real world" of agency practice in their teaching or keep abreast of changing social needs and conditions.

Most field instructors are employed by agencies and continue to provide social services while supervising one or two students. The teaching role is often added to a full workload without compensation by either the employing agency or the social work program. However, even in a period of heavy service demand and reduced resources, it is generally possible to recruit field instructors. Their availability suggests the satisfactions associated with the role, including the opportunity to teach, to facilitate the developing competence of another practitioner, to gain new skills, and to contribute to the profession (Marshack, 1984, pp. 115–18;

Strom, 1991, p. 190). For many social workers, field instruction provides entry to a supervisory role.

Estimates of field instructor turnover range from 20 to 50 percent annually. Schools offer limited benefits to field staff: most commonly, use of library holdings or equipment, free workshop attendance or reduced tuition for advanced education, designation as adjunct faculty, use of a school's recreational facilities, opportunities to teach in the classroom, and recognition ceremonies and certificates (Lacerte, Ray, and Irwin, 1989; Rohrer, Smith, and Peterson, 1992).

LIAISON BETWEEN SCHOOL AND FIELD

A major mechanism for connecting school and agency has been the designation by educational programs of liaisons charged to maintain linkage and to monitor both the practicum learning opportunities and the performance of students in practice. Liaisons might additionally provide consultation to field instructors and might assist students in integrating theory and practice.

Despite the centrality of the liaison function to the articulation of class and field education, liaisons surveyed in the late 1980s ranked this role as less important than classroom teaching or scholarship/research activities (Brownstein, Harrison, and Faria, 1990, p. 243). The responses were reflective of the status accorded liaison activity within most schools of social work and universities. Lower rank faculty predominate as liaisons, and the role is not generally considered in tenure decisions. University administrators often equate it with academic advising and question its relatively higher costs. As scholarship and both professional and community services have assumed increasing importance in evaluations of faculty, there has been greater variation in expectations and implementation of the liaison function. Integration seminars for students and group meetings for field instructors increasingly supplant and reduce more individualized activities. A problem-focused or residual model of response to practicum issues reduces the volume of activity but is less effective in early identification of problems than an institutional model would be that assumes ongoing contact betwen liaison, field instructor, and student.

STUDENTS

The diversity in the social work student body reflects the pluralism of social work's activities and clientele. Women have predominated over men throughout the history of the field, contributing to the public image of social work as a female profession; however, the gender proportions have varied with such factors as comparative occupational salary levels. In 1960, slightly less than half (43 percent) of the entering M.S.W. students were male; in 1990, the proportions of men had declined to 18 percent at a time when social work salaries had declined in relation to other occupations. The *Wall Street Journal* (February 10, 1992) reported that "those serving the needy are increasingly becoming impoverished themselves—a new class of genteel poor, in a sense" (p. 1). Among social work practitioners, men are disproportionately represented in administration and on faculties of social work programs (Curlee and Raymond, 1979, p. 308).

The proportion of M.S.W. students drawn from ethnic minority populations has fluctuated over thirty years. Twelve percent of the entering M.S.W. students in 1960 were described as "Negro," the only racial or ethnic minority cited by Pins (1964). After reaching a high point of 18.3 percent in 1976, the proportion declined in the mid-1980s (Rosen, 1987, p. 118). In 1990, 18 percent of M.S.W. students were described as African American, Puerto Rican, Chicano, Asian American, Native American, or other ethnic minority (Spaulding, 1991, p. 28). Since service to immigrant and economically disadvantaged populations has always been a major focus for social work, M.S.W. programs have attempted through recruitment and financial aid to attract students who are themselves members of ethnic minorities or who speak the primary languages of recent arrivals.

The ages of M.S.W. students have fluctuated over time but are now substantially higher than in 1960 when 68 percent of the entering class were under 30 (Pins, 1964). In 1990, 45 percent of M.S.W. students were 30 or younger (Spaulding, 1991, p. 27). Female applicants have typically come from more advantaged backgrounds than their male counterparts (Golden, 1972). Social work could now be competing for younger female students who can afford and have access to formerly male-dominated professions.

Life experience tends to be viewed as a valuable resource in a field dealing with complex social problems, often making older applicants especially welcome. Older students in M.S.W. education are drawn from three major constituencies. The numbers of women returning to education after child rearing may be diminishing, but the proportions of students making career changes or seeking the M.S.W. after preprofessional employment in social work have grown.

Part-time and work-study programs attract higher proportions of ethnic minority and older students to M.S.W. education than do full-time programs (ethnic minority students constituted 18.8 percent of all part-time students and 15.7 percent of the full-time group in 1990); students over 30 years of age accounted for 65 percent of part-time and 50 percent of full-time students.

15

ISSUES, QUESTIONS, SUGGESTIONS

The practice of social work and, consequently, the education for social workers have changed from their beginnings in the philanthropic movement of the nineteenth century. Changes have occurred in objectives, services performed, technologies and processes involved, the theories on which these are based, and the populations served. Changes in education have both followed and preceded changes in practice, but the relationships have been close. To an important degree this has followed from the educational practice of combining classroom learning of theory and learning from experience in practice in the field. The relations between the schools and the service agencies have been closer in social work than in any other professional field. As distinct from medicine where the teaching hospitals have become the dominant educational venue, the schools of social work have remained the educational focal point. However, in its approaching hundredth year social work education may have to face up to a number of problems and issues. Some have been identified but waved aside. And some are appearing on the horizon.

LEARNING APPROACH

Social work education has remained committed throughout its history to natural experiential learning as a vital component of professional education. Since practice was first specified as a basic component of social work education in 1932, six ensuing curriculum policy statements have continued to reflect "the perception of field as the educational component which implements and integrates the academic curriculum" (Skolnick, 1985, p. 4). A challenge is to maintain quality and consistency in learning across the broad range of organizations that provide the practice experience. The fact that social work relies, to an increasing extent, on organizations that it does not control to provide practice experiences for students and staff members could pose a threat to traditional field education, especially since student education is not usually cost-effective.

A primary one-to-one teaching relationship between a field instructor and a student has also remained the predominant educational form in the field. At a time of increasing diversity in social work practice, reliance on a single field teacher who might teach only a limited range of skills can severely limit the breadth and quality of a student's field education.

While social work education at the M.S.W. and B.S.W. levels makes extensive use of a natural experiential approach, integration of class and field learning is not entirely satisfactory. Several factors contribute: schools and social services have different primary objectives; communication between field and school is often less than perfect; and faculty advising has lower status in social work programs than teaching, research, and publication—a fact that is seldom confronted but favors ignoring situations that are not presented as problems by the student or field instructor. One consequence is that ties between theory and practice are not as uniformly strong as they could be. Another is insufficient encouragement of student's use of reflective analysis to extend and reinforce learning and to develop lifelong learning skills.

CURRICULUM CONTENT

Both B.S.W. and M.S.W. programs are mandated to educate students in a broad range of social work practice responding to changing social needs and problems. Students are expected to be exposed, in both class and field, to practice with individuals, families, groups, and communities as well as to social policy and planning. M.S.W. programs are mandated to offer opportunities for specialization in the second year. It is a challenge to combine breadth in the whole field with depth in a specialty. Skills in helping clients to identify and negotiate the baffling range of social service programs that now exist should be a primary component of social work education. Case management and family preservation programs have demonstrated the value of intensive, integrated services for clients confronting multiple problems such as the persistently mentally ill and families at risk of dissolution.

A large proportion of social workers become independent or private practitioners, often in conjunction with organizational practice. Preparation for intensive clinical practice is provided predominantly by certificate courses, many outside of social work programs. Do social work programs need to take more responsibility for postgraduate education of individuals entering independent practice?

THE PROFESSION

A challenge to professional social work comes from a proliferation of new "human service" programs. Social work, education, and religion have always had overlapping domains with respect to such activities as counseling and human services. Now numerous new programs, inside the university and outside, degree and certificate, train practitioners in these and other recognized social work areas. Some are helping crime victims, substance abusers, or families seeking counseling. The training tends to be narrower and more specialized than that for either the B.S.W. or M.S.W degree. The pressure from these occupations is forcing social workers to define their domain more precisely and to demonstrate its distinct competency more strongly. The development of B.S.W. programs that provide underpinning to the more specialized M.S.W. degree represents one approach. Another is seen in the effort to achieve legal regulation of social work practice throughout the United States.

CONTINUING EDUCATION

The need for lifelong education is recognized in every profession. Social work programs have tried to encourage lifelong learning by offering certificate courses in specialized areas under the assumption that professionals working in a specialty will seek more learning in that area. Recognition by the Academy of Certified Social Workers is another means. While useful, are these approaches adequate for the need? A partial answer is given by the large number of programs offered by individuals and organizations not part of social work academia. But beyond this evidence is there nothing to be learned from the incidence of burnout among social workers and by the fragmented character of isolated workshops and even "certificate" programs? Is there need for profession-wide efforts to develop advanced curricula for continuing education?

THE B.S.W.

After many years of deprecating undergraduate social work education, the National Association of Social Workers embraced the B.S.W. degree. This action might have been largely an effort to ward off encroachment on the social work domain by persons trained in other fields at a time of exploding need for personnel. But now the degree is well established, and there is need to legitimize it in all respects. Most M.S.W. programs give persons with a B.S.W. a year's credit for the M.S.W., but others argue that there is not equivalency. One approach to standardizing curriculum and field experience has been the development of accreditation standards for B.S.W. programs by the Council on Social Work Education. But competencies of the B.S.W.-level worker still need clearer definition so that the degree will be recognized as equivalent to one year of M.S.W. education.

STUDENTS

Some social work programs admit bachelor-level employees who perform social work tasks into special programs that recognize and make use of the student's employment while permitting the student to continue to work almost full-time during M.S.W. education. Some schools require a signed agreement with the employer that spells out the experience and other conditions needed for good experiential learning. Often these students remain with the same organizations after graduation so that the employers have more competent professionals. Students who have performed social work–related tasks for several years may be more committed to agency practice and less subject to burnout, so that perhaps this model should be further encouraged. We need more comparative analysis.

To a greater extent than any other profession, social work is subject to the claim that the most effective social workers come from the populations to be served. The rationale is simple and direct. The personal experiences of these workers with the cultures, and often the primary languages, of the client populations are expected to enhance their understanding and abilities to provide helpful services. Commonality may also be defined in the context of the problem to be met; many social workers have struggled with issues that they now confront in their clients, such as histories of parental mistreatment or substance abuse. Sometimes the similarity in experience can enhance empathy, while at other times it makes it more difficult for a worker to maintain essential objectivity. Gender is another salient characteristic. There always has been a preponderance of female students; the proportion of males increases at times when social work salaries are more competitive with other fields. Programs for experienced preprofessionals attract higher proportions of males and students of color.

FACULTY

There are many unresolved, perhaps unresolvable, issues related to the selection, tenuring, and promotion of faculty. I will only touch on three. Selection and promotion on the basis of research and publications reflect broader university policy but may have less validity in social work than in other areas. The role of faculty as a teaching body—rather than as researchers—with close ties to practice may be more important. A second issue is selection on the basis of current or past identification with a population served by social workers, with arguments paralleling those discussed for students.

The effect on education of the separation between school-based faculty and field instructors has been touched on. Improved communication would have a beneficial effect on both education and provision of social services. More exchanges of class and field teachers and joint meetings with students could be useful. While the field instructor plays a central role in individualized teaching, the liaison or faculty advisor is crucial in spanning the gulf between school and agency and in helping the student to integrate the entire learning experience. Despite its saliency, this function tends to be equated with academic advising and given minimal support or recognition.

SPECIALIZATION

There is a commonality in the approaches of all social work services; nevertheless, there are distinct specialities that require specific knowledge and skills. While these are not as sharply defined as in medicine, the special competencies are important for providing superior services. The one area of the profession in which there are established, although varied, criteria for advanced practice is clinical social work, largely in response to standards for third-party reimbursement. Otherwise social work leaves the achievement of specialized skills to the individual. Advanced training is widely available but is not standardized and often leads to certificates of completion rather than tests of competence. Should there be some standardization and test of competence for a school to issue a certificate in a speciality? It would not be a degree. But then there are none in graduate medical education. It might also make it easier to define the function of a doctorate in social work.

CONCLUDING REMARK

Responding to social, political, and economic change has been a hallmark of social work practice. It is to be anticipated that the schools of social work will be no less responsive.

SECTION V: MANAGEMENT EDUCATION

Solomon Hoberman and Sidney Mailick

16

HISTORY AND STATUS OF MANAGEMENT EDUCATION

INTRODUCTION

Management is an old activity. Martin (1989) traces management theory back to comments by Confucius (551–479 B.C.). Others go even earlier to the Egyptians and the Sumerians (George, 1972). But only in the past hundred years has there been formal education for private sector managers and a resurgence of training for public managers. In this chapter, we describe the status and nature of the managerial job and how these have affected management education.

THE MANAGEMENT PROFESSION

Questions often asked are, "Does management meet the criteria for a profession?" and "What sort of a profession is this occupation?" Criteria for recognition as a profession include:

- generally accepted theory and research relating to the occupation
- performance requiring special skills and judgment
- postsecondary, generally graduate, study for practitioners
- a process for credentialing practitioners

Management does not satisfy the last of these. A major reason is that there is no agreement on the specifics of the other criteria; management's characteristics are dependent on the parameters relating to the culture, structure, and functioning of the organization. In Simon's "man-made"/"natural," classification, it is "man-made" (1976).

When practitioners determined the content of management education, management was not considered to be a profession. Economists, who made little effort to put their theories to use in the business world, tended to ignore management and business schools, which they disparaged as "trade schools." Although respected thinkers such as Adam Smith and Carl von Clausewitz wrote extensively on management (George, 1972), academics viewed "management" as a set of unrelated techniques without a theoretical basis. Before the 1960s management was not considered to have significant intellectual content. Added content from economics, statistics, social psychology, and mathematical modeling has led to increased recognition as a profession.

WHAT IS MANAGEMENT?

Meaningful management education depends on agreement on the tasks of the manager. We categorize these tasks as "people-oriented," "other-than-people–oriented," and "general," and refer to them as "instrumental," "expressive," and "general." Examples of content in each of these categories are:

- instrumental—planning, financial analysis, evaluation
- expressive—leading, communicating, and motivating
- general—problem solving and decision making

Managerial tasks and competencies are functions of the work venue. We will illustrate the dependence with one variable: culture.

A "culture" is defined by the way in which people in one "culture" behave differently from people in another "culture." Cultural determinants include values, technology, conflict resolution, relationships, communication, decision making, as well as political, economic, and social practices, symbols, and rites. These determinants are passed from generation to generation and reinforced by socialization, rules, and education.

Japanese and German cultures foster managerial styles different from ours (Locke, 1989). Managers in Japan and Germany are taught to see making money as secondary to providing a good product. Managers in the United States learn that making as much money as possible for their companies and themselves is primary and that making the best product is secondary (Locke, 1989). Managers in the United States tend to be considered "equal" if they are paid equal amounts. In Germany and Japan, managers are considered "equal" if they are equally competent (Locke, 1989). When Japanese critics say that American managers don't "work hard," they miss the point. American managers work hard to make more money, not better products, unless the former is a positive function of the latter.

In America, the structure of organizations has a greater effect, than in other countries, on techniques, processes, practices, and theory—and, consequently, on management education. In other countries, cultural values tend to determine business practices and, ultimately, structure and education. The Japanese *rigi* is a formal process for collective bottom-up consultation within a strict seniority (hierarchical) structure with top-down control. The French have formal, structured, top-down decision making and control. This is a consequence of impersonal relationships; rules; well-defined, carefully bounded occupational groups with high cohesion within and separation between groups; and a central authority to decide exceptions, resolve ambiguities and uncertainties, and change the rules (Crozier, 1964; Locke, 1989). Different expressive tasks are consequences of different ideals; American individualism, British loyalty to a class, French loyalty to the school, and the Japanese and German loyalty to the organization.

There is a preponderance of technical people in the senior management ranks in Germany and of financial, marketing, and legal people in the United States. Americans tend to assume that all issues can be converted into well-defined problems and that all problems would be solvable if we had enough information and were sufficiently competent problem solvers. Corollaries are that clear-cut decisions and directions are necessary and confronting problems is good. These lead to greater dependence on agreements and problem solving and analytic techniques than in other countries (Locke, 1989).

The interplay between managers' and workers' expectations has a strong effect on managers' styles. Workers in a culture expect managers to behave in a given way. American managers are expected to be considerate of subordinates and to confront differences with both subordinates and superiors. French managers are expected to ignore, on a one-to-one basis, differences with subordinates (Crozier, 1964). In Europe, "technical" training is related to production. In the United States it refers to mathematical modeling, finance, and marketing.

Indicative of the American love of models is the prescription that managerial behavior leading to more effective organizations be modeled on our presumed "democratic" and "egalitarian" society. The research supporting this hypothetical society is generally ancedotal—and where it is not anecdotal, the literature does not provide reliable and valid tests of this hypothetical assumption. The hypothesis about a democratic and egalitarian society are based rather on old American values (noted by Tocqueville [1945] more than 150 years ago) and Kantian and Utilitarian thought. Elements of the model include:

- opportunities for individuals to pursue their happiness should be as equal as possible;
- individual and organizational goals should not conflict;
- total involvement and participation by individuals, both managers and other workers, is desirable;
- behavior leading to a culture of trust, openness, and confrontation of issues should be maintained;
- "power" should be "equalized" and decision making devolved as far down the hierarchy as possible.

It is clear that the answer to "What is management?" is a function of many variables, one of which is national culture.

MANAGERIAL FUNCTIONS

Tasks of managers are defined differently by different observers. Gulick (1937) defined seven general management functions: planning, organizing, staffing, directing, coordinating, reporting, and budgeting. While few continue to depend entirely on this neat classification, it is a base even for writers who disagree.

Managers' tasks in complex organizations are in part scheduled and in part random. Sometimes reactive and sometimes proactive actions are called for. Sometimes it is desirable to minimize risk and sometimes to maximize potential gains. Tasks and information are disjointed and interdependent, sometimes simultaneously. Some actions are programmed, some not. Some functions, such as budgeting, are instrumental and call for technical competencies. Others, such as "directing" (now "leading"), are expressive.

In this confusing, ambiguous situation, a manager is responsible for organizing the fragments into meaningful patterns so that subordinates will understand what they are to do and why they are expected to do it.

Some observers believe computer generated feedback and information systems will eliminate many management tasks (Zuboff, 1988). Others, including the authors, believe that expressive tasks will remain.

THE STATE OF AMERICAN MANAGEMENT

Dissatisfaction with performance of American managers compared to that of Japanese and German managers is indicated by the tone of studies to improve management. While these studies make more recommendations relating to the structure and culture of organizations than to managerial tasks and style, emphasis in respect to performance is on expressive tasks. Recommendations in "Made in America: Regaining the Productive Edge," the 1989 report of the M.I.T. Commission of Industrial Productivity are typical. The report calls for

- better cooperation between individuals and between organizations
- elimination of rigid hierarchies and tight unit boundaries
- increase in technological and knowledge transfers
- increase in employee participation in decision making
- industry-wide programs for training, research, and standards

In a study of changes that could affect management education McLagan (1989) identified pressure for productivity and for flatter and more flexible organization designs. Others have noted increases in the pace of change, customer and worker expectations, and "globalization" of operations and have called for changes in the expressive roles of managers (Stumpf and Mullen, 1992).

SCHOOLS OF ADMINISTRATION

Modern, formal management education began with education for officers in European armies. The British Royal Military College senior division was founded in 1799. Every major European country had a staff-and-command school by the early nineteenth century.

Schools of business arose about a hundred years later. By the 1920s it was possible to obtain a baccalaureate degree in business in most countries in the Western world. Graduates of the "écoles supérieures de commerce" dominated French finance, business, and industry (Locke, 1989).

Leipzig's Handelshochschule, at the turn of the twentieth century, was the first German school of business. Others followed in rapid succession. Management was an engineering specialty. Faculty members were experienced businessmen with little academic training in disciplines such as political science, law, and economics. Within twenty years, there was academic acceptance, and undergraduate and graduate curriculums were developed. In Eastern Europe, the engineering model persisted to the end of the communist regimes.

Wharton, founded in 1880, was the first school of business in the United States. Principal departments were accounting, finance, and marketing.

British business education lagged behind that in other countries. Business degrees were granted by the Universities of Birmingham and Manchester in 1910 and by London in the early twenties. The degrees were not highly regarded, either in the academic or business world.

In all countries there was conflict between businesspeople who wanted schools to prepare students for business and academics who sought to emphasize the development of the theory and science of business.

From the end of World War II until recently, the United States was the undisputed leader in management education. Countries impressed by the role of American management in achieving industrial goals during the war thought that the American type of management would dominate the future. The scene has changed. Although the number of foreigners in American schools has not decreased, these foreigners no longer come from Europe. The greatest number come from Japan. A high percentage of the rest come from less developed countries and countries without a tradition of advanced business education. The major interests seem to be to learn how to succeed in the American market, obtain an international point of view, and learn analytic techniques.

Britain continued to lag well after World War II. An institution of higher learning, Henley, was established long after other countries had business programs. Henley focused on preparing technical professionals for management. The 1963 Robbins Committee study led to the establishment of two major postgraduate schools, the London School of Management Studies and the Manchester Business School. While supporting the study, few British companies seem to have been interested in sending employees to the schools or employing their graduates (Locke, 1989).

European business schools in the 1990s are exploding the way that American schools exploded in the 1960s (Greenhouse, 1991). The disparagement of business schools—and in particular the M.B.A.—by European academic circles as having little intellectual content is changing. The strongholds of academic purity are falling into line: Cambridge in

1991 and Oxford in 1993. Some European schools such as the International Institute of Management Development (IIMD) are private with no university connections. These tend to have an international student body and faculty. Most schools have English-language programs, even the elite French schools l'École des Hautes Études Commerciales and l'École des Ponts et Chaussées.

While American schools led in mathematical modeling and analysis, the French and Germans, building on their prewar academic structures, adopted the American mathematical approaches easily, facilitated by the mathematical and engineering backgrounds of many managers. In no foreign country are expressive tasks taken seriously as academic management disciplines. If considered, these tasks are elements of company-sponsored management development.

The internationalization of business has led to a melding of approaches. Anticipation of barrier-free Europe is increasing the importance of managers who are generalists and who speak a common management language. Although considerably later than the Europeans, American schools are beginning to respond.

European schools emphasize experience prior to management education and the use of natural experiential learning. There is preference for approaches similar to Revan's "action learning" (Mailick, 1974; McNulty, 1979) and joint firm-school programs for management development. Even so, a survey showed 84 percent of European employers are dissatisfied with the insufficiency of natural experiential learning. Many are instituting their own programs to control "quality and relevance of employee education" (*Training and Development Journal*, December 1991, pp. 14, 15).

Some schools responded with increased natural experiential approaches. In the Cambridge three-year program for the M.B.A., students go to school for ten weeks, work for a year, return to school for ten weeks, work for another year, and return to school for a final ten weeks. Continued contact with the school is expected for data gathering, analysis, and contemplation relating theory to work. The Japanese are even more work and task oriented than the Europeans. The Japanese do not sponsor business education unrelated to jobs.

EFFECT OF MANAGEMENT STYLES ON EDUCATION

Competencies that are criteria for selection and advancement strongly influence curriculum. In the United States in the second half of the twentieth century the criteria are finance and marketing. In Germany, the criterion is production. In Japan, the criteria are political relations and networking. German emphasis on production directly influences the curricula of the schools. In Stuttgart University, business majors, without respect to area of emphasis, must take fully 25 percent of their courses in engineering-technical services (Locke, 1989). American focus on the "bottom-line" objective and problem solving emphasizes technique, short-term planning, and assessment. People who go back to school for the M.B.A. both in the United States and Europe are specialists who feel that they would do better financially as generalists. Japanese tend to start as generalists who are trained as specialists as need and assignments are changed.

American schools have tried to maintain relations with business organizations. The primary approach used for strengthening these relations has been to establish business advisory councils. The councils do not seem to have much influence on curriculum and educational approaches. Their major functions relate to raising funds and improving the image of the school. In the Porter and McKibbin (1988) study, 70 percent of council members contacted had little knowledge of the activities of the schools with which they were associated. Academics and businesspeople were, in general, satisfied with the existing limited relations. The academics feared that increased contacts would give the business community undue influence on academic programs.

PUBLIC ADMINISTRATION

France has for more than a century been a leader in management development for public servants. The model of the staff colleges and the increasing complexity of governmental affairs led the French government to found the National School of Administration in 1848, designed to teach "principles of administration" to potential and new managers. "The French emphasized practical education reinforced with 'political economy, statistics, and parliamentary eloquence'" and "adjunct faculty . . . supplement[ed] legal instruction with day-to-day application" (Martin, 1987).

In Britain, the influential Northcote-Trevelyan Report in the 1850s led to a "merit" civil service and the concept of the ideal government executive as a gentleman who was a graduate of a liberal arts university. The United States followed the lead of the British with "merit" civil service systems. Unlike the British system, executive positions in the United States remained patronage appointments. One result has been weak educational programs for civil service managers.

After World War II, France redesigned and renamed its school the École Nationale d'Administration. The emphasis on theory, deductive analysis, and legal studies—the mark of French academic programs—was retained. Senior managers in the civil service are virtually all graduates of the school, as are many managers in the former French colonies. Many graduates have risen to the level of cabinet minister. Michel Rocard, a graduate, was appointed prime minister by President François Mitterrand. Graduates dominate in the private sector as well. The school has had greater influence on management in France than any institution has had in other countries, except possibly the University of Tokyo in Japan. "Virtually every significant concept . . . in the American [public administration] literature as late as 1937 had already been published in France by 1859; most of it had been published by 1812" (Martin, 1987). The only management element lacking in the French literature was "the focus on supervisor-worker relationships that Taylor brought to American theorists" (Martin, 1987).

U.S. schools are not rated high. The Chapman and Cleaveland report states that "current programs of education for public administration are not meeting present professional needs" (1973). President Johnson's executive order of April 20, 1967, directed the Civil Service Commission to establish a Center for Advanced Study for executives in the highest grades of the civil service. There are no equivalent programs for management at the state and local levels. No institution plays the role of the École Nationale.

Not only do American schools have different curricula and criteria for the master's degree, but there is also wide variation with respect to location of public administration within universities. Kristal (1988) found four arrangements: the free-standing professional school (e.g., Harvard), the so-called generic school of administration (e.g., Yale), the separate department within a school (e.g., the Institute of Public Policy Studies, Michigan), a program within a department of government or political science (e.g., American University). Along with these structural variations, schools grant different degrees. These and other variations indicate greater difference of opinion than exists among schools of business administration with respect to the nature of public administration, appropriate student body, and role of the university.

RECOMMENDATIONS FOR IMPROVING MANAGEMENT EDUCATION

The 1959 studies supported by the Ford Foundation and the Carnegie Corporation (Pierson, 1959; Gordon and Howell, 1959) recommended adding liberal arts and management tool subjects such as decision making and quantitative analysis to the curriculum and increasing the use of "experiential" approaches such as case studies. The increased emphasis on quantitative analysis and use of case studies may be a consequence of these studies.

To answer criticism, deans of business schools sponsored a series of conferences. Discussion centered on "future educational needs" and "lifelong learning." The only tangible outcome was the Porter and McKibbin study that produced the report titled "Future of Management Education and Development Project" (1988). The following are some findings of the Porter and McKibbin study (1988).

- Faculties of business schools are complacent and satisfied with passive educational approaches.
- Corporate executives like the "idea" of research relating to business but seem to make no use of the research findings.
- There is insufficient interaction between academics and managers in business organizations.

THE STATE OF MANAGEMENT EDUCATION

On both the undergraduate and M.B.A. levels, business "management" education in the United States is successful in training specialists in such areas as accounting, marketing, and finance. "Management" education is less successful. In countries other than America, there is far greater emphasis on personal experiences and natural experiential approaches. There is more expressive content in American programs than there is in programs in other countries, where it is believed that expressive competencies can only be learned on the job. Perhaps for the same reason, the expressive content in American programs has been decreasing.

There are three other differences. First, European schools integrate "international" management throughout the course of study. American schools, generally, have isolated courses; the need for integration is recognized but remains a continuing agenda item. Second, the emphasis in the United States is on finance, marketing, and analytic techniques compared to an emphasis on production in other countries, particularly Germany. Third, American schools lead in faculty-conducted research.

The standing of American schools of public administration is tied to the low standing, in public eyes, of civil service generally and of managers in particular. These disadvantages are compounded by lower managerial salaries and the practice of filling more levels of managerial positions with persons from outside the civil service than is done in other advanced countries. Additional handicaps are little recognition of preemployment education for job placement and the failure of governments to sponsor significant postentry graduate education. Civil service unions seem to be stronger supporters of postentry management education than government is. Consequences include lower prestige for schools of public administration compared to business schools, decreasing registration, and a change in emphasis from "public" content to that of the business schools.

17

CONTENT AND EDUCATIONAL APPROACHES

INTRODUCTION

Focus in this chapter is on content and educational approaches. Although our primary concern is with the effectiveness of learning, content is important both in itself and in its relation to effective approach. We assume that the connection between learning and use venues has a decisive effect on the transfer of learning. There is a third, "personal venue"—namely, life outside of school and work. This is not included in our analysis, although what happens in this venue strongly affects both learning and use.

OBJECTIVES OF MANAGEMENT EDUCATION

Schools have both research and educational objectives. Our focus is on the latter. Objectives in areas such as accounting and finance are not hard to define. Defining objectives for educating managers is more difficult. What does it mean "to educate managers"? How should management research affect education? Should schools prepare students to understand current management theory and research or to become competent managers in specific industries? What does "competent manager" mean? How is competence determined? Objectives for managers in the business sector are easy to define when compared to the public sector. The "bottom line" is a good starting point for the private sector, not the public. Satisfying public need, public good, and political expediency are a few of the public criteria. How are performance and learning to be measured? We found no "school" answers to these questions. Yet we must assume that they have been thought through. We will estimate answers by examining content, approach, and other factors involved in the educational process.

CONTENT

Many concepts and techniques related to management in the private sector were developed before the twentieth century. At the beginning of the twentieth century, emphasis was on functional activities such as accounting, finance, and marketing. Production was rarely considered in business schools. It was more related to engineering. As new production techniques led to "scientific management" and other management theory, "management" became of greater interest to schools of business. Building on the work of the earlier empiricists, Mary Parker Follett, Chester Barnard, Lyndall Urwick, and Luther Gulick developed a comprehensive body of theory in the period before World War II (George, 1972).

While there was resistance to a thoroughgoing overhaul, some content that was derived from the work of these theorists was added to curricula. Except for courses in "industrial psychology," curricula consisted primarily of courses in instrumental areas. The World War II experience led to a significant enrichment of the curricula, which were enhanced by courses in broad areas related to the expressive and general tasks of management and by specialized studies employing quantitative and research techniques, involving the use of computers.

As the content of American management education becomes more and more based on recondite theory, fragmented and inconclusive research, and specialized techniques, critics charge that the education is not applicable in practice (Clement and Stevens, 1989). A major problem is that there is little agreement on what a manager, as distinct from a staff person, should be able to do.

Based on empirical studies of tasks that managers perform, Mintzberg (1973) gave failing marks to academic curricula for lack of such courses as conflict resolution, negotiation, leadership, information processing, management in unstructured situations, allocation of resources, entrepreneurship, and ability to learn from experience.

Porter and McKibbin (1988) identified specific instrumental areas that were underrepresented in the curricula. Some of these areas were consideration of the organizational environment, international considerations, information systems, and coordination and integration of specialized functional disciplines. They noted, in passing, a shortcoming in "people" skills.

Michael Levine (1992), dean of the Yale School of Organization and Management, observed that providing "education of [the] kind [needed by] the next generation of managers is not easy, and management schools are still groping for answers" (p. 20). The competencies that Levine thought were needed included the formulation of "management strategies in a confused and complicated world," an "intuitive understanding of fundamental theories that will help shape . . . messy, formless problems," and "an understanding of human motivations and culture."

More recently, there has been less emphasis on expressive tasks. The publicized conflict, a few years ago, in the Yale School of Organization and Management illustrates this. The school, to meet its objective of "preparing people to manage in public service and the private business," had been a leading proponent of the importance of the expressive role. Nevertheless, after a number of years of leadership in this area, it decimated its department of organizational behavior by not renewing the contracts of about three-quarters of the faculty members teaching these subjects.

There is a tendency to add and drop isolated courses in response to current issues, rather than to consider an overhaul of the curriculum. Thus, "deans and faculty of graduate business schools all over the country are scrambling to keep up with the fast-changing world. That means changing programs, adding courses, hiring different types of faculty." Deans see greater need to update their curricula than faculty members do. They are adding new elective courses ranging from ethics to advanced computer skills (Fowler, June 21, 1991).

Levine (1992) questions whether management schools can "through a two-years master's degree help men and women prepare to become management leaders" (p. 18). At the same time, some see no need for would-be managers to attend a school. *The Portable MBA*, edited by Collins and Devanna (1990), claims that "you can master the complete MBA curriculum at home, at your own pace, in your own time and save the expense of a formal program." The differences indicate different concepts of tasks of management and the difficulty of learning to be a manager.

Despite agreement on need, Porter and McKibben (1988) found resistance to basic change among key stakeholders. A summary of their findings follows.

Stakeholder Action to Take with Respect to Change in Curriculum

	Broaden	Specialize	No Change
Deans	27%	8%	65%
Faculty	23%	21%	56%
Students	7%	31%	60%
Alumni	13%	34%	53%

Later, Fowler (April 7, 1992) stated, "Graduate business schools . . . are revising and updating M.B.A. programs to meet changing business needs. They are integrating programs to include international aspects, ethics, and crisis management, while stressing total quality management, as well as adding new courses and seminars to treat new subjects." The Fuqua School of Business at Duke University, Fowler continued, has "four special weeks during the two-year program . . . called integrative learning experiences. . . . Team building and leadership development is the first. It includes one day of an Outward Bound experience in a wilderness setting, doing rope climbing." It is not clear how this "integrates" learning. Dean Meyer Feldman of Columbia, "called Outward Bound experiences 'flaky.' " The Columbia University business school is introducing courses such as globalization anad ethics (Fowler, April 7, 1992).

Problems of content in public administration programs differ from those in the business programs. This stems from significant differences between public and private organizations. There are differences in objectives, values, authority, and employee and client relationships. Recognition of these differences made public administration education for a long time the domain of political scientists. This changed in the immediate post–World War II period; functional programs such as personnel management, budgeting, and labor relations were introduced. This was followed by adding courses of schools of business such as economics and quantitative analysis. More recently, functional areas have been replaced by general management and public policy courses and area programs, such as those regarding health, policing, housing, and international organizations. The specific areas offered at a school seem to be happenstance.

There is some agreement on the core courses. These include (not all in any one school) administrative and organizational theory, research methodology, finance (sometimes limited to budgeting), policy analysis, politics, and economics. Many include human resources, information systems, and ethics.

There are two conflicting tendencies in curriculum development. In efforts to provide a rationale for employing "research" faculty and to gain status for faculty research, schools seek to emulate the "rigor" of the business schools by increasing "quantitative" courses. In efforts to increase registration and relevance of education, courses like accounting and computer literacy are offered (Kraemer and Northrop, 1989).

EDUCATIONAL APPROACHES

There is extensive use of traditional lecture and discussion and praxis-formulated passive education, that is, case studies. To a lesser extent synthetic experiential educational approaches are employed. There is almost no natural experiential learning. This flies in the face of the preference for experiential learning approaches expressed by corporate executives and educational theorists. Both groups see experiential learning as more effective for motivating change, integrating and freezing learning in managers' life banks, and transferring learning to the work venue.

Many school leaders agree and have sought ways to provide this learning within the restrictions of the classroom and library. The case study is seen as a substitute for natural experiential learning. Unable to bring the work venue into the classroom or to move the classroom, "real" cases are brought into the classroom. The attraction is that cases mimic experience and give students a feeling of being involved with the "real thing." However, case analysis is passive, not experiential, learning. It has limited value for transfer of learning to the workplace. Recognizing this, some schools go beyond cases to use elaborate simulation exercises and other synthetic experiential approaches.

Experiential learning is particularly appropriate for American managers. Pragmatism, the philosophic base of natural experiential learning, is the philosophy that most Americans absorb in the course of living. Two learning assumptions supporting experiential learning for managers are that (1) learning is most effective when it leads to use and (2) managers, more than most others, want evidence that learning is of use (Kolb, 1984).

Unfortunately, management is the only profession in which there are so few opportunities for learning in a natural setting. Where there are opportunities, it is difficult to arrange for sequential learning in which successive experiences require understanding and competence gained in earlier learning. This may be the major reason that advocates for changes in the educational approaches of business schools tend to play down the use of natural experiential education. Schon (1992) has recommended the use of more elaborate case studies in the education of professionals as one way to resolve the "rigor-relevance" dilemma. Mintzberg (1973) also has ignored natural experiential learning as an appropriate mode for the schools.

Natural experiential approaches in nondegree management development programs are used by a number of business schools that are not bound by full-time attendance, classroom base, and discipline straight jackets. However, only a few schools in America, compared to many in Europe, have been able to use natural experiential approaches effectively in degree programs.

Three degree programs that have used natural experiential approaches are the New York University program for the public administration doctorate in mental health (Hoberman and Mailick, 1992), the New School master's program in urban affairs, and Revans's interuniversity program (Revans, 1972).

In the New York University program, participants were managers in mental health systems. The program included plenary meetings to introduce, review, and integrate content with earlier and future modules in order to provide a holistic experience, independent reading and work assignments, and preceptoral sessions in which two or three students discussed learning and their use of learning, with a preceptor serving as resource and gadfly. The focus was on practicing and strengthening reflection and encouraging independent learning. The program was organized in modules, but holistic learning was strengthened by natural experiential learning, holistic exercises, and integration of content.

Revans (Mailick, 1974; McNulty, 1979) uses several natural experiential approaches. In one version, students work on a real time-management project useful to a host organization (other than their own) and receive feedback from managers in the host organization.

The New School's Graduate School of Management and Urban Professions employs a variation of the Revans design. Students work, in public and private organizations, in teams under the direction of a faculty member. In one course they conduct field research, collect and analyze data, and make reports. In another, they design and apply methodology and criteria for assessing a program and, given an issue by the host organization, develop and present a proposal for dealing with it.

The cost of natural experiential learning is higher than for other learning approaches. After sixteen or so years, the experiential component of the New School "career-entry" program was cut in half and case studies were substituted for experiential learning in the "midcareer" program. The high cost limited the New York University program to five classes.

In Harvard's Advanced Management summer program participants record what they have learned each day and indicate how the learning could be applied "back home." In another program, teams of managers come with a change issue from their workplace to serve as the basis for the application of learning. They are expected to leave with a detailed plan for dealing with the issue (Hollenbeck and Ingols, 1990).

ASSESSMENT OF MANAGEMENT PROGRAMS

Gordon and Howell (1959) and Porter and McKibbin (1988) found that schools do not meet the management needs of business. Porter and McKibbin found that employers were satisfied with graduates' technical skills but not with their expressive and communication skills. Employers wanted graduates with hands-on management experience.

There is insufficient emphasis on integration across disciplines to help students use learning in practice. Attempts to use "integrative courses" have not been very successful. Integration in public administration is no better since political science, the binding discipline, receives less emphasis.

Livingston (1971) claimed that "preoccupation with problem solving and decision making . . . overdevelops . . . analytic ability, but leaves . . . ability to take action . . . underdeveloped" (p. 82).

Supporters of case studies and of snythetic over natural experiential learning argue that with proper selection of cases, use follows when there are opportunities to practice technique (*Harvard Business Review*, March–April 1971) and that management in the work venue involves so many variables that there are no identifiable relevant variables for learning, no determinable relations between action and outcomes, and no adequate density of learning and reinforcement that could have a significant effect on managers' behavior. Supporters of case studies claim that synthetic experiential exercises can include elements of chance, ambiguity, and uncertainty. Their strong point is that failure in synthetic experience does not have the deadly effect of failure in the natural venue since students have opportunities to improve.

Critics claim that synthetic experiential approaches and case studies do not help learners to use knowledge. These critics note that synthetic experiential exercises are such simplified versions of experience, that participants are misled into believing that the proposed actions will work just as well in real life. This can lead to limiting analysis, oversimplifying relationships with people, reinforcing a belief that diagnosis is the remedy, and overemphasizing the role of managers as problem solvers. The experience downplays the importance of sensitivity to problems and opportunities and of risk and the will to accept risk.

Studies of schools focus on input and management research, not graduates' competence. There has been no significant research to improve transfer of learning. We need studies of managers' performance four or five years after graduation (Bowen, 1987).

SUMMARY

Few organizations define managers' tasks in the same way. Without well-defined tasks and required competencies, objectives for management education cannot be defined. A result is that schools emphasize different areas and define courses differently. We have incoherent, faculty-dictated curricula. Increase in quantitative analysis content is, in part, a consequence of research-oriented faculty. The American Assembly of Collegiate Schools of Business (AACSB) has proposed eliminating review of schools' curricula (Conry, 1990).

Deans want to be seen as top-notch money-making administrators. Faculty members want to be seen as innovators and researchers in their specialties. Students want well-paying jobs after graduation. Providing and getting a "good" education is secondary.

The simplicity and explicitness of much management theory and quantitative models makes them easier to learn. Models are used as if they were real life. Cases and exercises are designed both to demonstrate usefulness and to provide practice in the use of the models. This can lead to mistaking "axioms" about human behavior as true psychological insights. Students who learn to work with these simplified pictures tend to produce answers that are "satisficing" (to coin a word) in a very narrow range. Management is more than using models and techniques in simulated managerial situations. To some extent, this is being recognized. However, as Levine (1992) has stated, the schools don't know what to do about it.

No one of the three learning approaches is most efficient and effective for all purposes. Passive approaches are efficient and more effective for transmitting information and reinforcing learning in fields such as financial analysis. Research-oriented faculty members are better prepared by training and experience to use passive learning and to play down the ambiguous, unpredictable behavior of individuals and environment. Synthetic learning is effective when the time span required for natural experience, for example, strategic management, is too great to develop a tight feedback loop from theory to performance, output, and analysis and back to theory.

Natural experiential opportunities in approaches such as rotation and project assignments are made less effective by failure to use learning theory. There is little analysis of experience and reflection. Learning depends on a frame of reference and ways of learning from disorganized experience.

Structuring education in subject courses makes integration an essential need. The modular structure is more effective for achieving, in a limited time frame, depth of learning and analysis of alternative approaches. It is not for transfer to practice where holistic, not modular, performance is needed. Students do not learn to integrate the competencies needed to run an organization and relate to people. These competencies are not easily or passively acquired. Reality is too confusing and unstable. The modular approach also leads to adding and subtracting courses rather than integrating new, needed learning.

Focus on discipline models, for example, finance and politics, along with the "success" factor, leads to suboptimization in practice. Experience and learning in general management is necessary for specialists and technicians in order to promote coordination and reduce suboptimization.

It may be unrealistic to expect schools to help students acquire general competencies, such as creativity and sensitivity to total work venues, or expressive competencies, such as leadership and motivating others. It may be that American schools should follow the foreign practice of limiting management to managers who can engage in natural experiential education. Perhaps formal professional education should be a continuous process during the course of a manager's working life.

18
OTHER ISSUES

In this chapter, we consider some other issues raised in Part One.

THE PROFESSION

Management is not universally regarded as a profession. There is no professional association with the influence of medical, legal, and accounting associations on schools' curricula or on standards for practitioners. There is no legally required or generally accepted set of tasks and standards for performance by managers. Ethical canons, except for recommendations by associations of public administrators, tend to be those in the law for all people.

The number and quality of students in business schools have gone up during the past twenty-five years. The number and quality in schools of public administration has not kept pace. Reasons advanced relate to the work venue. Some are: low status of government; dominance of political executives and managers; low pay and prestige of public service; and irrelevance of the education.

SCHOOL ADMINISTRATION

American schools of business administration have had more applicants than those schools accept. The schools have been operating at a profit. Many universities regard schools of business as cash cows to support other university activities. A consequence is little pressure from university officials for change. Porter and McKibbin (1988) found a general air of complacency. As curricula of schools of public administration move closer to those of the business schools, there is a movement to join the two schools. Although this would increase offerings in specialized areas and reduce costs and deficits, it would be at the cost of emphasis on the distinctive character of public administration.

There is occasional administrative recognition in both types of schools that faculty members are teachers and that income from the "teaching activity" pays the bills. Thus, R. R. West, dean of the Stern Graduate School of Business at New York University is reported (Fowler, March 24, 1992) to have decried the lack of discussion of the failure of faculty members "to become more interested in the interdisciplinary aspects" and to have recommended that they "become skilled as teachers of the M.B.A." We have found no indication that administrators have taken concrete steps to improve teaching.

FACULTY

The primary objective of schools of management in selecting and promoting faculty is to increase the schools' prestige and meet accreditation criteria. Accreditation agencies emphasize hiring full-time faculty with Ph.D. degrees and frown on using working managers and specialists as part-time faculty.

According to Fowler (March 24, 1992), West stated that theory is overemphasized at expense of practice; faculty members are prepared to conduct research, not to teach; many faculty members have no experience in managing or in business; and some feel that teaching is only an evil, acceptable only because it is the reason that they are paid. A related issue is that a faculty of "experts" feels no desire to engage in give-and-take with students. Faculty specialization reinforces division of education into "courses," making it difficult to provide holistic management education dealing with real-life issues and problems. There seems to be little administrative influence over faculty classroom performance.

Faculty members educated in specialties and lacking management experience do not see themselves as professional managers, in the same way in which faculty members in other schools think of themselves as lawyers, social workers, and medical doctors (Porter and McKibbin, 1988).

Selecting and promoting faculty on the basis of published research might be excusable if the research led to advances in practice. But it has not in either business or public administration. In discussions with company executive officers, Porter and McKibbin found no evidence that the research has had a significant effect on business organizations.

Bailey (1992) notes that

separation of theory and practice neatly distinguishes between the skills required of doctoral research and the management skills possessed by the practitioner. Unfortunately, . . . theoretical scholars may not be equipped to be teachers of practitioners. If the masters [sic] is to have a focus on skills development, where are the faculty who possess these skills to come from if not from the doctoral programs in public administration? Although "acquaintance with" practice is not a sufficient criterion for doctoral programs and research, neither is "knowledge of" theory alone sufficient for teaching masters [sic] degree students. (p. 49)

It is ironic that the status of managers is questioned by faculty with, at most, experience as consultants but not as managers (Pugh, 1989; Hummel, 1991).

Faculty members are the key to effective education. Their role is to help students to learn to use knowledge, to learn from the use, and to integrate new learning as active life-bank elements, that is, to refreeze and use new learning. Faculty members have to be catalytic agents, sounding boards, mentors, coaches, resource consultants, counselors and integrators. Few play or accept these roles.

At the present time, more than ever before, there is a need for a clear statement of criteria for evaluating faculty performance and a need for more effective evaluation of faculty performance in developing practitioners. Despite the importance that some deans of schools of administration ascribe to teaching, students' ratings are the only basis for evaluation of teaching that is in general use (Clement and Stevens, 1989).

STUDENTS

The number, quality, and motivation of students are indicators of the status of a profession and of professional education. More students are enrolled in American business schools than in any other country. About 25 percent come from abroad primarily to learn specialized, quantitative, mathematical techniques. Most are full time. Many enter from undergraduate school, without business experience. This is a major difference between American and European students. Some programs consider students' experiences. Columbia University's "weekend" program for managers requires students to be managers.

The report entitled "The American Freshman: Twenty-Five Year Trends" issued by the Higher Education Research Institute (1990) stated that while the percentage of students seeking business careers increased from 11.6 percent in 1966 to 24.1 percent in 1986, it fell to 18.4 percent in 1990. The choice of business as a major followed a similar trend. However, the attraction of the M.B.A. as a more "employable" degree than specialized degrees remains strong and becomes stronger in depressed job markets for college graduates (Fuchsberg, 1992).

A survey of American M.B.A. candidates found that by far the greatest number, about one-third, concentrate in general management, followed by finance, marketing, and management information systems. Only one of these, management-information systems was rated in the first five of the "most marketable" (*Training and Development Journal*, December 1991, p. 15).

Business administration students are motivated by expectations of high salaries after receiving the M.B.A. Schools recruit students by reporting the incomes of graduates. This is not the case in public administration.

CERTIFICATION

While there is no certification for managers, there are accrediting agencies for the schools. Evaluation tends to be based on input. Oversight by AACSB accreditation standards remains and perhaps is growing stronger with respect to the academic credentials for faculty and the restriction on the employment of part-time faculty. AACSB standards require 75 percent of school faculty to be doctoral qualified. "These days, very few schools that want to maintain or increase their academic credibility choose to hire anyone without a doctorate" (Porter and McKibbin, 1988).

CONTENT

Interaction with others is almost totally ignored in management education. When considered, it is usually in content areas, such as negotiating, using passive or synthetic experiential learning. This is a recognized shortcoming (Porter and McKibbin, 1988).

ASSESSMENT OF MANAGEMENT EDUCATION

There has been more management theory and more techniques proposed and more management research conducted in the past fifty years than in the preceding four thousand. The techniques have affected practice much more than the theory. The research seems to have had little effect. Many question the usefulness of much of the research (Locke, 1989). Schon (1992) has claimed that "in recent years there has been a growing perception that researchers . . . have less and less to say that practitioners find useful" (p. 10). The Porter and McKibbin study (1988) found no chief executive officer who could identify any research that was used in the organization. Porter and McKibbin have noted that the audience for research is academia, not business. White (1986) has tracked the effect of research publications and has concluded that most research from the 305 dissertations reviewed was not communicated beyond a small group of people, namely, the dissertation committee. Bailey (1992), reviewing several studies of research literature in public administration, including White's, has come to a similar conclusion. Little research relates to the effectiveness of education. Based on anecdotal evidence, there are as many who claim that the schools do not educate as who claim that they do.

Porter and McKibbin (1988) asked chief executive officers to assess recently hired M.B.A.s. "Analytic" skills and "motivation" were identified as the major strengths. At the low end of the scale were knowledge of how the business world really operates, understanding of the environment, and leadership and interpersonal skills. The chief executive officers did not think that schools were places to learn how to manage. They felt that management education was drifting and that action was needed to avoid serious consequences. Two recommendations were (1) to integrate learning from different disciplines and apply it to real situations and (2) to adapt education to changing management needs. As noted earlier, the findings had little effect on education.

Some schools responded to findings that M.B.A.s lack communication and leadership skills by testing students for the skills and providing special training for those who do not measure up (Fowler, January 12, 1991). There is no evidence of effectiveness.

The University of Chicago's Graduate School of Business has students evaluate content. Students can take a one-credit course in auditing and assessing value of a specific course. Assessment is based on observation and participation. Instructors get feedback weekly, "in time for them to make mid-course corrections" (Deutsch, 1991). There is little evidence to determine the reliability, validity, meaning, or effectiveness of this approach.

There is no significant evidence that schools of administration produce managers or improve managerial competence. There is no significant research assessing the value of management education. It may be that there are no operationally quantifiable hypotheses that can be tested empirically. But should the effort not be made?

Most "marketable" specialties identified by students in a Lake Forest Graduate School of Management study (*Training and Development Journal*, December 1991, pp. 15–16) were (in approximate order) computer sciences, management information systems, international business and marketing, waste management, environmental management, finance, marketing, general management, and behavioral sciences. Choices for study, in order, were general management, finance, marketing, and management information systems.

The students' evaluations are by Porter and McKibbin (1988). Unseem's (1989) and other studies indicate that executives are satisfied with the education of specialists in such fields as accounting and financial analysis. There is no evidence that graduates get jobs as managers. This may be the most valid assessment of management education!

19

CONCLUSIONS, QUESTIONS, SUGGESTIONS

INTRODUCTION

The purpose of graduate education is to help students learn to be effective managers. Schools attempt to do this by helping students acquire information about management techniques, problem analysis, the functioning of complex organizations, the role of the manager, and appropriate managerial behavior under different circumstances. Unfortunately, the acquisition of this information does not necessarily lead to use of the learning on the job.

Learning to manage, or to manage better, must be based on experience as a manager. While learning to manage can only be based on experience, experience alone does not necessarily lead to managerial competence. Without concrete theory and concepts to provide the basis for organizing, analyzing, and generalizing from experience, learning from experience is minimal and sometimes counterproductive. Consequently, there is a need for both education and experience in learning managerial competencies.

There is acceptance that a manager's job is not as well defined as the jobs of other professionals and that few management theories and "good management" practices are universally applicable. These characteristics of management account to a great extent for the differences in curricula between schools, greater dependence on passive learning, failure of graduates to transfer classroom learning to the workplace, and the difficulty in evaluating management education. However, these difficulties must be overcome; if they are not, management education will never be of great value.

CONTENT AND EDUCATIONAL APPROACHES

Emphasis in management education is on general theory and models rather than on unique practice. The explicitness of much of management theory makes it so easy to present that it is the basis of virtually all the academic content. Most models studied have a limited number of variables and present very simplified pictures of complex systems. This makes text writing and lecturing easy. It also permits students—few of whom have experience in dealing with the doubt and impermanence, characteristic of contingency models—to be comfortable in dealing with cases and in "solving problems." Working even with probabilistic models is far different from assessing and taking risks in practice. This reduces the usefulness of the education to the point of questioning its practical value.

The way chosen to increase usefulness has been to teach technique. But is the technical specialization worth the cost if it is not used? Management education in Germany and Japan does not emphasize specialized techniques. "German firms can send their people abroad to get proper education [in these areas] or recruit people from abroad [as needed]" (Locke, 1989). The Japanese follow a similar policy. Other countries seem to assume that paying for learning that will not be used is wasteful.

Some important managerial roles are minimized. The importance of the boundary-spanning role and the need for managers to be able to scan, enact, and respond to their environments are widely recognized. These competencies are crucial in reactive and turbulent environments. Competencies gained in real, "normal" environments can be extended, by passive and synthetic learning, to learn to function in more difficult environments. Natural, experiential learning may be the only way to help to prepare students for this vital, boundary-spanning, managerial role.

One response to recognition that there is need for integration across functional disciplines has been to establish new "integrative" courses. While better than nothing, these courses are not opportunities for holistic learning, nor are they the same as integration into real-life experience. The greater use of problem solving and analytic techniques in management education in the United States compared to other countries (Locke, 1989) is further emphasized in "integrative" courses. This is counterproductive if "preoccupation with problem solving and decision making . . . tends to distort management growth because it overdevelops an individual's analytic ability, but leaves his ability to take action and to get things done underdeveloped" (Livingston, 1971, p. 82).

When management education focuses on "practice" there is a tendency to teach the use of superior instruments and techniques and to use case studies and synthetic experiential exercises to provide practice in their use. The content and educational approarches are counterproductive to the extent that they reinforce the tendency of students to see all interactions as win/lose and to see systemic closure as being preferable to investing and taking risk for possible win/win actions while living with ambiguity.

Experiential education for practicing managers needs to be concerned with the shortcomings of the experience opportunities of lower- and middle-level managers. These tend to consist of management practices in closed systems which deal with the internal venue. For the most part there is little experience in dealing with the external environment and working in a wide-open system. The managers tend to have experience in using internal information but little experience and competence in converting partial and ambiguous evidence, obtained from environmental scanning and reporting, into signals for specific actions. These managers need to acquire sensitivity, awareness, and the ability to analyze environmental factors. It is rare that these competencies are acquired in degree programs.

Simulation and other types of synthetic experiential learning are used in the best designed programs. They are better focused, safer, less costly, more intensive, and less time consuming than natural experiential learning. But there are significant drawbacks. Some were noted in the use of simulation in the training of airplane pilots (Fisher, 1989). These drawbacks include:

- distrusting normal approaches that worked in practice
- focusing on "beating" the problem to get good grades or win in the competition
- learning to respond to the variables on which the simulation is based rather than to those in the actual situation
- discounting the space-time differentials between successive events based on the simulation rather than the real situation
- responding to planted cues instead of seeking and identifying cues

Synthetic experiential approaches can be of great value, but only if used appropriately and if the negative nonlinear consequences are avoided.

In every professional field, except management, natural experiential learning opportunities exist or can be developed. It is not too difficult in specialized administrative areas, such as finance. But it is very difficult to provide opportunities for managers, unless students are working managers. Decreased emphasis on "expressive" content seems to be a consequence of the difficulty of using natural experiential learning and of the ineffectiveness of other learning approaches. It is not from failure to appreciate the importance of expressive tasks. This is a crucial barrier to effective management education. Emphasis on theory, abstraction, and generalization, without the leavening effect of learning through the experience of working with others, does not lead to effective human relationships and concern with others. Effective managerial behavior is rarely the result of simple reiteration—using passive and synthetic experiential approaches—as to why others are important and of practice in techniques for developing effective human relations.

With no anchor in defined tasks and no anchor in required competencies for managers, curricula are adrift with few specific program objectives. This should have led to "contingency management" curricula. But this is not possible when the curricula are modular rather than holistic, when there are no strong integrating activities, when faculty members are specialists, and when there is little use of natural experiential learning.

Management education might benefit by use of "learning contracts" in which faculty and students agree on roles, objectives, and their commitments. This could strengthen independent learning and could provide experiential learning in gaining lifelong learning competencies.

STATE OF THE SCHOOLS

Conant (1992), in a study of schools of public administration from 1972 to 1989, found rapid growth to 1979, sharp decline from 1979 to 1983, and a mixed situation from 1983 to 1989. While generic management programs were the program type least adversely affected in the period of sharp decline, in the last period enrollments declined 73.3 percent and "four of the five generic schools [went] out of the public . . . administration business" (p. 294). Private universities lost most. Conant notes that this was predictable "given the tuition costs at private universities and low wages for public sector entry positions" (p. 294). Another factor is "the government bashing begun in the Carter administration and continued with great passion during the Reagan administration" (p. 296). Conant warns that "schools or programs located in private universities have particular reason for concern about the future."

Factors in addition to those noted by Conant have been responsible for growth and decline. There was artificial growth in the earlier period owing to students who were not accepted in the M.B.A. program and enrolled for the Master of Public Administration (M.P.A.) as second best; a decrease in the number of entry management–related jobs; and decline in government funding for graduate study by employees.

There has been a decline in the number of applicants for M.B.A. programs, although not nearly as serious as the decline in applicants for the M.P.A. Whatever the causes of the declines, it is clear that many traditional public administration programs and weaker business school programs for full-time American students may not survive far into the twenty-first century.

FACULTY

Many faculty members cannot play the dual roles of teacher and researcher. Is it time to reconsider competent researchers who are poor teachers and failing to give tenure to good teachers who are mediocre researchers? Is it desirable to assign outstanding researchers—who have no wish, or are unable, to become good teachers—to full-time research and to replace the merely competent researchers with good teachers?

STUDENTS

Most M.B.A. students indicate that their primary reason for studying management is to obtain a well-paying job. However, there is no direct relation between the M.B.A. degree and future work as a professional, as there is in the other professions. This is a consequence of the ambiguity of managerial tasks and absence of academic qualifications for managers.

The decrease in applicants may indicate a decrease in the perceived value of the degree. "Business schools are experiencing a drop in male [as well as female] applicants because of the economy and a growing feeling that the schools have failed to teach the right skills, recession has made pricey business schools a dubious luxury" (Cowan, 1992).

It is even less clear why students not sent by their government employers want to study for the M.P.A. Durant and Taggart (1985) studied midcareer and "the more traditioinal pre-service clientele of MPA programs." Pre-service students felt that midcareerists had unfavorable attitudes toward public-sector employment and had decreased optimism about their ability to make a contribution to society as a public manager. Under these conditions, one can expect that there will be fewer and fewer government employees seeking management education.

CRITICS

Critics point out a number of shortcomings in management education. Some examples are Mintzberg (1973) in the expressive area, Porter and McKibbin (1988) in integration of content, and Levine (1992) in dealing with ambiguity and risk. Corporate managers generally wanted more "realistic, practical, hands-on" education with greater emphasis on human relationships, for example, leadership and training subordinates (Porter and McKibbin, 1988). However, the critics have had little influence on education regarding either the M.P.A. or the M.B.A. This is not to say that there have been no changes in these programs. But the changes have not been in response to the criticism but have consisted of adding and dropping courses as issues develop and wane, recruiting outstanding faculty, and demonstrating to potential students the depth of course offerings.

Porter and McKibbin (1988) found that neither the board of directors of AACSB nor most deans thought that the criticisms required direct response. The researchers attributed this to the complacency of faculties. Few schools have made efforts to provide hands-on experience or to require students to be practicing managers. The Porter and McKibbin findings indicate that few faculty members have had sufficient managerial experience to be able to provide insight for students from their own experiences to make up for the lack of experiential learning.

The United States no longer is seen as having the best trained managers in the world. The United States will slip even farther in the economic hierarchy unless business schools start preparing managers to lead on the international "corporate battle fields" (Wolniansky, 1990). This is more than a "school" issue.

OBJECTIVES

Excellence in research is the primary objective for natural and social science faculties. This may be desirable in the "knowledge" disciplines where the objective of practitioners is to increase knowledge. But excellence in research is not an objective of managers. Consequently, it is doubtful that it should be the primary objective of the schools.

We have argued that if students do not have opportunities to use and test learning during the educational process, there will be little transfer of learning to practice. Acceptance of this point of view would call for admitting to management programs only those students who will be able to use the learning during the educational process. It would also suggest that schools have as a major objective providing formal continuing management education.

HOW CAN MANAGEMENT EDUCATION BE IMPROVED?

There is need for research relating education and managerial competence. A crucial question is how to improve transfer of learning. There should be research and systematic, periodic review and revision of the curriculum and structure of M.B.A. and M.P.A. programs in order to meet current and projected needs. It is essential to make conscious use of learning theory in the design and conduct of management and related specialist education.

Although we do not believe in a universally applicable management theory or set of managerial competencies, there is value in learning theory. Such theory could be the "given" to be tested in practice rather than the eternal truth. It could provide a frame-of-reference criteria for choosing from an arsenal of models, techniques, and general concepts for guiding students' reflection on experience.

Some advocates for changes in management education tend to play down the use of natural experiential learning. Thus, Schon (1992), after presenting strong arguments for natural experiential learning, recommends the use of elaborate case studies to increase relevance of learning. From our point of view, this would be an improvement but would be insufficient in the management field. It is crucial to provide students with natural, experiential learning opportunities similar to those in the Revans, New York University, and New School programs.

Recognizing that there are different needs, some schools are tailoring the M.B.A. to the needs of working managers and specific companies and are instituting programs for lifelong learning. The programs of the Darden Graduate School of Business Administration of the University of Virginia with Hercules, Inc., and Barcardi are examples of programs to meet specific organizational needs. Carnegie-Mellon's individual assignments and conferences with faculty is a program tailored to the needs of participants. The Columbia Business School M.B.A. programs for experienced managers meets on weekends. Some programs offer experienced managers help in dealing with specific problems and opportunities.

Dean John Rosenblum of the Darden School recognized the need for systemic change by advocating increased experience before training managers and by proposing a "curriculum with three study sequences [ten years apart] evolving over a lifetime of learning rather than during a traditional M.B.A. program. . . . [His] dream is to move toward continuing education and to see . . . business schools helping businesses and individuals over a lifetime" (Fowler, May 14, 1991).

It may be time for some dreams to be put into practice.

Part Three

SECTION VI: SUMMING UP

Solomon Hoberman

20
CONCLUSIONS

While education for only four professions was discussed in the preceding sections, the four are representative of the service professions, and a large part of all professional degrees are granted in these four. Consequently, in this final section not only will we integrate the findings in the earlier sections, but we will also attempt to generalize our conclusions for education of professionals generally. In addition, we will briefly discuss other issues related to professional education and will make recommendations for improving professional education.

OBJECTIVES OF PROFESSIONAL EDUCATION

Society has a great stake in the education of its professional class but has surprisingly little input in determining the objectives of professional schools other than to expect that the schools will prepare students to become competent practitioners. Schools have other objectives as well. In addition, paralleling research professions, they make research and the education of researchers more important objectives. Few question the value of linking research/scholarship and teaching in the research professions. Not only is this advance in knowledge and technology beneficial to society, but the linkage provides financial and human resources for research and scholarship, training the next generation of researchers and keeping educational content current for all students. Nevertheless, in these fields, there is recognition of the need to separate research and teaching and to relieve researchers of the burden of scheduled classes. Thus, there are fewer teaching hours for faculty and research institutes with programs for full-time researchers and postdoctoral students.

The function of the service professions is to provide professional services. The objectives of the schools have to be tightly linked to preparing students to become competent practitioners. There are few chairs for scholars and researchers in the professional schools; the teaching faculty does almost all scholarship and research. The "publish or perish" criterion for evaluating faculty is detrimental to both teaching and research/scholarship objectives. The time may have come for the professional schools to have different priorities and standards than the graduate schools of arts and sciences.

CONTENT

Two issues relating to content are emphasized. These are the importance of interpersonal relationships and of preparation for holistic practice. No professional can provide effective services to clients without establishing relationships with the client and other providers. Although most often such relationships are with others in the same profession, not infrequently they are with persons in other occupations. Little professional education includes content relating to clients and providers in the same service area, and none includes content relating to providers in other service areas.

The almost exclusive use of the modular approach results in failure to prepare students to be effective boundary spanners. In an era of specialization, this is a serious shortcoming. Experiential education could provide appropriate learning opportunities. A related content area that is neglected is preparing professionals to be case managers. There is little training in coordinating related professional services, necessitated by specialization within a profession and services provided by different professions.

Professional education curricula follow the undergraduate and the research and professional school practice of dividing education into distinct courses and sequences of modules in specialties. Advantages are that

- content is well defined
- use of learning is made clear
- competencies are related to specific tasks
- facts and techniques are learned rapidly
- teaching is easier
- subject specialists can be recruited

- faculty prefers the modular structure

Disadvantages are that

- transfer of learning to service practice is difficult
- much learning tends to be inactive and easily lost
- focus tends to be on specific, instrumental tasks
- techniques are emphasized
- natural experiential learning is rarely possible
- educating top-notch generalist faculty is difficult

LEARNING APPROACH

Emphasis on passive learning followed growth of the academic professional school with a full-time faculty. Critics very early pointed out that formal passive education has limited effectiveness for transfer of learning to practice. The case method of teaching was advanced as a solution and is still advocated by some (Schon, 1992). The case approach is an academic substitute for experience. Case analysis focuses learning on solving well-defined problems. It does not provide learning that deals with real situations that are ill defined and indeterminate, that have numerous intervening variables, and that are always subject to risk and the unpredictable behaviors of others.

The components of experiential learning are identified as knowledge of theory, identification of the need for action, action that uses theory, and feedback and reflection on the relations between theory, action, and outcome. Learning—that is, inducing new theory and revision of life-bank elements—stems from analysis, reflection, and revision or reinforcement of theory. Reflection can occur during or after an activity. The reflection turns the learner into a researcher in the context of practice (Schon, 1983, 1992; Cervero, 1988; Hoberman and Mailick, 1991; Center on Education and Training, 1992).

The importance of experiential learning is accepted in all fields. However, use is spotty and its potential is rarely achieved owing to limited content, inappropriate experience, confusion of "experience" and "experiential learning," failure to emphasize the role of "reflection," poor linkage between classroom and experiential learning, and, most important, inadequately trained faculty.

The limited, learning research available indicates that cognitive learning improves when learning is in the actual work venue. This learning is more effective for transferring learning, particularly for developing effective relationships with others and responding to new situations. The approach has shortcomings. The work experience available for students tends to be limited and few faculty are prepared to serve as mentors and help students gain competence in "practical research" and reflection. Moreover, good experiential learning tends to be "deep" rather than "broad." Narrow experience in practice coupled with the explosion in knowledge and technology can lead to narrow specialization.

There are natural experiential-learning venues, in addition to the actual work venue. Two of these natural venues are (1) specially developed venues, for example, school-developed and school-directed activities, and (2) special tasks performed in a real work venue, for example, special projects. There are programs with a kind of a sandwich structure. Students have practical experience before entry and have directed, planned experience for one or two years between formal parts of the educational program, with faculty contact throughout. These approaches could be used in almost all professional education. Synthetic experiential learning is an important educational approach. It can be used to deal with problems and shortcomings in natural experiential opportunities. But it is an error to believe that it can replace natural experiential learning. It does not present the same complexities, risk, feedback, or opportunities for reflection and learning.

Learning can be the outcome of a conscious effort to learn, or it can be the serendipitous result of a review of an action or consequences or of a rearrangement of life-bank elements in order to achieve a new objective. Experiential education uses all of these. Students are motivated to ponder situations, not to give expeditious "right answers." This is necessary for the education of service professionals.

FACULTY

In the early development of professional education, most faculty members were either part-time teachers and practitioners or recent practitioners. The practical bent of faculty members, the focus on preparing students for practice, and limited university affiliation were taken as proof that faculty members in professional schools were not engaged in an appropriately "high level" of intellectual activity. To bring professional school faculties up to the academic standards of other colleges, studies of professional education have recommended that professional schools employ only full-time faculty and select and evaluate faculty members on the basis of published research. Desire and ability to teach are now rarely decisive factors in selection or promotion. Even when faculty members practice, they have little in common with everyday practitioners; their practice is institutionalized into a distinctly academic profession of consultation. Few have current practice experience or an interest in natural experiential education in the venue in which practice will take place.

There is a need to provide education for both faculty members and students in relating effectively with others in supplying professional services. But without faculty sensitivity and effective mentoring, much of the potential value of experiential learning is lost.

STUDENTS

Professionals constitute the "upper class" in the United States. Emphasis on college, graduate, and professional education by government, educational authorities, the press, and career counselors lead people ambitious for their children and the children themselves to fight to enter that upper class. Prior to World War II, most students entered professional school after fewer than four years of college. Only after the war and the great increase in applicants did a baccalaureate become a general requirement for entry. While this delays and makes entry more difficult, there is no evidence that it leads to greater professional competence. It retards maturation and increases costs. Undergraduate and professional content overlap. Students and education would benefit by shortening the length and reducing the cost of education and by integrating content.

Professional school students are younger and less apt to be married than other postbaccalaureate students. More than 75 percent were younger than 30, and less than 30 percent were married in 1989–1990. Most professional, service students were studying law or medicine (or another health profession). The health area, including related professions, was by far the greatest for any postbaccalaureate degree (National Center for Educational Statistics, 1992, 1993).

The continuation of "classroom" education means that these professional-school students have had little respite from the passive "student" role. Few have had significant experience in relating to people in an important work setting or as service providers. Both of these factors increase the need for professional education to move the students out of the classroom and into the working world and to provide extensive, varied, natural experiential education under the tutoring of a qualified mentor.

21
OTHER ISSUES

Some issues and some aspects of issues discussed in earlier chapters that were not in the design for the book surfaced in reviewing the literature and in our discussions. In this chapter we touch upon some of these: impact of the environment, assessment of professional performance, use of new technologies, quality and cost of services, the structure of education, continuing education, and specialization. Many deserve full-blown discussion and analysis, which we hope our brief descriptions will encourage others to undertake.

ENVIRONMENT

Public support for professional education is both direct and indirect. There are state-supported schools, and state support for private professional schools; there are federal and state scholarships and an extensive loan program to help pay tuition and living expenses. Federally directed research pays part of faculty salaries. Subsidizing medical research has indirectly led to increased specialization and a reluctance to practice in areas without facilities and support for advanced technologies. This may have led to increases in medical costs.

Although we already have too many professionals as far as absolute need is concerned, there are unmet service needs for poor and rural populations. Efforts to limit funding for professional education will be resisted by those seeking to enter the professional class.

Societal views are unfocused. However, they are indicated by critical articles, books, and movies and by decreased public support for professional schools and research. A *Business Week* editorial of May 20, 1991 (quoted in Bonser, 1992) stated, "It's time for universities to reenter the real world. They can no longer assume that taxpayers will foot the bill for endless expansion, more empire building, or lavish perks. It's a time for more accountability and a return to basics."

Public scrutiny is focused on the behavior of professionals. Films such as *The Firm*, *The Fugitive*, and *Dr. Giggles* portray lawyers and physicians as scheming, greedy, and incompetent. Most books and articles describe professionals, not as honest, concerned, and competent, but as dishonest, antisocial, and incompetent. It is one step to move from focus on performance to focus on professional education.

At present, the call for accountability is directed toward precollegiate education and public two- and four-year colleges. There are some demands for assessment of outcomes and use of resources in medical education (Jonas, Etzel, and Barzansky, 1991). However, other than that of acreditation boards there is no systematic assessment of professional schools. Because these schools tend to assess input, not output, they do not satisfy the demands.

The oversupply of professionals is related to the number of available seats in the professional schools. There may be too many schools. Publicly supported schools are at risk.

PROFESSIONAL SERVICES

A number of problems connected with provision of professional services may have their roots in professional education. Among these are fragmentation, the cost of services, and large populations with insufficient access to services.

America supports more professionals per capita than any other country does. The ratio of lawyers to population in America is 1 to 250. In Japan, it is 1 to 7,500 (*New York Times*, November 12, 1992). The differences in ratios, though not as great, are similar in other professions. Although these ratios are not as different from other Western countries as they are from Japan, they are nevertheless startling. More does not always lead to increased and better professional services, to lower costs, or to increased services for underserved populations. The contrary may be the case. Most professionals have a target standard of living based on factors such as cost and length of education, living standards of current practitioners, and maintenance of status. Service rates and populations served tend to be determined by these factors. The more professionals there are, the more the professionals find a need for professional services. The recognized propensity of Americans to take legal action may, in part, be due to the great number of lawyers. The cost of medical services may in part be due to the great number of medical specialists.

Sociopolitical forces have for some time been directed toward reducing the cost and increasing the availability of professional services. This is perhaps most easily seen in medical services. There are demands for controlling costs, reducing unessential services, equalizing access, and increasing public health activities. The solutions involve an increase in government intervention in funding, resource allocation, and delivery of health care services. (See the many proposals for national health in Leichter, 1992, and Martini, 1991.) Clients are asking law firms to utilize the services of paralegals rather than higher priced lawyers (Feder, 1993).

Specialization and services from different disciplines makes coordination a necessity. The tendency of each provider to achieve a specific objective leads to suboptimization. This is diffiuclt to overcome, but must be if the client is to be served. The services of one professional may influence, to an unpredictable degree, the services of another.

Except for malpractice suits, there is little assessment of delivery of professional services. Medicine is virtually alone in concern for formal assessment of performance. While assessments of quality of care provided by individual physicians is generally not available, there are evaluations of care provided by health maintenance organizations (HMOs). Freudenheim (1992) has reported on several of these. They tend to depend on subscribers' assessments. Some studies are by employers checking on the benefits received by their employees.

Critics point out that the choice of professional provider (a key element in satisfaction) does not enhance quality. Consumers are rarely qualified to evaluate professional competence. And evaluation without a basis for comparison is meaningless.

In the past, extending well beyond the middle of the century, professional services were provided by individuals or small partnerships with occasional support from other professionals. The trend is now toward services provided by large groups of specialists, with a supporting cast of paraprofessionals with related competencies and of professionals from other professions. There are organized service teams, using common data banks and administrative, technical, and equipment services. In some cases the professionals own the organization and share in the profits. In others they are employed by the service company. The method used to pay for services affects relationships. The alternatives include fee for individual services, single payment for multiple services, and insurance to pay for future needs. The new conditions tend to further fragment and impersonalize professional services.

Increasing costs and underserved populations have led to an increase in alternative service providers. Sometimes these are new professionals or existing professionals assuming new tasks, and sometimes they are paraprofessionals. Some states have enlarged the domains of paraprofessionals at the expense of professionals and have established overlapping professional domains.

Partly in response to the cost issue, there is increased training and employment of paraprofessionals in professional fields. There were an estimated 100,000 paralegals in 1993. Many paraprofessionals work without professional supervision. In social work, they are admitted into the professional organization. In some fields they have set up their own organizations. The ABA was sufficiently concerned to establish a Commission on Non-Lawyer Practice to study the situation and make recommendations.

CONTENT

The effects of rapid changes in technology and the consequent specialization were only touched upon in earlier chapters. The increases in theory, research, and technology and the number of practitioners make "specialization" a law of development in every profession. It is so extensive in some professions that practitioners in different specialties require quite different competencies. In the "hard sciences," professionals in different specialties, have not talked the same language for fifty years. A similar condition now exists in some service professions. This issue does not have to be completely resolved in the hard sciences for professionals to work together. It is in service professions that the focus must be on the person or system served and not on the service provided. Not only do services for a client provided by practitioners in the same profession have to be coordinated, but coordination is also needed between practitioners in different professions.

Most managers of professional service organizations are not trained as managers. Nothing in their professional education prepares them. Social work schools are the only professional schools that include supervision in their curricula. But supervision is only part of management. There is an assumption, without evidence to support it, that professionals are qualified to administer programs in their professional areas.

Schools are concerned that there is a public perception that many professionals engage in unethical practices. Some schools include a course or two on morality and ethics in their curricula. As Plato noted some thousands of years ago, this passive learning has had no significant effect. Hart and Norwood have indicated that clinical learning, which provides both real-life practice and a mentor/model, is more effective (see Section III of this volume on Legal Education).

LEARNING APPROACHES

The learning approach that is used affects more than transfer of learning. Some see natural experiential learning as a way for schools to provide quality services to persons with limited access to services by reason of poverty, race, ethnicity, health, mental condition, or lifestyle. Others, as far back as the Flexner report, have recognized that linking learning and service in this way may reduce the value of experiential learning. Another caution is to ensure that achieving the objectives of the organization that provides the experiential opportunities are not given priority over students' education.

In the course of their practice, professionals must be able to adapt learning to new and ambiguous situations, note cause-effect relationships, and reflect on the expected and unexpected. They must acquire the ability to learn from practice. Natural experiential learning is the most effective way for students to acquire

- competencies for independent study and lifelong learning
- appropriate ethical and professional standards
- the will to contribute to society

One might ask, "If natural experiential education is superior, why isn't there more of it?" An easy answer is that it is an approach with which academics are uncomfortable. A more important reason was given by David S. Walker, dean of the Drake Law School: "We have much to praise clinical education for. We have every reason to pursue it. Why don't we do more of it? The reason is obvious. It is very expensive" (Power, 1991, p. 10).

In only one professional field has natural experiential education been supported by the federal government. Several million dollars of federal subsidies have been given to clinical legal education each year. This twenty-year program has never been assessed. Support has been fostered by Congress. Based on my review of its annual reports, the Department of Education's attitude has varied from indifference to outright opposition.

FACULTY

There is general agreement that professional education should be improved, but there is little evidence that tenured faculty are concerned about the issue or motivated to make any serious efforts to make teaching more effective. Each profession has one or more journals devoted to education. The journal articles deal mainly with content, faculty benefits, case studies, and synthetic experiential learning. Many general periodicals publish articles on education in the profession. Publication of an article on professional education rarely counts in the "publish-or-perish" game.

Part-time faculty members responsible for experiential education tend to have lower academic status than other teaching faculty, except in medicine. Graduate medical education (GME) faculty members are an exception. The dominance of the practitioners makes services the objective, and clinical teaching of medical students is shifted to residents. This does not benefit the education of either group.

A consequence of specialization has been a radical increase in faculty members in different disciplines. This has tended to improve research and enrich offerings and teaching in specialty areas. But it also has fostered the modular approach; compartmentalized faculty, learning, and services; and tended to focus practitioner attention on a specific problem rather than on client's needs. It increases the gap between education and practice.

There are attempts to consider teaching competence in the selection and promotion of faculty members, at least in the undergraduate schools. DePalma (1992) has reported that Cornell makes formal evaluations of teaching an essential element of tenure decisions. "The evaluations will make use of student critiques, peer review and syllabuses, tests and lesson materials. Such materials have long been required to evaluate a professor's performance in research." DePalma has quoted the dean of the university faculty as saying that "teaching is just as important to one's success as faculty members at Cornell as is research." DePalma has reported that, according to E. Benjamin, general secretary of the American Association of University Professors, Stanford University's effort to improve teaching, "higher salaries for successful teachers, special teaching prizes and opportunities for undergraduate research," is the strongest of any university. There are Doctor of Arts Degree programs to prepare for college teaching, none for professional schools.

STUDENTS

Competition to enter most professional schools is intense. Admission is most often based on factors such as grade averages and test scores. While these may have predictive value for success in school, they are not predictive of success as a practitioner.

The cost of education has increased most sharply for professionals. Students' expectations for income as practitioners are dependent on the length and cost of their education. Average cost for medical education in 1989–1990 was $13,866 in a public school and $23,558 in a private, not-for-profit school; for legal education the average cost was $14,572 and $20,812, respectively (National Center for Educational Statistics, 1992, 1993). Income for medical students during their residencies hardly pays their living expenses. Other professional education costs are less but still high. Almost 75 percent of full-time professional students received some sort of financial aid. The average aid in 1989–1990 was $12,310. While this is an investment by society, by far the greatest amount of aid was in the form of loans, which have to be repaid (National Center for Educational Statistics, 1992, 1993).

Society's objective of redressing injury to populations that have been discriminated against in access to professional education has in the past twenty years led to significant changes in the characteristics of the student population. After massive increases for more than a century, the number of graduates has stabilized. Conflicting forces have been at play. Some forces directed toward reducing applicants are a decline in the number of 16- to 24-year-olds during the period 1975 to 1993 and a recognition of oversupply in some professions. Increases in applicants are due to greater numbers of women, African Americans, Hispanics, and Asians who are seeking to enter the professions. The number of degrees, defined as "first professional" by the Office of Educational Research and Improvement (almost all law and medicine/health related), granted to men declined from 52,194 to 43,819; the number granted to women increased from 19,146 to 26,917 from 1950 to 1980. Among men, only Asian Americans showed a significant increase in degrees granted. Although there was an increase in the percentage of African American, non-Hispanic, and Hispanic men who received first professional degrees from 1950 to 1980, there was no significant increase from 1980 to 1990. However the percentage of degrees granted to minority women doubled (National Center for Educational Statistics, 1992).

The number of 16- to 24-year-olds will increase 5 percent by the year 2000 and another 5 percent by the year 2005. It can be expected that at least the same percentage of these young people will seek professional education as the present cohorts, and a far higher percentage of these will be women. If the entry demands of professional schools are met, the increase in professionals will be far greater than the expected increase in population.

Graduates in most professions have to be certified on the basis of a qualifying competence examination. This usually includes oral and written tests or papers. Unfortunately, these tests do not reliably and validly assess competence in practice. Further, written tests encourage passive-learning approaches. The most advanced performance assessment is in medical education. Langley (1973) has reported that license boards are developing tests for cognitive processes used by experienced clinicians. Specialty boards review standardized evaluations of residency performance. "The National Board of Medical Examiners . . . and the Educational Commission for Foreign School Graduates . . . are developing tests of clinical skills. . . . As recertification moves toward an evaluation of practice, there is a call for competence evaluations that will also examine practice performance."

Medical schools are accredited by the Liaison Committee for Medical Education. The current standards for accreditation include requirements for evaluating students' performance that determine whether students have acquired the core clinical skills and behaviors needed for subsequent medical training. Langsley (1991) has noted that the evaluations for entry to a residency and for a license to practice in a state do not claim to predict physician performance. Calls for performance assessment have been accompanied by proposals for practice guidelines and standards. Synthetic experiential tests have been developed in which actors and raters simulate patient behavior. "The process of clinical skills assessment is . . . being explored by the Clinical Skills Assessment Alliance, . . . [which] represents all the major groups concerned with the evaluation of clinical competence at medical school, graduate medical education, and practitioner levels." Approaches include peer ratings, audit of charts from a physician's own practice, cognitive tests, and structured oral tests. Similar approaches would be desirable in other service professions.

There are more than fifty distinct sets of criteria and certifications in the United States. This tends to reduce professional mobility. Although there are individual agreements among states to recognize each other's certifications, the problem remains.

ADMINISTRATION

Few schools have continuing programs to control costs. Few administrators have had any management education. This is true even in schools of administration. And there is little attempt to help administrators improve on the job.

There is a movement to make faculty at public universities account for hours worked and for research, teaching, and service performed. The University of Connecticut has devised a plan to measure the productivity of faculty members. Departments are to be scored on a scale from zero to five in ten categories, which include research productivity, service to the state, national reputation, and undergraduate and graduate teaching (*New York Times*, January 10, 1993). There is no measure of quality of ouptut.

Professional schools have gained in status by affiliation with universities. However, it is not at all clear that the relation has been beneficial from the viewpoint of quality and cost of professional education.

ORGANIZATION AND STRUCTURE OF PROFESSIONAL EDUCATION

Structural issues include relations between undergraduate and professional education, the modular nature of education compared to the holistic nature of practice, and education for practitioners and researchers in the same program.

Entry requirements link undergraduate and graduate education. Except for professions such as engineering and accounting, professional schools expect students to have a baccalaureate degree. The justification is that students will be more mature, "better rounded," and better prepared. Academics disparage "preparation for a trade" and claim that it dilutes and diminishes "liberal" education as "education for life." Professional-school faculties tend to feel that an emphasis on "liberal" education diminishes in value as a preparation for professional education. It would make "liberal" education more meaningful if educators could demonstrate to students that humanities provide learning useful for their careers (Saunders, 1982). The requirement of a baccalaureate may be more a financial benefit for universities than preparation for a profession.

ACCREDITATION

To a great extent school associations have been allowed to deal with accreditation of professional schools. Some question whether the associations have the will and competence and whether they should have the authority to determine the salient societal goals and the ability of schools to achieve these. Professional associations have not been strong advocates for changes in educational practices that are not seen as beneficial to their members.

INFLUENCE OF TECHNOLOGY

Electronic technologies and data banks are changing the nature of professional services. But these may have an even greater influence on professional education. The new technologies reduce the need for class-rooms, school buildings, libraries, and teachers. Individual instruction may become easier. Lectures by outstanding teachers can be provided in hundreds of locations by satellite. "Instruction on demand, at an individual's desktop workstation, will . . . supplement the group methods we now employ" (Baldwin, 1991, p. 90). Electronically mediated learning environments can replace many on-site synthetic and observational experiential-learning approaches. Interactive group participation, such as the preceptoral sessions discussed in the LIFE approach (Hoberman and Mailick, 1992), can take place without either participants or the preceptor moving from their home bases. Students can observe services being performed. Their performances can be observed, feedback provided, and the details of performance discussed with "mentors at a distance" and with outstanding teachers (Baldwin, 1991; Dede, 1991; Hawkins, 1991; Pis-kurich, 1993). Opportunities for mentoring and cooperative learning are increased.

Computer-based data systems can facilitate the coordination of profes-sional services in every professional field. Central data banks can contain all the information needed to diagnose and to provide a specific profes-sional service.

While these advances could have a positive effect on education, there are problems that include developing, paying for, and maintaining the networks; compensating for more impersonal instruction and reduced interaction between faculty members and students; learning the nature of education that is effective using distance-learning channels; identifying activities in which there can be effective learning through collaboration and communication with others across a distance; training teachers to use the new technologies effectively; obtaining feedback from students; and limiting the use of the approach to where it is efficient and effective (Hawkins, 1991; Piskurich, 1993; Johnstone, 1991; Bruce, Katz, and Tomsic, 1991).

CONTINUING PROFESSIONAL EDUCATION

The rapidity with which much of professional education is superseded is the basis for formal requirements for continuing professional education (CPE) and periodic recertification. In surgery, the problem is so acute that "the New York State Health Department . . . has directed hospitals to be stricter in deciding which surgeons can perform the procedure and to pay more attention to their results" (Altman, 1992).

It may be desirable to do away with lifetime professional licensing and to institute periodic recertification on the basis of performance assessment. State legislatures have tended to avoid conflict by mandating less threatening CPE (Stern and Queeny, 1992). Although there is no reliable evidence that CPE programs increase professional competence, it is accepted that CPE is necessary for all professionals.

For many years there was little practitioner interest and participation in formal CPE. This has changed in the past twenty-five years as a consequence of practitioners' recognizing the need to acquire new knowledge and competencies, programs publicized by aggressive providers, new requirements instituted by regulatory agencies, and employer and professional support. Although professional journals and conferences that were major sources for CPE in the past continue, they are no longer the chief providers. New important providers include consultants, professional associations, regulatory agencies, and entrepreneurial educational institutions.

Recently, professional schools, mostly in medicine, realizing the status and money involved, have become providers. "The 1991 list of [Accreditation Council for Continuing Medical Education] accredited institutions and organizations consists of 489 entries, including 121 medical schools and 166 specialty societies [35 hospitals, 20 state medical societies, 13 voluntary health organizations and 134 'other']. . . . State medical societies accredited 1826 CME-sponsoring organizations in 1991" (Wentz, Osteen, and Gannon, 1991, pp. 953–56). In law, education for a specialized, new practice is conducted by organizations such as the National Institute for Trial Advocacy and the Practicing Law Institute. In management, consultant firms and nonprofit organizations, such as the American Management Association, are principal providers. Some schools of social work sponsor courses in specialized areas. More often faculty members freelance courses.

In less than two decades, CPE has become an industry with its own professionals. Papers dealing with CPE as a distinct field first appeared in the 1970s. Houle's (1980) was the first major text. The Council for the Improvement of Continuing Education for the Professions has as its objectives to identify and solve CPE problems across professions, provide networking opportunities, share ideas and programs, and assess and improve CPE's effect on performance. Studies to develop "a set of standards to help distinguish between good and poor quality programs has met with resistance among college and university-based providers" (Azzaretto, 1992). There are professional periodicals, for example, *The Journal of Continuing Education in the Health Professions.*

Studies indicate that although integrated and systematic CPE is needed, most programs are segmented and fragmented. Azzaretto (1992) has ascribed this to competition among providers. There is recognition that the most common approach—passive learning—is inadequate. The value of isolated lectures not related to assessment of individual needs is questioned (Stern and Queeny, 1992). But, as in other educational fields, there is little reliable and valid research addressed to key questions of the usefulness and quality of CPE (Hunt, 1992). Azzaretto (1992) has indicated that some reasons for this are lack of agreement on a standard of quality, methodological obstacles to defining and measuring quality, and defensiveness in the face of criticism.

In a study of CPE in four European countries, Lynton (1992) found that there was an acceptance that professionals have to deal with changes in fundamentals of professionals expertise, a strong trend toward practice-based continuing education rather than knowledge accumulation, and a shift to programs tailored to needs of organizations and individuals. The British, French, Germans, and Dutch believe that making good CPE available and affordable is in the interest of both the public and the individual. Responsibility is shared between state, employers, professional associations, and individuals. The state's share includes start-up costs, setting up information networks, staff development, and catalytic and leveraging activities.

RESEARCH TO IMPROVE PROFESSIONAL EDUCATION

There has been only limited research on the relation between education, on the one hand, and practice directed toward improving practice, on the other. In his influential study, Flexner (1925) simply assumed that all that was needed was to adopt the "German" educational model. There is no generally accepted superior model at the present time that could serve as a prototype. We first need to identify criteria for superior practice and work back to superior education. And if this is accomplished, would the findings have influence? The effect of the Flexner report is unique. No other research on the effectiveness of professional education has had any significant effect. Federal support may be required in order for studies to improve professional education and CPE.

22
RECOMMENDATIONS

For these general recommendations, we have drawn on and extrapolated from the analysis and recommendations of all the contributors. However, we are solely responsible for the specific comments and recommendations.

OBJECTIVES

If professional education is to continue to receive public support, faculties have to become more sensitive and responsive to societal needs and expectations. There are demands for increasing quality of services, sensitivity to clients' needs, and availability of services while decreasing their cost. Although education's potential effect on these services characteristics is limited, it is not insignificant.

Schools can help providers meet these service demands by

- reducing the time and cost of professional education by using new communication means, separating teaching and research, and telescoping undergraduate and professional education;
- providing and integrating graduate and continuing professional education;
- participating in planning to train paraprofessionals and technicians to qualify them to perform increased tasks;
- including education for case management and the supervision and utilization of paraprofessionals;

- budgeting educational resources to make the number and types of professionals compatible with societal needs;
- providing learning for integrating and coordinating services;
- integrating and rationalizing the undergraduate and professional educational sequence and structure;
- inculcating professional ethics throughout professional education, particularly through experience, role modeling, and mentoring.

Achievement of this complex set of objectives necessitates continual self-assessment and involvement in research to improve professional education.

CONTENT

In the short term, changes in courses and the addition and deletion of courses may suffice. But there must be periodic assessment and revision of an entire curriculum. Accreditation organizations should mandate periodic review and revision of curricula.

While specialization enriches offerings, it fosters the modular approach and focuses practitioners' attention on specific needs. Relationships with other people, clients, support staff, colleagues, and persons in the service network tend to be ignored. To counteract the fragmentation from specialization, education should include an integrative sequence to bring the full picture of the profession's services into focus for students.

Students should be helped to acquire research skills not to become researchers but to become practitioners who can learn from their practice. Reflection in experiential learning and in research analysis are similar. The skill transfers to practice.

LEARNING APPROACHES

Natural experiential learning in venues similar to those in which professionals practice should be increased and improved. Difficulties in implementation are outweighed by the superiority of the natural experiential approach with respect to transferring learning, continuing to learn from experience, learning to relate effectively to others, and dealing with the unexpected. Integration with well-designed, synthetic experiential education can increase the breadth of learning and reduce the time and cost of learning. Achieving these objectives requires that students learn and use experiential-learning theory to reflect on the learning process and the enhancement of learning by linking theory, practice, feedback, analysis, and reflection.

Where it is too difficult to provide satisfactory natural experiential education in a venue similar to that in which students will practice, alternative learning venues include school-based professional service organizations, consulting services, and project assignment.

It is to be hoped that there will be renewed support by the U.S. Department of Education for natural experiential learning in professional education.

FACULTY

Faculty members have to be motivated and helped to be more open to change to make conscious use of learning theory, and to make greater and more effective use of experiential-learning approaches.

"Experiential" faculty should be as carefully selected and have the same status as other faculty members. All faculty members should be responsible for coordinating and integrating school and work-based learning. Increased use of teaching teams consisting of classroom and field faculty members is essential for natural-experiential learning to be effective.

Teaching should be given priority over research. Faculty members should be trained and recognized as teachers.

STUDENTS

Admission to professional schools should take into account the values and needs of society. The criteria should be made public. There is a movement to establish national voluntary standards for elementary and secondary teachers. The associations of the various professional schools should assess the cost/benefits of establishing standards for graduation and certification in their professions. This is in line with the recommendation to "create a National Board for Professional and Technical Standards . . . [funded by] Congress, private foundations, [et al.] to work collaboratively with states and cities involved in . . . development of standards" (National Center on Education and the Economy, 1993, p. 11).

The importance of written and oral test scores for entry and graduation should be reduced. Tests of competence as a professional call for assessment over a period of time. Natural experiential learning could provide the portfolio of information needed for competency-based assessment. At least one year of clinical education under the mentorship of a qualified professional should be required before taking the test for a professional license.

We can expect the number of applicants for entry to professional schools to increase. There are in many professions already more practitioners than are needed to provide adequate services. Consequently, consideration should be taken to avoid actions that would increase the number of students. In particular, additional schools should be discouraged.

ADMINISTRATION

"Most university administrative systems today are overly political, reactive, and based on a hodgepodge of outmoded concepts and philosophies of management and leadership, if a concept exists at all" (Bonser, 1992, p. 506). We believe that this comment about universities applies and is compounded in professional-school administration. Some of the adverse effects would be lessened if university oversight were directed toward improving the administration and output of the professional schools rather than imposing counterproductive criteria selection of faculty.

ORGANIZATION OF PROFESSIONAL EDUCATION

Many have recommended telescoping undergraduate and professional education (Cantrall, 1952; Pincus, 1980). It would be desirable to improve and adopt the model that is used by some medical and law schools to telescope undergraduate and professional education. The Association of American Medical Colleges lists twenty-five medical schools that combine liberal arts and M.D. programs leading to the award of combined baccalaureate and M.D. degrees. The University of Missouri School of Medicine integrated courses for baccalaureate and M.D. degrees can be completed in six years (Martini, 1991). Telescoping would provide time for one year of natural experiential education without increasing the length of education. The one year could be in the form of two years of integrated half-experiential and half-classroom education, with some of the experiential education linked to the liberal-arts curriculum.

Professional schools should consider providing both graduate professional and continuing professional education. Their failure to do this insulates crucial specialty education and lifelong education from critical review. The situation is similar to what existed when professional education was the domain of proprietary schools. There is need to motivate and make it possible for professional schools to extend their domains to these postgraduate activities.

ACCREDITATION

Criteria for accreditation of professional schools should emphasize curriculum, educational approaches, competence of graduates, periodic self-assessment and revision of curriculum, and postgraduate programs. Postgraduate programs should be a more important criterion for full accreditation than the number of papers published by faculty. A statement by accreditation organizations of general criteria for continuing self-assessment—with stated, self-imposed standards—could have a significant beneficial effect.

NEW TECHNOLOGIES

There should be more experimentation with new educational technologies, particularly for continuing professional education. We have to learn how to use distance-learning channels effectively, identifying the kinds of activities in which there can be effective learning through collaboration and communication with others across a distance (Hawkins, 1991; Piskurich, 1993). Distance-learning techniques should be employed to increase the quality and reduce the cost of class and experiential learning. Consortia of schools, similar to those in engineering, could use the techniques to provide graduate and continuing professional education.

Instruction in use of data banks and other computer technologies should be a mandatory subject in every school and included in experiential education.

CONTINUING PROFESSIONAL EDUCATION

Specialization and the need for lifelong learning present challenges and opportunities for professional schools. These schools should develop graduate education programs in interspecialty areas and grant a certificate to practitioners who meet competency criteria. With the use of the new technologies, many of these programs could be at the learner's convenience.

RESEARCH

There is no significant exploratory research relating to professional education. Consequently, it is not possible to make meaningful research recommendations. Studies are needed to identify and define learning variables and posit relations on which to base hypotheses that can be subjected to test. The activities should provide insight into the learning process and the conditions under which the use of learning is increased.

The U.S. Department of Education lost an opportunity to contribute to learning in this area by its indifference to the clinical legal education program. It is to be hoped that such opportunities will not be lost in the future.

CHANGE

In the past, significant changes in higher education have been sudden rather than incremental and have rarely been initiated from within the educational system (Hartle, 1977). Change in any activity calls for change in the behavior of the principal stakeholders. Studies will be a waste of time as long as administrators and faculties ignore or respond defensively to criticism. Many reasons can be given for not acting on recommendations. The most common reasons include unsatisfactory past experience, the high cost of change, and disruption in education and research. Inertia and interest in maintaining the status quo are never mentioned.

However, social, economic, and political forces for change are stronger than at any time since the beginning of the century (the last time at which major changes were made in professional education). Further, Hart and Norwood's description of law schools' responsiveness to internal criticism of the case approach and of the willingness of many law schools to introduce and extend clinical education in response to student and faculty advocacy indicate that, although systemic change may require significant external pressure, there can be effective internal change agents (see Section III of this volume on Legal Education).

In an issue of the *Annals of the American Academy of Political and Social Science* devoted to "American Higher Education: Prospects and Choices," Ladd (1972) has reported that demands for change include

the three-year degree, more emphasis on teaching, a $10 billion cut in expenditures by 1980. Change is sought on two rather different levels. One level involves policies and procedures—curriculum, faculty qualifications, admissions, and so on. Change at this level can and does occur quite regularly. The other level of change relates to basic goals and objectives—such as . . . discovering, preserving, and transmitting knowledge or actively applying knowledge on society's behalf. Change at this level occurs infrequently, if at all, in most social institutions. (pp. 207–16)

While we agree with Ladd that development of a new consensus about the goals of higher education is a societal and political task, not a professional school responsibility, we note that few of the changes that he saw occurring have materialized.

Jonas, Etzel, and Barzansky (1991) have claimed that assessment has led to changes in medical education, including "fewer didactic lectures, more small-group teaching, increased supervision of students learning clinical skills, more interdisciplinary efforts that emphasize making basic science components of the curriculum relevant to the clinical practice of medicine, a greater emphasis on social and ethical issues, and a renewed effort to evaluate student performance" (p. 913).

We hope, at the minimum, that our presentation will lead to the type of change reported by Hart and Norwood (in this book) and by Jonas, Etzel and Barzansky (1991) and to increased and better use of natural experiential education. Beyond that, we hope that our efforts will, to some extent, disrupt complacency and lead to creative controversy, more extensive innovation by the educators responsible, and increased national concern for educating the next generation of professionals.

GLOSSARY

Academic health center (AHC) is a consortium of a medical school, one or more other health professional schools, a university hospital, and one or more other teaching hospitals.

Academic medical center (AMC) may be synonymous with AHC, but does not necessarily include professional schools other than medicine.

Active learning is learning that can be usefully and directly applied or whose future application can be clearly foreseen.

Behavior refers to the activities (primarily observable) of a person.

Boundary is the set of criteria for distinguishing tasks performed by the focal profession and other workers. Boundary refers to the limit of the profession's domain.

Change, also referred to as "moving," is a stage in the Lewin model in which new learning is defined and accepted.

Clinical education is the term most often used in legal education for natural-experiential education, but occasionally for synthetic methods.

Closure is skill in completing and making sense of incomplete and ambiguous information. Closure is related to skill-retrieving, life-bank elements on the basis of limited information for identification of desired elements.

Coaching is helping a student to learn from practice in a one-to-one relationship. The focus is on the whole person and uses such techniques as feedback, consultation, and task analysis.

Cognitive apprenticeship is an approach that simulates natural-experiential learning by providing students with opportunities (1) to learn by getting to know and reflect on the thought processes and activities of skilled practitioners and (2) to apply, test, and reflect on learning, working on complex occupational tasks as one of a team of students. It is similar to an experiential approach proposed by Schon (1983).

Community Hospital. See *hospital.*

Competencies are both the behavior and thought processes needed to perform a task and the tasks that the individual can perform. We distinguish five categories:

1. Knowledge—useful information
2. Skill—competence to use information to perform tasks not involving others, for example, analyzing data, reviewing a medical chart, designing a course of study, and developing a legal brief
3. Ability—competence in relating to other people, for example, as a student, client, associate, superior, subordinate, and mentor
4. Judgment—competence in identifying issues and opportunities, in developing and identifying reasonable alternative solutions and decisions, in anticipating consequences, and in selecting an appropriate alternative
5. Will—motivation, determination, and persistence in undertaking to complete a task and achieve an objective.

Content is the learning that participants are expected to gain by participating in a professional education program.

Continuing professional education (CPE) is organized learning that is recognized by an appropriate authority as contributing to the knowledge, competence, development, and performance of individual professionals after they have been licensed as practitioners (Hunt, 1992).

Culture, in an operational sense, consists of those factors that characterize and influence the members of an identifiable population to exhibit thought and behavior patterns different from those of other populations.

Design is the completed plan for a program, including objectives, resources, activities, and assessment and feedback techniques.

Domain is the set of activities recognized as appropriate for a profession or system and for which a profession or system has a special and distinctive competence.

Element is the individual unit in a person's life bank. Among the elements are components of specific competencies. There are active elements that can readily be employed alone or in combination, less active elements that require an effort to retrieve and employ but that are of potential use, and inactive (or inert) elements that were once learned but are of no potential use.

Experiential learning is learning stemming from an analysis of past learning and current experience. It is an activity that involves observing, interacting with others, acting derived from past learning and new hypotheses, experiencing the consequences of actions, noting the effect on others and their responses, reflecting, and learning derived from the reflection on the cause/effect relationship. The experience is sometimes preceded and sometimes followed by consideration of theory or models related to the activity and its effect. Based on the analysis, new theory may be developed (usually when the experience precedes), or theory might be modified, discarded, or reinforced. The result is the addition of new elements or a modification of existing elements in the person's life bank. The learning provides raw material and opportunities for generalization. Some definitions limit "experiential learning" to learning that takes place in a venue different from a specifically educational venue, that is, classroom. This is not our position. However, we do distinguish between experiential learning that takes place in the work venue and other venues. We categorize experiential learning as either synthetic or natural. See the definitions of these terms.

Expressive role refers to the set of social-emotive tasks in which relationships with others are of primary importance. Examples of these tasks are advising, informing, leading, motivating, resolving conflict, and coaching.

Feedback is information about behavior and its effect. The objectives of feedback include providing the information for learning, modifying goals, models, and activities, and assessing and improving performance. In communications, feedback is information that completes the communication loop by indicating what the designated receiver understood and is doing about the message sent by the transmitter.

"Freeze." See *refreeze.*

Function in management is a set of related tasks covering a recognized major area of managerial work.

Graduate medical education is education following medical school. It includes residency and fellowship training, which is mostly hospital based. It would be more accurate to call it postgraduate education, since it follows medical school (a graduate school). But it has come to be called graduate medical education.

Hard money in faculty salaries refers to money from continuing sources of university income, such as tuition, interest on endowment, and, for state schools, line-item budget support.

Health maintenance organization (HMO) describes at least three different types of prepaid health plans. In the group model, a group of physicians contracts with the HMO to provide services to a patient population at a negotiated cost per member or per family (the group of physicians is at risk if the cost exceeds the negotiated contract). In the staff model, the physicians are salaried by the HMO. In the independent physician association (IPA), the HMO contracts with individual physicians to provide care for members of the HMO.

Holistic refers to the educational approach directed toward integrating learning in order to facilitate the performance of a set of professional tasks. Content is presented as a complete professional activity rather than as specialties in separate sessions or modules.

Hospital refers to three types. University hospitals are owned or affiliated with universities, so that all staff appointments are made jointly. These are the principal medical school teaching hospitals. Teaching hospitals are affiliated with a university for teaching purposes. Nonuniversity hospitals have more autonomy than university hospitals. Community hospitals are voluntary hospitals that may be teaching hospitals.

Indemnity insurance pays for all or part of the cost of each illness.

Inert learning is learning for which the student has no immediate use or sees any future use in relationship to professional practice. Learning that might be inert in one situation might not be in another.

Instrumental role refers to the set of professional tasks that do not involve extensive relationships with other people. Examples are planning, collecting data, analyzing data, writing a brief, and making a report.

Learning style is the set of processes by which individuals incorporate new elements into their life banks.

Life bank is the totality of values, assumptions, competencies, habits, expectations, motivators, concerns, thought patterns, learning style, attitudes, worldview and other behavioral determinants with which a person is born, develops through growth, or acquires in some manner over a lifetime. It includes sets of elements that determine interpretations and responses in situations, as well as processes and criteria for responding to and accepting, acquiring, and integrating new experiences and learning into itself. Dewey (1938) has referred to a similar construct in the realm of purely personal events that are always at the individual's command and that are his or hers exclusively. Weick (1969), extending an assumption of George Mead (1956) has suggested that each person has unique response repertoires that control perception and, consequently, affect all thought.

Lifelong learning is the continuation during a person's lifetime of a planned, directed process for adding active learning to one's lifebank.

Managed care is a health care system in which one person, usually a primary care physician, is responsible for all referrals to specialists or for admission to a hospital. HMO care is an example.

Medical sects were a characteristic of nineteenth-century American medicine. Each sect had a distinct philosophy. In the 1870s about 13 percent of physicians were in nonmainstream sects. Mainstream physicians were referred to as "allopathic doctors" by others. Thomasonians believed that cold caused disease and that heat was the cure. Botanical products were held to have medicinal power. "Physiomedicals" were descendants of

Thomasonians who emphasized the medicinal use of botanical products. Homeopaths believed that "cure" was possible by using drugs that caused the same symptoms in a healthy person, that very small doses of medicine enhanced the therapeutic effect, and that most disease was caused by a suppressed itch. Eclectics accepted traditional medical science but opposed excessive medication and bleeding. Osteopaths saw the human body as a machine, the parts of which lost proper alignment as a consequence of disease.

Meta-element is a set of life-bank elements that function together to utilize other elements in the life bank. Meta-element includes establishing new sequences and patterns, discarding or changing elements, and converting and organizing experience and elements into new learning (creativity).

Model is a specific application of a set of assumptions (i.e. the parameters are assigned values).

Modular design is an educational design in which courses of study focus on a single area (e.g., in management or human resources) to the virtual exclusion of other areas related to the profession. The "modular" design is the opposite of "holistic" design.

Module is a unit of an educational program devoted to a single area of study.

Natural experiential learning is experiential learning that takes place in the venue in which the learning is expected to be used or in a very similar venue. The activity is real time and with real relationships. Activities are of consequence to the individual and others involved.

Needs analysis includes both the process and the findings of the process for determining desirable educational objectives, content, and learning approaches.

Passive learning is a learning methodology in which students do not actively engage in implementing a decision and dealing with the consequences. Passive learning includes readings, lectures, discussions, and case analyses.

Preceptor in the LIFE approach is a faculty member who is a consultant, mentor, role model, and gadfly in the formal small-group sessions.

Preceptoral sessions are formal sessions in the LIFE approach that are the integrating venues for natural experiential learning. Objectives are to help students learn to reflect and induct learning from their experience.

Prepaid care is insurance, in contrast to indemnity, that pays a set amount for care, no matter the actual cost.

Primary care specialties include family medicine, general internal medicine, general pediatrics, and sometimes obstetrics and gynecology.

Reflective practice is a learning mode to integrate and link thought and action through reflection. It involves analyzing theory, actions, and consequences with the goal of improving practice.

Refreeze is the stage in the Lewin model at which change is stable.

Risk and *uncertainty* are used interchangeably to mean that the consequences of alternative actions are uncertain.

Role conflict is a state, leading to cognitive dissonance, that arises when there are two or more role expectations—for example, responsibility to a client and a governing institution—such that carrying out one would make it difficult, if not impossible, to carry out one or more of the others.

Self-directed (or independent) learning is a process in which one takes the initiative, without the help of others, to determine learning needs and to actively engage in learning activities in order to achieve a specific objective.

Soft money is money for support of faculty salaries from grants, contracts, and faculty-practice plans.

Specialty refers to a branch of medicine. The major specialties are medicine, surgery, pediatrics, obstetrics, gynecology, and psychiatry. Recently, family medicine has been added.

Subspecialty refers to subdivisions of a major branch. For example, gastroenterology and cardiology are subspecialties of internal medicine.

Synthetic experiential learning is learning derived from engaging in physical activities that have real and observable consequences. Activities are designed to provide an occasion for learning and usually do not involve real time and continuing relationships. Some examples are managerial games, moot courts, and dissection.

Teaching hospital. See *hospital.*

Unfreezing, along with *moving* (or *changing*) and *refreezing,* are three stages of a change model (Lewin, 1951): motivating to change, gaining acceptance for the change, and fixing the change in the life bank.

Utility is the value assigned by an individual to one of a set of alternative consequences.

Venue includes the physical, economic, and social elements (or variables) in the place where activitites occur. Two venues are intrinsic to the learning process: the educational venue, wherein "teaching" and "learning" take place, and the work venue wherein learning is used.

Work up on a patient involves a history of illness, a physical examination, some routine laboratory work, a differential diagnosis, and a list of tests to be considered.

BIBLIOGRAPHY

Abramson, J., and A. E. Fortune. "Improving Field Instruction: An Evaluation of a Seminar for New Field Instructors." *Journal of Social Work Education*, Fall 1990.

Adelman, C., ed. *Assessment in American Higher Education: Issues and Contexts.* Washington, D.C.: U.S. Department of Education, 1985.

Allison, G. T. *Essence of Decision: Explaining the Cuban Missile Crisis.* Boston: Little, Brown, 1971.

Altman, L. K. "The Doctor's World." *New York Times*, June 23, 1992.

———. "U.S. Doctors Said to Be Hesitant on AIDS Care." *New York Times*, July 19, 1992.

American Bar Association. *Standards for Approval of Law Schools and Interpretations.* Indianapolis: Office of the Consultant on Legal Education, 1973–1993.

———. *Report and Recommendations of the Task Force on Lawyer Competency.* Chicago: ABA, 1979.

———. *Clinical Legal Education: Report of the Association of American Law Schools.* 1980.

———. *Special Committee for a Study of Legal Education, Law Schools and Professional Education.* 1980.

———. *Final Report and Recommendations of the Task Force on Professional Competence.* 1983.

———. *Comprehensive Guide to Bar Admission Requirements, 1991–92.* 1991.

———. *Pro Bono in Law Schools.* 1991.

———. *Report of the Task Force on Law Schools and the Profession.* 1992.

American Law Institute—American Bar Association Committee on Continuing Professional Education. *A Practical Guide to Achieving Excellence in the Practice of Law: Standards, Methods, and Self-Evaluation.* Philadelphia, PA: American Law Institute, 1992.

American Society for Training and Development. *The Learning Enterprise*. Washington, DC, 1989.

Annan, N. "Hint: It's More Than One Idea." *New York Times Book Review*, May 24, 1992.

Ansberry, C. "The Genteel Poor: Social Service Workers Moonlight and Scrimp to Make Ends Meet." *Wall Street Journal*, February 10, 1992, Western edition.

Appleby, P. H. *Big Democracy*. New York: Alfred Knopf, 1945.

Argyris, C. *Integrating the Individual and the Organization*. New York: Wiley, 1964.

——— . *Reasoning, Learning and Action*. San Francisco: Jossey-Bass, 1982.

Argyris, C., and D. A. Schon. *Organizational Learning: A Theory of Action Perspective*. Reading, MA: Addison-Wesley, 1978.

Association of American Law Schools. *Report of the Association of American Law Schools—ABA Committee on Guidelines for Clinical Legal Education*. 1980.

——— . *Final Report of the Committete on the Future of the In-House Clinic*. 1991.

Azzaretto, J. F. "Quality Control in Continuing Professional Education: Accountability, Effectiveness, and Regulation." In *Professional Workers as Learners*, edited by E. S. Hunt. Washington, DC: U.S. Department of Education, 1992.

Bahrick, H. P. "Psychologist Examines Retention of Mathematical Knowledge." *Education Week*, January 9, 1991.

Bailey, M. T. "Do Physicists Use Case Studies? Thoughts on Public Administration Research." *Public Administration Review*, January–February 1992.

Baldwin, J. N. "Comparison of Perceived Effectiveness of MPA Programs Administered under Different Institutional Arrangements." *Public Administration Review*, September–October 1988.

Baldwin, L. V. "Higher-Education Partnerships in Engineering and Science." *Annals of the American Academy of Political and Social Science*, March 1991.

Balfour, D. L., and F. Marini. "Child and Adult, X and Y : Reflections on the Process of Public Administration Education." *Public Administration Review*, November–December 1991.

Bandura, A. *The Social Foundations of Thought and Action*. Englewood Cliffs, NJ: Prentice-Hall, 1988.

Barker, M., and P. Hardiker. *Theories of Practice in Social Work*. London: Academic Press, 1981.

Barker, R. L. "Private and Proprietary Services." In *Social Work Encyclopedia*, 18th ed., vol. 2, edited by A. Minahan. Silver Spring, MD: National Association of Social Workers, 1987.

Barnard, C. I. *The Functions of the Executive*. Cambridge: Harvard University Press, 1938.

——— . *Organizations and Management*. Cambridge: Harvard University Press, 1948.

Barnhizer, D. "The University Ideal and Clinical Legal Education." *New York Law School Review* 87 (1990).

Befort, S. "Musings on a Clinic Report: A Selective Agenda for Clinical Legal Education in the 1990s." *Minnesota Law Review* 75 (February 1991).

Behrman, J. N., and R. I. Levin. "Are Business Schools Doing Their Job?" *Harvard Business Review*, January–February 1984.

Bell, E. T. *Men of Mathematics*. New York: Simon and Schuster, 1937.

Bellah, R. N. *Habits of the Heart: Individualism and Commitment in American Culture*. Berkeley: University of California Press, 1985.

Bellow, G., and E. Johnson. "Reflections on the University of Southern California Clinical Semester." *University of Southern California Law Review* 664 (1971).

Bellow, G., and B. Mouton. *The Lawyering Process: Materials for Clinical Instruction in Advocacy*. Mineola, NY: Foundation Press, 1978.

Bennis, W. *Why Leaders Can't Lead: The Unconscious Conspiracy Continues*. San Francisco: Jossey-Bass, 1989.

Bennis, W., and B. Nanus. *Leaders: The Strategies for Taking Charge*. New York: Harper and Row, 1985.

Berger, W. "The Special Skills of Advocacy: Are Specialized Training and Certification of Advocates Essential to Our System of Justice?" Fordham University School of Law Annual Sonnet Memorial Lecture, New York, 1973.

Berkman, B., and T. O. Carlton, eds. *The Development of Health Social Work Curricula: Patterns and Process in Three Programs of Social Work Education*. Boston, MA: General Hospital Institute of Health Professions, 1985.

Berlin, I., and N. Gardels. "Two Concepts of Nationalism: An Interview with Isaiah Berlin." *New York Review of Books*, November 21, 1991.

Berman-Rossi, T. "The Early History of Social Work Education and Its Ties to the Society in Which It Emerged." Doctoral dissertation, Yeshiva University School of Social Work, New York, January 1981.

Bernard, L. D. "Education for Social Work." In *Social Work Encyclopedia*, 18th ed., vol. 2, edited by A. Minahan. Silver Spring, MD: National Association of Social Workers, 1987.

Berry, F. S. "State Regulation of Occupations and Professions." In *The Book of the States: 1986–1987*. Lexington, KY: Council of State Governments, 1986.

Berryman, S. E. "Breaking Out of the Circle: Rethinking Our Assumptions about Education and the Economy." Paper presented at the Conference of the American Society for Training and Development, June 21–26, 1987.

Betters-Reed, B. L. "Search for Integration of Theory and Practice: The Early History and Analysis of Three Innovative Graduate Institutions." Paper presented at the annual meeting of the Association for the Study of Higher Education, San Antonio, February 1986.

Bickerstaffe, G. "Crisis of Confidence in the Business Schools." *International Management*, August 1981.

Biggs, W. D. "Functional Business Games." *Simulations and Games*, June 1987.

Black, J. "Convenience vs. Educational Integrity: The Agency of Employment as a Field Work Site." Paper presented at the American Council on Social Work Education, Chicago, 1989.

Blank, R. H., and J. M. Ostheim. "An Overview of Biomedical Policy: Life and Death Issues." *Policy Studies Journal*, Winter 1979.

Block, P. *The Empowered Manager: Positive Political Skills at Work*. San Francisco: Jossey-Bass, 1988.

Bloom, H. *The American Religion*. New York: Simon and Schuster, 1992.

Bogo, M., and E. Vayda. *The Practice of Field Instruction in Social Work*. Toronto: University of Toronto Press, 1987.

Bok, D. C. *Universities and the Future of America*. Durham, NC: Duke University Press, 1990.

Bonser, C. F. "Total Quality Education?" *Public Administration Review*, September–October 1992.

Boorstin, D. J. *The New Americans: The Colonial Experience*. New York: Random House, 1958.

Bowen, D. D. "Developing a Personal Theory of Experiential Learning." *Simulation and Games*, June 1987.

Bowman, J. S. "Admission Practices in Master of Public Administration Programs: A Nationwide Study." *Public Administration Review*, September–October 1988.

Bretz, R. D. "College Grade Point Average as a Predictor of Adult Success: A Meta-Analytic Review and Some Additional Evidence." *Public Personnel Management*, Spring 1989.

Bridgeman, D. S. "Company Management Development Programs." In *The Education of American Businessmen*, by F. C. Pierson. New York: McGraw-Hill, 1959.

Brieland, D. "History and Evolution of Social Work Practice." In *Social Work Encyclopedia*, 18th ed., vol. 2, edited by A. Minahan. Silver Spring, MD: National Association of Social Workers, 1987.

Brown, B. "The Search for Public Administration: Roads Not Followed." *Public Administration Review*, March–April 1989.

Brown, S. J., and J. W. Wilson. "Cooperative Education for Graduate Students." In *Developing and Expanding Cooperative Education*, by J. W. Wilson. San Francisco: Jossey-Bass, 1978.

Brownstein, C., Y. Harrison, and G. Faria. "The Liaison Role: A Three Phase Study of the Schools, the Field, the Faculty." In *Field Education for Social Work: Contemporary Issues and Trends*, edited by D. Schneck, B. Grossman, and U. Glassman. Dubuque, IA: Kendall/Hunt, 1990.

Bruce, C. L., E. J. Katz, and J. A. Tomsic. "Industry Training and Education at a Distance: The IBM Approach." *Annals of the American Academy of Political and Social Science*, March 1991.

Bruner, J. *Acts of Meaning*. Cambridge: Harvard University Press, 1991.

Bruno, F. J. "Twenty-Five Years of Schools of Social Work." *Social Service Review*, June 1944.

Bryant, A. L., J. O. Jensen, M. Z. Thompson, and R. G. Miletich. *Management and Executive Development in Industry, Universities, and the Federal Government*. Washington, DC: U.S. Army Management Engineering, 1978.

Budziszewski, J. *The Nearest Coast of Darkness: The Vindication of the Politics of Virtues*. Ithaca, NY: Cornell University Press, 1988.

Bureau of Labor Statistics. *How Workers Get Their Training*. Washington, DC: U.S. Government Printing Office, 1985.

Burger, W. "The Special Skills of Advocacy: Are Specialized Training and Certification of Advocates Essential to Our System of Justice?" Fordham University School of Law Annual Sonnet Memorial Lecture, November 26, 1973.

Callahan, D. *What Kind of Life? The Limits of Medical Progress*. New York: Simon and Schuster, 1990.

Campbell, C. Report of the President, Northeastern Ohio Universities College of Medicine, Rootstown, Ohio, 1991.

Campbell, J. P., M. D. Dunnette, E. E. Lawler III, and K. E. Weick. *Managerial Behavior, Performance, and Effectiveness*. New York: McGraw-Hill, 1970.

Cantrall, A. M. "Law Schools and the Layman: Is the Law Education Doing Its Job?" *American Bar Association Journal*, November 1952.

Carlton, T. O. "The Relationship of Practice to Education: Past Constraints and Present Opportunities Shaping Professional Preparation for Health Social Work." In *The Development of Health Social Work Curricula: Patterns and Process in Three Programs of Social Work Education*, edited by B. Berkman and T. O. Carlton. Boston, MA: General Hospital Institute of Health Professions, 1985.

Carnegie Council on Policy Studies in Higher Education. *Progress and Problems in Medical and Dental Education: Federal Support Versus Federal Control*. San Francisco: Jossey-Bass, 1976.

———. *A Summary of Reports and Recommendations*. San Francisco: Jossey-Bass, 1980.

Carnegie Foundation for the Advancement of Teaching. *Governance of Higher Education: Six Priority Problems*. New York: McGraw-Hill, 1973.

———. *Priorities for Action: Final Report of the Carnegie Commission on Higher Education*. New York: McGraw-Hill, 1973.

———. *More Than Survival: Prospect for Higher Education in a Period of Uncertainty*. San Francisco: Jossey-Bass, 1975.

Carnevale, A. "Management Training Today and Tomorrow." *Training and Development Journal*, December 1989.

———. "The Learning Enterprise." *Training and Development Journal*, January 1986.

Center on Education and Training for Employment. *Reflective Practice in Adult Education*. Digest 122. Columbus, OH: Center on Education and Training for Employment, Ohio State University, 1992.

Cervero, R. M. *Effective Continuing Education for Professionals*. San Francisco: Jossey-Bass, 1988.

———. "Cooperation and Collaboration in the Field of Continuing Professional Education." In *Professional Workers as Learners*, edited by E. S. Hunt. Washington, DC: U.S. Department of Education, 1992.

Cervero, R. M., and J. F. Azzaretto, eds. *Visions for the Future of Continuing Professional Education*. Athens: University of Georgia, 1990.

Chapman, R. L., and F. N. Cleaveland. "Reply to a Critique." *Public Administration Review*, March–April 1975.

———. *Meeting the Needs of Tomorrow's Public Services*. Washington, DC: National Academy of Public Administration, 1973.

Charlton, K. *Education in Renaissance England*. London: Routledge and Kegan, 1965.

Claxton, C. S., and P. H. Murrell. *Learning Styles: Implications for Improving Educational Practices*. Washington, DC: George Washington University, 1987.

Cleary, R. E. "What Do Public Administration Master's Programs Look Like? Do They Do What is Needed?" *Public Administration Review*, November–December 1990.

———. "Revisiting the Doctoral Dissertation in Public Administration: An Examination of the Dissertations of 1990." *Public Administration Review*, January–February 1992.

Clement, R. W., and G. E. Stevens. "Performance Appraisal in Higher Education: Comparing Departments of Management with other Business Units." *Public Personnel Management*, Fall 1989.

Coates, J. F. "Tomorrow's Leader: MBAs Need Not Apply." *Across the Board*, May 1990.

Coggeshall, L. T. "Planning for Medical Progress through Education." A Report Submitted to the Executive Council of the Association of American Medical Colleges, Evanston, Illinois, 1965.

Collins, E.G.C., and A. M. Devanna. *The Portable MBA*. New York: Wiley, 1990.

Commission on Medical Education. "Final Report of the Commission on Medical Education." New York: Office of the Director of Study, 1932.

Conant, J. K. "Enrollment Trends in Schools of Public Affairs and Administration: A Search for Winners and Losers." *Public Administration Review*, May–June 1992.

Conference on Legal Education in the 1980s. *ABA Law Conference on Education*. New York, 1981. (8 sound cassettes)

Conrad, D., and D. Hedin. "Are Experiential Learning Programs Effective?" *National Association of Secondary School Principals Bulletin* 62 (1978).

Conry, E. J. "The Deregulation of Business Schools." *New York Times*, December 23, 1990.

Cooper, P. J. "Public Administration Review: The First Fifty Years." *Public Administration Review*, March–April, 1990.

Corcoran, E. "Robots for the Operating Room." *New York Times*, July 19, 1992.

Council on Legal Education for Professional Responsibility (CLEPR). Newsletters, 1969–1972.

Council on Social Work Education. Commission on Accreditation. *Handbook of Accreditation Standards and Procedures*. New York: Council on Social Work Education, 1984.

Council on Social Work Education. *Curriculum Policy Statement for Master's Degree Programs in Social Work Education*. Alexandria, VA: Council on Social Work Education, 1992.

Cowan, A. L. "For Women, Fewer M.B.A.'s." *New York Times*, September 27, 1992.

Crozier, M. *The Bureaucratic Phenomenon*. Chicago: University of Chicago Press, 1964.

Curlee, M. B., and F. B. Raymond. "The Female Administrator: Who Is She?" *Administration in Social Work*, Fall 1979.

Dahl, R. A. "The Science of Public Administration: Three Problems." *Public Administration Review*, Winter 1947.

Deal, T. E., and A. A. Kennedy. *Corporate Cultures: The Rites and Rituals of Corporate Life*. Reading, MA: Addison-Wesley, 1982.

DeBaggis, A. M. "Systems of Theological Education in the United States." In *Education for the Professions of Medicine, Law, Theology, and Social Welfare*, edited by E. C. Hughes, B. Thorne, A. M. DeBaggis, A. Gurin, and D. Williams. New York: McGraw-Hill, 1973.

Dede, C. J. "Emerging Technologies: Impacts on Distance Learning." *Annals of the American Academy of Political and Social Science*, March 1991.

Deming, W. E. "The Deming Theory of Management." *Academy of Management Review*, January 1988.

Denhardt, R. B. "The Contemporary Critique of Management Education; Lessons for Business and Public Administration." *Public Administration Quarterly*, Summer 1987.

DePalma, A. "Cornell to Evaluate Teaching Ability in Tenure Decisions." *New York Times*, November 4, 1992.

De Pree, M. *Leadership Is an Art*. New York: Doubleday, 1989.

Dewey, J. *How We Think*. New York: D. C. Heath, 1910.

———. *Experience and Education*. New York: Collier Books, 1938.

———. *John Dewey on Education: Selected Writings*. Edited by R. D. Archambault. Chicago: University of Chicago Press, 1974.

Deutch, C. H. "Getting Credit for Correcting the Professor." *New York Times*, Special Education Section, November 3, 1991.

Dickerton, D. *Language and Species*. Chicago: University of Chicago Press, 1991.

Dolgoff, R. *Report to the Task Force on Social Work Practice and Education*. New York: Council on Social Work Education, 1974.

Dressel, P. L., and M. Thompson. "A Degree for College Teachers: The Doctor of Arts." In *Carnegie Council on Policy Studies in Higher Education*. Berkeley, CA, 1977.

Drucker, P. F. *The Practice of Management*. New York: Harper, 1954.

———. *The Effective Manager*. New York: Harper and Row, 1966.

———. *Management: Tasks, Responsibilities, Practices*. New York: Harper and Row, 1974.

———. *Managing for the Future: The 1990s and Beyond*. New York: Truman Talley Books/Dutton, 1992.

Dubin, S. S. *Professional Obsolescence*. London, England: English Universities Press, 1971.

Durant, R. F., and W. A. Taggart. "Mid-Career Students in MPA Programs: Implications for Pre-Service Student Education." *Public Administration Review*, March–April 1985.

Dye, D. A., and M. Reck. "College Point Average as a Predictor of Adult Success: A Reply." *Public Personnel Management*, Summer 1989.

Dymsza, W. A. "The Education and Development of Managers for Future Decades." *Journal of International Business Studies*, Winter 1982.

Ebert, R. H. "Can the Education of the Physician Be Made More Rational?" *New England Journal of Medicine*, November 26, 1981.

———. "Medical Education at the Peak of the Era of Experimental Medicine." *Daedalus*, Spring 1986.

Ebert, R. H., and S. Brown. "Academic Health Centers." *New England Journal of Medicine*, May 19, 1983.

Eisenger, J. "Nonlawyers Claim a Growing Swath of Legal Turf." *New York Times*, July 16, 1993.

Elman, S. E., and E. A. Lynton. "Assessment in Professional Education." Paper presented at the National Conference on Assessment in Higher Education, Columbia, South Carolina, October 1985.

Etzioni, A. "Mixed Scanning Revisited." *Public Administration Review*, January–February 1986.

Etzioni, A., ed. *The Semi-Professions and Their Organizations*. New York: Free Press, 1969.

Faerman, S. R., R. E. Quinn, and M. P. Thompson. "Bridging Management Practice and Theory: New York State's Public Service Training Program." *Public Administration Review*, July–August 1987.

Feder, B. J. "Finding a Lifeboat in a Flood of Asbestos Litigation." *New York Times*, Business Section, July 4, 1993.

Ferguson, E. S. "Engineering and the Mind's Eye." Cambridge: M.I.T. Press, 1992.

Ferren, J. "The Teaching Mission of the Legal Aid Clinic." *Arizona State Law Journal* 37 (1969).

Finestone, S. "Selected Features of Professional Field Instruction." *Journal of Education for Social Work*, Fall 1967.

Fisher, L. M. "Sickness in the Cockpit Simulator." *New York Times*, February 20, 1989.

Flexner, A. *Medical Education in the United States and Canada: A Report to the Carnegie Foundation for the Advancement of Teaching, Bulletin No. 4*. Boston: Updyke, 1910.

——— . "Is Social Work a Profession?" In *Proceedings of the National Conference of Charities and Correction*. Chicago: Hildman Printing, 1915.

——— . *A Modern College and a Modern School*. New York: Doubleday, Page, 1923.

——— . *Medical Education: A Comparative Study*. New York: Macmillan, 1925.

Follett, M. P. *Freedom and Coordination, Management Publications Trust*. London: Management Publication Trust, 1949.

Fowler, E. M. "Carrers." *New York Times*, March 28, 1989.

——— . "Careers." *New York Times*, June 20, 1989.

——— . "Careers." *New York Times*, October 10, 1989.

——— . "Careers." *New York Times*, February 27, 1990.

——— . "Careers." *New York Times*, March 6, 1990.

——— . "Careers." *New York Times*, March 20, 1990.

——— . "Careers." *New York Times*, March 22, 1990.

——— . "Careers." *New York Times*, May 22, 1990.

——— . "Careers." *New York Times*, June 19, 1990.

——— . "Careers." *New York Times*, January 12, 1991.

——— . "Careers." *New York Times*, May 14, 1991.

——— . "Careers." *New York Times*, June 21, 1991.

——— . "Careers." *New York Times*, March 24, 1992.

——— . "Careers." *New York Times*, April 7, 1992.

Frank, J. "Why Not a Clinical Lawyer-School." *University of Pennsylvania Law Review*, June 1933.

Frank, R. H . *Passions within Reason: The Strategic Role of the Emotions*. New York: Norton, 1988.

Freamon, B. "A Blueprint for a Center for Social Justice." *Seton Hall Law Review*, Fall 1992.

Freedman, L. *Quality in Continuing Education*. San Francisco: Jossey-Bass, 1987.

Freudenheim, M. "Business and Health." *New York Times*, July 21, 1992.

Fuchsberg, G. "Depressed Job Market Prompts Paradox: Upsurge of Interest in M.B.A. Programs." *Wall Street Journal*, February 2, 1992.

Fuller, T., ed. *The Voice of Liberal Learning: Michael Oakeshott on Education*. New Haven: Yale University Press, 1990.

Galagan, P. A. "Execs Go Global, Literally." *Training and Development Journal*, June 1990.

——— . "Executive Development in a Changing World." *Training and Development Journal*, June 1990.

Galbraith, M. W., and J . W. Gilley. *Professional Certification: Implications for Adult Education and HRD*. Columbus, OH: Center on Education and Training for Employment, 1986.

Gartner, A. *The Preparation of Human Service Professionals*. New York: Human Service Press, 1976.

George, A. "A History of Social Work Field Instruction." In *Quality Field Instruction in Social Work*, edited by B. W. Sheafor and L. E. Jenkins. New York: Longman, 1982.

George, C. S. *The History of Management Thought*. Englewood Cliffs, NJ: Prentice-Hall, 1972.

Germain, C. "Casework and Science: A Historical Encounter." In *Theories of Social Casework*, edited by R. W. Roberts and R. H. Nee. Chicago: University of Chicago Press, 1970.

Germain, C., and A. Gitterman. *The Life Model of Social Work Practice*. New York: Columbia University Press, 1980.

Gibelman, M., and P. H. Schervish. *Who We Are: The Social Work Labor Force as Reflected in the NASW Membership*. Washington, DC: National Association of Social Workers, 1993.

Gilbreth, F. B. *Motion Study*. New York: Van Nostrand, 1911.

Glaser, R., and M. Bassok. "Learning Theory and the Study of Instruction." *Annual Review of Psychology*, 1989.

Gless, D. L., and B. H. Smith, eds. *The Politics of Liberal Education*. Durham, NC: Duke University Press, 1990.

Gold, K. A. "Managing for Success: A Comparison of the Private and Public Sectors." *Public Administration Review*, November–December 1982.

Golden, D., A. Pins, and W. Jones. *Students in Schools of Social Work: A Study of Characteristics and Factors Affecting Career Choice and Practice Concentration*. New York: Council on Social Work Education, 1972.

Golembiewski, R. T. "Organization as a Moral Problem." *Public Administration Review*, Spring 1962.

————. "Excerpts from 'Organization as a Moral Problem.'" *Public Administration Review*, March–April 1992.

Goleman, D. "Social Workers Vault into a Leading Role in Psychotherapy." *New York Times*, April 30, 1985.

Gollub, J. O. *The Decade Matrix*. Reading, MA: Addison-Wesley, 1991.

Gordon, R. A., and J. E. Howell. *Higher Education for Business*. New York: Columbia University Press, 1959.

Gove, S. K., and T. M. Stauffer, eds. *Public Controversies in Higher Education*. New York: Greenwood Press, 1986.

Gray, B. H. *The Profit Motive of Patient Care: The Changing Accountability of Doctors and Hospitals*. Cambridge: Harvard University Press, 1991.

Greenhouse, S. "In Europe, a Boom in M.B.A.'s." *New York Times*, May 29, 1991.

Greenwood, E. "Attributes of a Profession." *Social Work*, July 1957.

Greer, W. *Western Reserve's Experiment in Medical Education and Its Outcome*. New York: Oxford University Press, 1980.

Gulick, L., and L. Urwick, eds. *Papers on the Science of Administration*. New York: Institute of Public Administration, Columbia University, 1937.

Gurin, A., and D. Williams. "Social Work Education." In *Education for the Professions of Medicine, Law, Theology and Social Welfare*, edited by E. C. Hughes, B. Thorne, A. M. DeBaggis, A. Gurin, and D. Williams. New York: McGraw-Hill, 1973.

Hall, R. H. "Professionalization and Bureaucraticization." *American Sociological Review*, February 1968.

Hamilton, S. F., and M. A. Hamilton. "Teaching and Learning on the Job: A Framework for Assessing the Workplaces as Learning Environments." Unpublished paper, Cornell University, Ithaca, New York, 1989.

Harno, A. J. *Legal Education in the United States*. San Francisco: Bancroft Whitney, 1953.

Hartle, T. W. "Public Policy and Higher Education." *Public Administration Review*, March–April 1977.

Hatala, R. J. "The Problem-Solving Model of Graduate Education." *Expanding the Missions of Graduate and Professional Education*, March 1982.

Hawkins, J. "Technology-Mediated Communities for Learning Design and Consequences." *Annals of the American Society of Political and Social Science*, March 1991.

Hebb, D. O. *The Organization of Behavior*. New York: Wiley, 1949.

Hedin, D., and D. Conrad. "The Impact of Experiential Education on Youth Development." In *Combining Service and Learning*, edited by J. C. Kendall and Associates. Raleigh, NC: National Society for Internships and Experiential Education, 1990.

Hoberman, S. "Current Concerns and Trends in Management Development." Paper given at a New York University workshop for training and development specialists, 1984.

————. "Organizational Variables and Management Development." *Public Personnel Management*, Summer 1990.

Hoberman, S., and S. Mailick. "Learning Inducted from Experience (LIFE)." In *The Practice of Management Development*, edited by S. Mailick, S. Hoberman, and S. Wall. New York: Praeger, 1988.

————. *Experiential Management Development: From Learning to Practice*. New York: Quorum, 1992.

Hollenbeck, G. P., and C. A. Ingols. "What's the Takeaway?" *Training and Development Journal*, July 1990.

Hollis, E. V., and A. L. Taylor. *Social Work Education in the United States*. New York: Columbia University Press, 1951.

Hopps, J. G., and E. B. Pinderhughes. "Profession of Social Work: Contemporary Characteristics." In *Social Work Encyclopedia*, 18th ed., vol. 2, edited by A. Minahan. Silver Spring, MD: National Association of Social Workers, 1987.

Houle, C. O. *Continuing Learning in the Professions*. San Francisco: Jossey-Bass, 1980.

Hornbeck, D. W., and L. M. Salamon. *Human Capital and America's Future: An Economic Strategy for the 90s*. Baltimore: Johns Hopkins University Press, 1992.

Howard, L. C. "Education for the Public's Interest: A Critique and a Projection of the National Academy of Public Administration View of Meeting the Needs of Tomorrow's Public Service." *Public Administration Review*, March–April 1975.

Hughes, E. C., B. Thorne, A. M. DeBaggis, A. Gurin, and D. Williams. *Education for the Professions of Medicine, Law, Theology and Social Welfare.* New York: McGraw-Hill, 1973.

Hummel, R. P. "Stories Managers Tell: Why They Are as Valid as Science." *Public Administration Review,* January–February 1991.

Hummel, R., and D. Carnevale. "Of Mice and Men." *Public Administration Review,* March–April 1992.

Hunt, E. S., ed. *Professional Workers as Learners.* Washington, DC: U.S. Department of Education, 1992.

Hutchings, P., and A. Wutzdorff, ed. *Knowing and Doing: Learning through Experience.* San Francisco: Jossey-Bass, 1988.

Imel, S. *Vocational Performance Standards.* Digest No. 96. Columbus, OH: Center on Education and Training for Employment, Ohio State University, 1990.

Jason, H. "The Relevance of Medical Education to Medical Practice." *Journal of the Medical Association,* June 1973.

Jennings, E. T. "Accountability, Program Quality, Outcome Assessment, and Graduate Education for Public Affairs and Administration." *Public Administration Review,* September–October 1989.

Johnson, G. *In the Palaces of Memory.* New York: Knopf, 1991.

Johnson, J. S., and Associates. *Educating Managers.* San Francisco: Jossey-Bass, 1986.

Johnstone, S. "Research on Telecommunicated Learning: Past, Present, and Future." *Annals of the American Academy of Political and Social Science,* March 1991.

Jonas, H. S., S. I. Etzel, and B. Barzansky. "Educational Programs in US Medical Schools." *Journal of the American Medical Association,* August 21, 1991.

Kakabadse, A., and S. Mukhi. *The Future of Management Education.* New York: Nichols, 1984.

Kass, H. D., and B. L. Catron, eds. *Images and Identities in Public Administration.* Newbury Park, CA: Sage, 1990.

Katsh, M. E. *The Electronic Media and the Transformation of Law.* New York: Oxford University Press, 1990.

Kendall, J. C., and Associates, eds. *Combining Service and Learning.* Raleigh, NC: National Society for Internships and Experiential Education.

Kendall, K. A. "Selected Issues in Field Instruction in Education for Social Work." *Social Service Review,* March 1959.

Kerka, S. *Life Cycles and Career Development: New Models.* Digest No. 119. Columbus, OH: Center on Education and Training for Employment, Ohio State University, 1992.

Kerr, C., and J. Rosow, eds. *Work in America.* New York: Van Nostrand Reinhold, 1979.

Keys, B. "Total Enterprise Business Games." *Simulation and Games,* June 1987.

Khinduka, S. K. "Social Work and the Human Service." In *Social Work Encyclopedia,* 18th ed., vol. 2, edited by A. Minahan. Silver Spring, MD: National Association of Social Workers, 1987.

Kitch, E. Foreword to *Clinical Education and the Law School of the Future,* edited by E. Kitch. University of Chicago Conference Series, no. 20. Chicago: University of Chicago Law School, 1971.

Kitch, E., ed. *Clinical Education and the Law School of the Future.* Chicago: University of Chicago Law School, 1970.

Klamer, A., and D. Colander. *The Making of an Economist*. Boulder, CO: Westview Press, 1990.

Knowles, M. S. *Self-directed Learning: A Guide for Learners and Teachers*. Chicago: Association Press, 1975.

———. *The Modern Practice of Adult Education: Andragogy vs. Pedagogy*. Rev. ed. New York: Association Press, 1980.

———. *Andragogy in Action: Applying Modern Principles of Adult Learning*. San Francisco: Jossey-Bass, 1984.

———. "The Magic of Contract Learning." *Training and Development Journal*, June 1980.

———. *The Making of an Adult Educator*. San Francisco: Jossey-Bass, 1989.

———. "Enhancing HRD with Contract Learning." *Training and Development Journal*, March 1987.

———. *The Adult Learner: A Neglected Species*. 3d ed. Houston: Gulf, 1984.

Kolb, D. A. *Experiential Learning*. Englewood Cliffs, NJ: Prentice-Hall, 1984.

Kominski, R., and R. Sutterlin. "What's It Worth?: Educational Background and Economic Status: Spring 1990." U.S. Department of Commerce, 1990.

Konner, M. "Becoming a Doctor." *New York Review of Books*, September 24, 1987.

Koontz, H., and C. O'Donnell. *Management: A Book of Readings*. New York: McGraw-Hill, 1976.

Kraemer, K. L., and A. Northrop. "Curriculum Recommendations for Public Management Education in Computing: An Update." *Public Administration Review*, September–October 1989.

Kramer, J. "Who Will Pay the Piper or Leave the Check on the Table for the Other Guy." *Journal of Legal Education* 39 (December 1989).

Kramlinger, T., and T. Huberty. "Behaviorism Versus Humanism." *Training and Development Journal*, December 1990.

Kristal, S. "Tying Theory to Practice in the Education of Public Administration." Master's thesis, New York University Graduate School of Public Administration, New York, 1988.

Kruzich, J. M., B. J. Friesen, and D. Van Soest. "Assessment of Student and Faculty Learning Styles: Research and Application." *Journal of Social Work Education*, Fall 1986.

Kuhn, J. W. *New York Times*, Special Education Section, November 3, 1991.

Lacerate, J., J. Ray, and L. Irwin. "Recognizing the Educational Contributions of Field Instructors." *Journal of Teaching in Social Work* 3, no. 2 (1989).

Ladd, D. R. "Achieving Change in Educational Policy in American Colleges and Universities." *Annals of the American Academy of Political and Social Science*, November 1972.

Lammers, C. J. "Sociology of Organizations around the Globe: Similarities and Differences between American, British, French, German, and Dutch Brands." *Organizational Studies* 11, no. 2 (1990).

Langdell, C. C. *A Selection of Cases on the Law of Contracts*. Birmingham, AL: Gryphon, 1970.

———. *A Summary of the Law on Contracts*. Boston: Little, Brown, 1980.

Langley, Donald G. *Mental Health Education in New Medical Schools*. San Francisco: Jossey-Bass, 1973.

Langsley, L. A. "Medical Competence and Performance Assessment." *Journal of the American Medical Association*, August 1991.

Laser, G. "Educating for Professional Competence in the Twenty-first Century: Educational Reform at Chicago-Kent College of Law." *Chicago-Kent Law Review* 69 (1993).

Leavitt, H. J. *Managerial Psychology*. Chicago: University of Chicago Press, 1958.

Leiby, J. "History of Social Welfare." In *Social Work Encyclopedia*, 18th ed., vol. 2, edited by A. Minahan. Silver Spring, MD: National Association of Social Workers, 1987.

Leichter, H. M. Review of *State Intervention in Medical Care: Consequences for Britain, France, Sweden, and the United States, 1890–1970*, by J. R. Hollingsworth, J. Hage, and R. A. Hanneman. *Annals of the American Academy of Political and Social Science*, July 1992.

Lessard, G. "Introduction: The Interuniversity Poverty Law Consortium." *Washington University Journal of Urban and Contemporary Law* 57 (Spring 1992).

Levering, R. *A Great Place to Work*. New York: Random House, 1988.

Levering, R., M. Moskovitz, and M. Katz. *The 100 Best Companies to Work for in America*. New York: New American Library, 1985.

Levine, M. E. "How Will We Ever Manage?" *New York Times Book Review*, March 8, 1992.

Levitt, B., and J. G. March. "Organizational Learning." *Annual Review of Sociology* 14 (1988).

Lewin, K. *Field Theory in Social Sciences*. New York: Harper and Row, 1951.

Likert, R. *New Patterns of Management*. New York: McGraw-Hill, 1961.

Little, J. W. "Norms of Collegiality and Experimentations: Workplace Conditions of School Success." *American Educational Research Journal*, Fall 1982.

Livingston, J. S. "The Myth of the Well-Educated Manager." *Harvard Business Review*, January–February 1971.

———. "New Trends in Applied Management Development." *Training and Development Journal*, January 1983.

Lloyd, G. A. "Social Work Education." In *Social Work Encyclopedia*, 18th ed., vol. 2, edited by A. Minahan. Silver Spring, MD: National Association of Social Workers, 1987.

Locke, R. R. *Management and Higher Education since 1940: The Influence of America and Japan on West Germany, Great Britain, and France*. New York: Cambridge University Press, 1989.

Lubove, R. *The Professional Altruist*. Cambridge: Harvard University Press, 1965.

Lusterman, S. *Education in Industry: A Research Report*. New York: Conference Board, 1977.

Lynn, K., ed. *The Professions in America*. Boston: Beacon Press, 1967.

Lynn, N. B., and A. Wildavsky, eds. *Public Administration: The State of the Art*. Chatham, NJ: Chatham House, 1990.

Lynton, E. A. "Continuing Professional Education: Comparative Approaches and Lessons." In *Professional Workers as Learners*, edited by E. S. Hunt. Washington, DC: U.S. Department of Education, 1992.

McDiarmid, M. "What's Going on Down There in the Basement: In-House Clinics Expand Their Beachhead." *New York Law School Law Review* 35, nos. 1-2 (1990).

McGarrah, R. E. "Restoring the University from within." *Educational Record*, Summer 1980.

McGee, H. "Universities, Law Schools, Communities: Learning of Service or Learning and Service?" *Journal of Legal Education* 22, no. 1 (1969).

McGregor, D. *The Human Side of Enterprise*. New York: McGraw-Hill, 1960.

McLagan, P. A. "Models for HRD Practice." *Training and Development Journal* 43 (1989).

McNulty, N. C. "Management Development by Action Learning." *Training and Development Journal*, March 1979.

McNulty, N. C., ed. *International Directory of Executive Education*. New York: Pergamon Press, 1985.

Machiavelli, N. *The Prince*. New York: Modern Library, 1940.

Maeroff, G. I. "Class Size as an Empowerment Issue." *Education Week*, January 9, 1991.

Macy Study Group. "Graduate Medical Education, Present and Prospective: A Call for Action." Report of the Josiah Macy, Jr. Foundation, New York, 1980.

Maher, S. "The Praise of Folly: A Defense of Practice Supervision in Clinical Legal Education." *Nebraska Law Review* 69 (1990).

Mailick, S., ed. *The Making of the Manager*. Garden City, NY: Anchor/Doubleday, 1974.

Mailick, S., and S. Hoberman. "General Considerations Regarding Managerial and Organizational Development." In *The Making of the Manager*, edited by S. Mailick. Garden City, NY: Anchor/Doubleday, 1974.

————. "New Techniques in Management Training." In *The Making of the Manager*, edited by S. Mailick. Garden City, NY: Anchor/Doubleday, 1974.

Mailick, S., S. Hoberman, and S. Wall, eds. *The Practice of Management Development*. New York: Praeger, 1988.

Major, R. A. *A History of Medicine*. Vol. 2. Springfield, IL: Charles C. Thomas, 1954.

March, J. G., and H. Simon. *Organizations*. New York: Wiley, 1958.

Marmor, T. R., and J. Godfrey. "Canada's Medical System Is a Model. That's a Fact." *New York Times*, July 23, 1992.

Marshack, E. F. "Task Supervision in Social Work Education." D.S.W. diss., Yeshiva University, New York, 1984.

Marshack, E. F., and U. Glassman. "Innovative Models for Field Instruction: Departing from Traditional Methods." In *Field Education for Social Work: Contemporary Issues and Trends*, edited by D. Schneck, B. Grossman, and U. Glassman. Dubuque, IA: Kendall/Hunt, 1990.

Martin, D. W. "Deja Vu: French Antecedents of American Public Administration." *Public Administration Review*, July–August 1987.

————. *The Guide to the Foundations of Public Administration*. New York: Marcel Dekker, 1989.

Martini, C.J.M. Editorial. *Journal of the American Medical Association*, August 21, 1991.

Maslow, A. *Motivation and Personality*. New York: Harper and Row, 1964.

Mayhew, L. B. *Graduate and Professional Education, 1980: A Survey of Institutional Plans*. New York: McGraw-Hill, 1970.

Merriam, S. B., and M. C. Clark. *Lifelines: Patterns of Work, Love, and Learning in Adulthood*. San Francisco: Jossey-Bass, 1991.

Middlebrook, B. J., and F. M. Rachel. "A Survey of Middle Management Training and Development Programs." *Personnel Administrator*, November 1983.

Mintzberg, H. *The Nature of Managerial Work.* New York: Harper and Row, 1973.
————. *Mintzberg on Management.* New York: Free Press, 1989.
Mitchell, J. "Educations and Skills for Public Authority Management." *Public Administration Review,* September–October 1991.
Mohl, R. A. "Three Centuries of American Public Welfare: 1600–1932." *Current History,* July 1973.
Moore, D. T. "Experiential Education as Critical Discourse." In *Combining Service and Learning,* edited by J. C. Kendall and Associates. Raleigh, NC: National Society for Internships and Experiential Education, 1990.
Moore, G. T. "The Case of the Disappearing Generalist: Does It Need to Be Solved?" *Milbank Quarterly* 70, no. 2 (1992).
Moore, W. E. *The Professional Roles and Rules.* New York: Russell Sage Foundation, 1970.
Morgan, B. C. "Patient Access to Magnetic Resonance Imaging Centers in Orange County, California." *New England Journal of Medicine,* March 25, 1993.
Mosher, F. E. *Democracy and the Public Service.* 2d ed. New York: Oxford University Press, 1982.
Moskovitz, M. "Beyond the Case Method: It's Time to Teach with Problems." *Journal of Legal Education* 42 (March 1993).
Myers, R. J. "The Indivisibility of Ethics." *New York Times,* March 3, 1991.
National Center for Educational Statistics. *Race and Ethnicity Trends in Degrees Conferred by Institutions of Higher Education: 1980–81 through 1989–90.* Washington, DC: U.S. Department of Education, 1992.
————. *Student Financing of Graduate and First-Professional Education.* Washington, DC: U.S. Department of Education, 1993a.
————. *120 Years of American Education: A Statistical Portrait.* Washington, DC: U.S. Department of Education, 1993b.
National Center on Education and the Economy. *A Human Resource Development Plan for the United States.* Rochester, NY, 1993.
National Commission on the Public Service. *Leadership for America: Rebuilding the Public Service.* Washington, DC, 1989.
NEOUCOM. *The Network,* 1993. Special inauguration section, p. 515.
Nigro, L. G., and W. D. Richardson. "Between Citizen and Administrator: Administrative Ethics and PAR." *Public Administration Review,* November–December 1990.
Norman, G. R., and H. G. Schmidt. "The Psychological Basis of Problem-based Learning: A Review of the Evidence." *Academic Medicine,* September 1992.
Norris, D. R. "External Validity of Business Games." *Simulation and Games,* December 1986.
Pais, A. *The Science and Life of Albert Einstein.* New York: Oxford University Press, 1982.
Papell, C. "Self-Profile of Learning Styles for Direct Social Work Practice." D.S.W. diss., Yeshiva University, New York, 1980.
Patel, V. L., G. J. Groen, and G. R. Norman. "Effects of Conventional and Problem Based Medical Curricula on Problem Solving." *Academic Medicine,* July 1991.
Payne, M. *Modern Social Work Theory.* Chicago: Lyceum, 1991.
Pelikan, J. *The Idea of the University.* New Haven: Yale University Press, 1992.

Perrow, C. *Complex Organizations: A Critical Essay.* 2d ed. Glenview, IL: Scott, Foresman, 1979.

Peters, T. *Thriving on Chaos: A Handbook for a Management Revolution.* New York: Knopf, 1987.

Peters, T., and N. Austin. *A Passion for Excellence: The Leadership Difference.* New York: Random House, 1985.

Pierson, F. C. *The Education of American Businessmen.* New York: McGraw-Hill, 1959.

Pincoffs, E. L. *Quandries and Virtues: Against Reductivism in Ethics.* Lawrence: University Press of Kansas, 1986.

Pincus, W. "The Clinical Component in University Professional Education." *Ohio State Law Journal* 32 (Spring 1971).

——— . *Clinical Education for Law Students.* New York: Meilen Press, 1980.

Pins, A. *Who Chooses Social Work: When and Why.* New York: Council on Social Work Education, 1964.

Piskurich, G. *Handbook of Instructional Technology.* New York: McGraw-Hill, 1993.

Pizer, H. F. *Boston Globe,* November 17, 1992.

Porter, L. W., and L. E. McKibbin. *Management Education and Development: Drift or Thrust into the 21st Century?* New York: McGraw-Hill, 1988.

Power, D. L. "Final Report to United States Department of Education on the Title IX Law School Clinical Experience Program, National Evaluation Conference." February 1991.

Public Law 88–129: Health Professions Educational Assistance Act of 1963.

Public Law 90–490: The Health Manpower Act of 1968.

Public Law 91–496: The Family Practice Act of 1970.

Public Law 92–157: The Comprehensive Health Manpower Training Act of 1971.

Public Law 94–484: The Health Professions Educational Assistance Act of 1976.

Pugh, D. L. "Professionalism in Public Administration: Problems, Perspectives, and the Role of ASPA." *Public Administration Review,* January–February 1989.

Ravitch, D. "Education in the 1980's: A Concern for 'Quality.' " *Education Week,* January 10, 1990.

Reynolds, B. *Learning and Teaching in the Practice of Social Work.* New York: Rinehart, 1942.

Revans, R. W. "The Project Method: Learning by Doing." In *The Making of the Manager—A World View,* edited by S. Mailick. Garden City, NY: Anchor/Doubleday, 1972.

——— . "Action Learning Projects." In *Management Development and Training Handbook,* by B. Taylor and G. L. Lippitt. New York: McGraw-Hill, 1984.

Rhinesmith, S. H. "Going Global from the Inside Out." *Training and Development Journal,* November 1991.

Riggs, F. W. "Public Administration: A Comparativist Framework." *Public Administration Review,* November–December 1991.

Roberts, R. W., and R. H. Nee, eds. *Theories of Social Casework.* Chicago: University of Chicago Press, 1970.

Rogers, C. R. *Freedom to Learn: A View of What Education Might Be.* Columbus, OH: Merrill, 1969.

Rohrer, G., W. Smith, and V. Peterson. "Field Instructor Benefits in Education: A National Survey." *Journal of Social Work Education,* Fall 1992.

Rosen, S. M., D. Fansheld, and M. E. Lutz. *Face of the Nation.* Silver Spring, MD: National Association of Social Workers, 1987.

Rosenthal, E. "That Person in the White Smock Is Not a Doctor." *New York Times,* January 10, 1991.

——— . "Medicine Suffers as Fewer Doctors Do General Work." *New York Times,* May 24, 1993.

Rothfeld, C. "What Do Law Schools Teach? Almost Anything." *New York Times,* December 23, 1988.

Rothwell, W. J. "The Case for External Peer Review." *Training and Development Journal,* June 1985.

Rubin, S. "Donald Schon's 'Reflective Artistry.'" In *Combining Service and Learning,* edited by J. C. Kendall and Associates. Raleigh, NC: National Society for Internships and Experiential Education, 1990.

Saunders, W. S. "The Humanities vs. Careerism." *Improving College and University Teaching,* Fall 1982.

Schein, E. H. *Professional Education: Some New Directions.* New York: McGraw-Hill, 1972.

——— . *Organizational Culture and Leadership.* San Francisco: Jossey-Bass, 1987.

Schneck, D., B. Grossman, and U. Glassman, eds. *Field Education for Social Work: Contemporary Issues and Trends.* Dubuque, IA: Kendall/Hunt, 1990.

Schneider, S. K. "Influences on State Professional Licensure Policy." *Public Administration Review,* November–December 1987.

Schon, D. A. *The Reflective Practitioner.* New York: Basic Books, 1983.

——— . *Educating the Reflective Practitioner.* San Francisco: Jossey-Bass, 1988.

——— . "The Crisis of Professional Knowledge and the Pursuit of an Epistemology of Practice." *Journal of Interprofessional Care,* January 1992. Reprint from C. R. Christensen, *Teaching by the Case Method* (Cambridge: Harvard Business School, 1987).

Schwartz, B. *The Battle for Human Nature.* New York: Norton, 1986.

Schwartz, W. B. "The Hard Choices in Health Care." *New York Times,* July 19, 1992.

Searle, J. "The Storm over the University." *New York Review of Books,* December 6, 1990.

Seligmen, J. *The High Citadel: The Influence of Harvard Law School.* Boston: Houghton Mifflin, 1978.

Seltzer, M. M., and J. Wayne. "Outcome Evaluation of the Part-time Program of the Boston University School of Social Work." *Newsletter of the National Committee on Part-time Social Work Education,* October 1985.

Selznick, P. *Leadership in Administration: A Sociological Interpretation.* Berkeley: University of California Press, 1984.

Shangraw, R. F., and M. M. Crow. "Public Administration as a Design Science." *Public Administration Review,* March–April 1989.

Sheafor, B. W., and L. E. Jenkins, eds. *Quality Field Instruction in Social Work.* New York: Longman, 1982.

Shuchman, H. L. *Self-Regulation in the Professions.* Glastonbury, CT: Futures Group, 1981.

Shulman, J. "Legal Education: A Selective Bibliography, 1991." Unpublished document, New York University Law Library, 1993.

Siegel, B. N. Review of *The Making of an Economist*, by A. Klamer and D. Colander. *Annals of the American Academy of Political and Social Science*, January 1992.

Simon, H. *Administrative Behavior: A Study of Decision-Making Processes in Administrative Organization*. New York: Macmillan, 1957.

————. *The Sciences of the Artificial*. Cambridge: M.I.T. Press, 1976.

Skinner, B. F. *Beyond Freedom and Dignity*. New York: Bantam/Vintage, 1971.

Skolnick, L. *Final Report: Field Education Project*. Washington, DC: Council on Social Work Education, 1985.

Smith, P. *Killing the Spirit: Higher Education in America*. New York: Viking, 1990.

Smothers, R. D. "A Shortage of Lawyers to Help the Condemned." *New York Times*, June 4, 1993.

Smythe, O. "Practical Experience and the Liberal Arts: A Philosophical Perspective." In *Combining Service and Learning*, edited by J. C. Kendall and Associates. Raleigh, NC: National Society for Internships and Experiential Education, 1990.

Social Work Encyclopedia, 18th ed., vol. 2, edited by A. Minahan. Silver Spring, MD: National Association of Social Workers, 1987.

Spaulding, E. C. *Statistics on Social Work Education in the United States, 1990*. Alexandria, VA: Council on Social Work Education, 1991.

Spaulding, R. M. *Imperial Japan's Higher Civil Service Examinations*. Princeton, NJ: Princeton University Press, 1967.

Speigel, M. "Theory and Practice in Legal Education: An Essay on Clinical Education." *UCLA Law Review* 34 (February 1987).

Spence, J. D. *The Memory Palace of Matteo Ricci*. New York: Viking, 1984.

Spiro, J. D. "Evaluation of the Modular Preceptor Training Method as in NYU's Doctoral Program in Mental Health Policy and Administration." Master's thesis, New York University, 1979.

Stamford Research Institute. *Anticipating Educational Issues over the Next Two Decades: Overview Report of Trend Analysis*. Washington, DC: U.S. Department of Education, 1973.

Stark, J. S., M. A. Lowther, and B.M.K. Hagerty. *Responsive Professional Education: Balancing Outcomes and Opportunities*. Washington, DC: George Washington University, 1986.

Starr, P. *The Social Transformation of American Medicine*. New York: Basic Books, 1982.

Stein, R. "The Future of Legal Education." *Minnesota Law Review*, February 1992.

Stern, M. R., and D. S. Queeney. "The Scope of Continuing Professional Education: Providers, Consumers, Issues." In *Professional Workers as Learners*, edited by E. S. Hunt. Washington, DC: U.S. Department of Education, 1992.

Stevens, R. *Law School Legal Education in America from the 1850s to the 1980s*. Chapel Hill: University of North Carolina Press, 1983.

Stillman, P. L., M. B. Regan, M. Philbin, and H. L. Halley. "Results of a Survey on the Use of Standardized Patients to Teach and Evaluate Clinical Skills." *Academic Medicine*, May 1990.

Stillman, P. L., M. Y. Burpeau-DiGregorio, G. L. Nicholson, D. L. Sabers, and A. E. Stillman. "Six Years of Experience Using Patient Instructors to Teach Interviewing Skills." *Journal of Medical Education*, March 1983.

Stone, A. "Legal Education on the Couch." *Harvard Law Review*, December 1971.

Strom, K. "Should Field Instructors Be Social Workers?" *Journal of Social Work Education*, Spring–Summer 1991.

Stumpf, A. S., and R.L.M. Dunbar. "Beyond Strategy Formulation and Implementation: Strategic Leadership Skills." *Journal of Management Education*, March 1992.

Stumpf, A. S., and T. P. Mullen. *Taking Charge: Strategic Management in the Middle Game*. Englewood Cliffs, NJ: Prentice-Hall, 1992.

Summer, C. E., R. A. Bettis, I. H. Duhaim, J. H. Grant, D. C. Hambrick, C. C. Snow, and C. P. Zeithaml. "Doctoral Education in the Field of Business Policy and Strategy." *Journal of Management*, June 1990.

Taylor, B., and G. L. Lippitt. *Management Development and Training Handbook*. New York: McGraw-Hill, 1984.

Taylor, F. W. *The Principles of Scientific Management*. New York: Harper, 1911.

Thomas, L. Review of *Becoming a Doctor*, by M. Konner. *New York Review of Books*, September 24, 1987.

Thomas, R. G., and L. Anderson. "Teaching for Transfer: Application of Cognitive Theory in Vocational Education." Paper presented at the American Vocational Association Convention, Los Angeles, December 1991.

Thompson, J. D. *Organizations in Action: Social Bases of Administrative Theory*. New York: McGraw-Hill, 1967.

Thorne, B. "Professional Education in Medicine." In *Education for the Professions of Medicine, Law, Theology and Social Welfare*, by E. C. Hughes, B. Thorne, A. M. DeBaggis, A. Gurin, and D. Williams. New York: McGraw-Hill, 1973.

Tifft, S. E. "Does Business Want What It Can't Use?" *America's Agenda*, Spring 1992.

Tocqueville, Alexis de. *Democracy in America*. New York: Knopf, 1945.

Toren, N. *Social Work: The Case of a Semi-Profession*. Beverly Hills, CA: Sage, 1972.

United States Department of Education. *Law School Clinical Experience Program: Guide for the Preparation of Applications Fiscal Year 1993*. Washington, DC: U.S. Department of Education, 1992.

————. *Digest of Educational Statistics*. Washington, DC: U.S. Department of Education, 1993.

University of Chicago Law School. *Clinical Education and the Law School of the Future*. University of Chicago Law School Conference, no. 20. Chicago: University of Chicago Press, 1970.

Unseem, M. *Liberal Education and the Corporation: The Hiring and Advancement of College Graduates*. Hawthorne, NY: Walter De Gruyter, 1989.

Ventriss, C. "Contemporary Issues in American Public Administration Education: The Search for an Educational Focus." *Public Administration Review*, January–February 1991.

Vocino, T., and R. Heimovics, eds. *Public Education in Transition*. New York: Marcel Dekker, 1982.

Waldo, D. "(Re)founding the Field." *Public Administration Review*, March–April 1991.

Watson, A. "Quest for Professional Competence: Psychiatric Aspects of Legal Education." *University of Cincinnati Law Review*, Winter 1968.

Weaver, R. "Langdell's Legacy: Living with the Case Method." *Villanova Law Review*, April 1991.

Wenocur, S., and M. Reisch. *From Charity to Enterprise: The Development of American Social Work in a Market Economy*. Chicago: University of Illinois, 1989.

Wentz, D. K., A. M. Osteen, and M. I. Gannon. "Continuing Education: Refocusing Support and Direction." *Journal of the American Medical Association*, August 1991.

Wheatley, W. J., R. W. Hornaday, and T. G. Hunt. "Developing Strategic Management Goal-Setting Skills." *Simulation and Games*, June 1988.

White, J. D. "Dissertations and Publications in Public Administration." *Public Administration Review*, January–February 1986.

Whitehead, A. N. *Science and the Modern World.* New York: New American Library, 1948.

——— . *The Aims of Education, and Other Essays.* New York: New American Library, 1955.

——— . *An Introduction to Mathematics.* New York: Oxford University Press, 1958.

Wiggenhorn, W. "Motorola U: When Training Becomes an Education." *Harvard Business Review*, July–August 1990.

Wijnberg, M. H., and M. C. Schwartz. "Models of Student Supervision: The Apprentice, Growth, and Role Systems Models." *Journal of Education for Social Work*, Fall 1977.

Wilensky, H. L., and C. H. Lebeaux. *Industrial Society and Social Welfare.* New York: Free Press, 1965.

Willis, S. L., and S. S. Dubin, eds. *Maintaining Professional Competence: Approaches to Career Enhancement, Vitality, and Success throughout a Work Life.* San Francisco: Jossey-Bass, 1990.

Wilson, J. W., ed. *Developing and Expanding Cooperative Education.* San Francisco: Jossey-Bass, 1978.

Wolf, J. F. "Careers in Public Administration Education." In *Public Education in Transition*, edited by T. Vocino and R. Heimovics. New York: Marcel Dekker, 1982.

Wohlking, W. "Management Training: Where Has It Gone Wrong." *Training and Development Journal*, December 1971.

Wolniansky, N. "International Training for Global Leadership." *Management Review*, May 1990.

Wooldridge, B. "Assessing the Professional Orientation of Public Personnel Administration Courses." *Public Personnel Management*, Fall 1989.

Young, S. D. *The Rule of Experts: Occupational Licensing in America.* Washington, DC: Cato Institute, 1987.

Younghouse, R. H., and W. H. Young. "Program Relationships of Community Hospitals and Medical Schools in CME." *Journal of Medical Education*, July 1984.

Zuboff, S. *In the Age of the Smart Machine: The Future of Work and Power.* New York: Basic Books, 1988.

INDEX

ABOUT THE EDITORS AND CONTRIBUTORS

ROBERT H. EBERT, M.D., is Caroline Shields Walker Professor of Medicine, Emeritus, and former Dean of the Faculty of Medicine, Harvard University. He has held professional appointments and shared responsibility for undergraduate and graduate medical education at the University of Chicago, Case Western Reserve University, and Harvard University as well as a board member or advisor to six private foundations having programs concerned with health manpower, health policy, or medical education.

FREDERICK M. HART is Professor of Law at the University of New Mexico school of law. He was President of the Law School Admission Council, on the Accreditation Committee of the Section on Legal Education and Admission to the Bar of the American Bar Association Accreditation, and served on the Law School Admission Council's Board of Trustees and Test Development and Research Committee.

SOLOMON HOBERMAN was a management consultant for government and private-sector organizations. He was former Personnel Director, Chair of the Civil Service Commission, and Director of Training for New York City and professor of administration. He has received awards for public service, administrative achievement, and contributions to experiential education and has published on such topics as mathematics, management, training and development, and experiential education. He was the author (with Sidney Mailick) of *Experiential Management Development: From*

Learning to Practice (Quorum Books, 1992) and *The Practice of Management Development* (Praeger, 1988).

SIDNEY MAILICK is Professor Emeritus of Public Administration at the Wagner School of Public Service of New York University where he served as director of the doctoral program in mental health policy and administration. He has directed executive development programs at the University of Chicago and New York University, and founded and directed Israel's Administrative Staff College, and served as a consultant on training and development for numerous organizations including the U.S. State Department and the United Nations.

ELAINE MARSHACK is Associate Professor at the Hunter College School of Social Work, City University of New York and has served as Director of the Field Practicum for twelve years. She is the author of numerous articles on field education in social work and has co-chaired the field work symposium for the Council of Social Work Education. She is a consulting editor for the *Journal of Teaching in Social Work*.

J. MICHAEL NORWOOD is Professor of Law at the University of New Mexico school of law. He served as Director of Clinical Programs, was a managing attorney for the Legal Aid Society of Albuquerque, and was a reporter to the American Bar Association Section on Legal Education and Admissions to the Bar.